Eliot's Early Years

Eliot's Early Years

LYNDALL GORDON

OXFORD UNIVERSITY PRESS
OXFORD AND NEW YORK
1977

ISBN 0 19 812078 8
Copyright © 1977 by Oxford University Press
Library of Congress Catalogue Card Number: 76-29809
Printed in the United States of America

Acknowledgements

I AM greatly indebted to my mother who has always spoken of the religious life with unusual clarity. I owe, too, special thanks to Siamon Gordon and Sacvan Bercovitch for detailed criticism at an early stage, and to A. Walton Litz and Helen Gardner for generous help later on. The book was also read in typescript by Jacques Barzun, Valerie Eliot, Ronald Schuchard, and Anne Elliott, and their corrections and suggestions are incorporated in the text. In New York, Marie Grossi typed with a critical eye, ably seconded by Audrey Richards in Oxford.

The notes do not acknowledge two books whose influence has lingered. One is Quentin Anderson's essay on nineteenth-century America, *The Imperial Self.* The other is *The Art of T. S. Eliot* by Helen Gardner, whose chapter on *The Waste Land* must remain the classic account of the continuity of Eliot's career.

I should finally like to thank the Rhodes Trust for a fellowship which enabled me to complete the book, and the Principal and Fellows of St. Hilda's College, Oxford, for their hospitality from 1973 to 1975.

Contents

List of Plates

Abbreviations

ASG   *After Strange Gods: A Primer of Modern Heresy.* The Page-
      Barbour Lectures at the University of Virginia, 1933.
      London: Faber, 1934; New York: Harcourt Brace, 1934*.

AW   'Ash Wednesday', 1930 (see *The Collected Poems*).

CC   *To Criticize the Critic and Other Writings.* London: Faber,
      1965; New York: Farrar Straus, 1965, rpr. Noonday–
      Farrar, 1968*.

CP   *The Collected Poems of T. S. Eliot 1909–1962.* London: Faber,
      1963; New York: Harcourt Brace, 1963*.

*facs. WL The Waste Land: A Facsimile and Transcript of the Original
      Drafts Including the Annotations of Ezra Pound,* ed.
      Valerie Eliot. London: Faber, 1971; New York: Harcourt
      Brace, 1971*.

FQ   *Four Quartets,* 1943 (see *The Collected Poems*).

ICS   *The Idea of a Christian Society.* London: Faber, 1939; New
      York: Harcourt Brace, 1940, rpr. in *Christianity and Culture*,
      Harvest-Harcourt, 1960*.

KE   *Knowledge and Experience in the Philosophy of F. H. Bradley.*
      London: Faber, 1964*; New York: Farrar Straus, 1964.

NDC   *Notes Towards the Definition of Culture.* London: Faber, 1948;
      New York: Harcourt Brace, 1949, rpr. in *Christianity and
      Culture**.

NEW   *New English Weekly.*

NYRB *New York Review of Books.*

OPP   *On Poetry and Poets.* London: Faber, 1957; New York:
      Farrar Straus, 1957, rpr. Noonday–Farrar, 1969*.

SE   *Selected Essays.* London: Faber, 1932; New York: Harcourt
      Brace, 1932, rpr. 1960*.

SW   *The Sacred Wood: Essays on Poetry and Criticism.* London:
      Methuen, 1920; New York: Alfred A. Knopf, 1920. Rpr.
      London: University Paperbacks, Methuen, 1967*.

* Editions used in text. In the footnotes and source notes, when both
English and American publishers of a book are cited, the first cited is
the one used in this book.

TLS   *Times Literary Supplement.*

UPUC   *The Use of Poetry and the Use of Criticism: Studies in the Relation
       of Criticism to Poetry in England.* Charles Eliot Norton
       Lectures for 1932–3 at Harvard University. London:
       Faber, 1933; Cambridge, Mass.: Harvard University
       Press, 1933, rpr. New York: Barnes & Noble, 1970*.

WL   *The Waste Land,* 1922 (see *The Collected Poems*).

Eliot's Early Years

1. Early Models

THOMAS STEARNS ELIOT was born in 1888 in St. Louis, Missouri, the son of a New England schoolteacher and a St. Louis merchant. Thirty-eight years later he was baptized as an Anglican in an English village. Such facts tell little of a man for whom there was usually a gap between his outward and his private life, the formulated, highly articulate surface and the inward ferment. Wyndham Lewis painted Eliot's face as if it were a mask, so that he might distinguish Eliot's formal surface from his hooded introspective eyes, and the severe dark lines of his suit from the flesh of his shoulders beneath. Virginia Woolf wrote that his hazel eyes seemed oddly lively and youthful in a pale, sculptured, even heavy face.[1]

Eliot was obsessed by his private experience and determined to guard it. He was barely famous in 1925 when he decided that there should be no biography.[2] He urged those close to him to keep silence. Many letters are shut away until the next century. Meanwhile, Eliot wrote his own biography, enlarging in poem after poem on the character of a man who conceives of his life as a religious quest despite the anti-religious mood of his age and the distracting claims of women, friends, and alternative careers. Eliot once spoke of the man who tries to explain to himself 'the sequence that culminates in faith'[3] and in a letter, written in 1930, mentioned his own long-cherished intention to explore a mode of writing neglected in the twentieth century, the spiritual autobiography.[4] Eliot's Notebook and other manuscript poems show that he began to measure his life by the divine goal as far back as his student days, in 1910 and 1911, and that the turning-point came not when he was baptized in 1927 but in 1914 when he first interested himself in the motives, the ordeals, and the achievements of saints. In his later years Eliot seemed to beg off personally in favour of a routine life of prayer and observance, but the early manuscripts suggest that for a time in his youth he dreamed of the saint's ambitious task, of living by his own vision beyond the imaginative frontiers of his civilization.

As more is gradually known of Eliot's life, the clearer it seems that the 'impersonal' façade of his poetry—the multiple faces and voices—masks an often quite literal reworking of personal experience. Eliot wrote that there is a 'transfusion of the personality or, in a deeper sense, the life of the author into the character.'[5] This book is an attempt to elicit the autobiographical element in Eliot's poetry by measuring the poetry against the life. It may be called a biography, but in Eliot's rather special sense of the genre. Whenever Eliot wrote about lives he was not so much concerned with formal history and circumstance as with what he called the 'unattended' moments. 'The awful daring of a moment's surrender', he wrote in *The Waste Land*. 'By this, and this only, we have existed.' The external facts of Eliot's life are here, but only to prop the record of the definitive inward experiences to the time of his conversion. By avoiding the traditional schema of an official biography and by limiting the amount of biographical trivia, it becomes possible to trace the continuity of Eliot's career and to see the poetry and the life as complementary parts of one design, a consuming search for salvation.

A poet, Yeats said, 'is never the bundle of accident and incoherence that sits down to breakfast; he has been reborn as an idea, something intended, complete.'[6] It is hard to say exactly how or when the commanding idea is born but, in Eliot's case, an obvious source suggests itself in the dramatic figures that surrounded his American youth. The shadowy exemplary figure that haunts Eliot's poetry may be traced back to the model grandfather, whom Emerson called 'the Saint of the West',[7] to the New England mother's heroes of truth and virtue, to the hardy fishermen of Cape Ann, Massachusetts, and the rockpool and the silences between the waves that shaped Eliot's religious imagination. Towards the end of his life Eliot came to see his poetry as more American than English: '. . . in its sources, in its emotional springs, it comes from America.'[8]

From the start, Eliot's family recognized him as exceptional, particularly his mother who would speak to him as an equal. He, in turn, was devoted to her. His strongest recorded expression of emotion is on the flyleaf of a copy of *Union Portraits* which he sent to her 'with infinite love'. High-minded and plain-living, Charlotte Champe Eliot taught her children to perfect themselves each day, 'to make the best of every faculty and control every tendency to evil'.[9] The father, Henry Ware Eliot, Sr., was a man of refined bearing, with a taste for art and music, and an acute sense of smell. He had a curious way of smelling his food before he ate it. Although he eventually made his success as a manufacturer of bricks, he lived under the shadow of his own father, William Greenleaf Eliot, a financial genius of whom it was said that, if he had not been called to the ministry, he might have owned nearly everything west of the Mississippi. There is little sign of imagination in Henry's autobiography; he presents himself as rather a plodder, proud of his industry and filial piety.[10] He could be, in a studied way, playful and liked to draw faces on his children's boiled eggs.[11]

T. S. Eliot spent his first sixteen years in a city distinguished at the turn of the century for the corruption of its businessmen, its inadequate sewers, and its sulphurous fumes. Yet Eliot could still say: 'I am very well satisfied with having been born in St. Louis.'[12] Whenever he recalled his St. Louis childhood in later life he did not think first of the city's blemishes but of the more personal memories that overrode them: the moods and rhythms of the great Mississippi ('the river is within us . . .'[13]); the steamboats blowing in the New Year;[14] the river in flood 'with its cargo of dead Negroes, cows and chicken coops';[15] his Irish nurse, Annie Dunne, and her prayers in the little Catholic Church on the corner of Locust Street and Jefferson Avenue; her discussing with him, at the age of six, the existence of God.[16] There is a photograph of Eliot, aged seven, with his dimpled nurse. His beret is perched jauntily on his head and his face is mischievous; Annie's lips are pursed, one hand on her hip.[17] Years later, Eliot wrote a rhyme about some naughty Jim Jum Bears who got up to tricks to exasperate their Nurse ('Was ever a Nurse so put about?').[18] It recalls the secure intimacy of his very early days with Annie to whom he said he was 'greatly attached'.

The Eliots lived in an unfashionable area of St. Louis at a time when most of their friends were moving to suburbs further west. Tom was the last of seven children, and his sisters and brother were relatively mature by the time he was born. He had few playmates and spent most of his time reading. He had a congenital double hernia and Charlotte, afraid it would rupture, forbade football and strenuous sports. During summers at Cape

Ann, when 'the Skipper' used to give him sailing lessons, Charlotte would go along, fortified by a guard of grown-up sisters,
to ensure that he did not get too wet or too hot or too tired.[19]
He accepted his mother's domination in good humour.[20]

There was in Eliot's mother a rare moral passion and a gift of
eloquence. She had the ardent, unsophisticated intellectual
energy of a Dorothea Brooke, a natural scholar whose sex and
circumstances debarred her from higher education. She set out to
be a poet, but when her youngest child showed talent, hoped
that he might redeem her sense of failure. She wrote in a letter to
Eliot at Harvard:

I hope in your literary work you will receive early the recognition
I strove for and failed. I should so have loved a college course, but was
obliged to teach before I was nineteen. I graduated with high rank,
'a young lady of unusual brilliancy as a scholar' my old yellow testi-
monial says, but when I was set to teaching young children, my Trigo-
nometry and Astronomy counted for nought, and I made a dead
failure.[21]

After several years as a teacher she married a handsome clerk
who dealt with groceries shipped on the Mississippi. She then
devoted much of her energies to her growing family and local
social reforms, particularly a house of detention for juveniles.
Her room displayed no sign of conventional femininity except for
a pincushion on the dresser. There was a comfortable armchair
next to a sunny window even though it blocked a chest of drawers.
The bed faced a mantlepiece draped with a velvet cloth on which
rested a painting of the madonna and child. On her wall there
hung an engraving of Theodosius and St. Ambrose, illustrating
the triumph of holy over temporal power.

After her death, when Henry Ware Eliot, Jr. placed Charlotte's
poems in Harvard's Eliot Collection, he wrote to the librarian:
'Perhaps a hundred years from now the connection with T. S.
Eliot will not seem so remote. Of all the family, my brother most
resembled my mother in features and . . . if there is anything in
heredity, it must have been from that side that T. S. Eliot got his
tastes.' Apart from Charlotte herself, there was no literary
tradition on the Stearns side, but there was, occasionally, a certain
moral fervour. The statue called 'The Puritan' in Springfield,
Massachusetts, shows one of the Stearns ancestors striding along
vigorously with his huge Bible grasped under one arm and, in

the other, a pilgrim's staff.* A reserved uncle, the Revd. Oliver Stearns, used to startle his students at Harvard Divinity School with sudden hot floods of eloquence. Whatever he saw to be true or right, that would he say and do, 'though the heavens fell'.[22]

It is curious to read Charlotte Champe Eliot's poetry in the context of her son's work. Charlotte writes habitually of 'the vision of the seer' and 'the prophet's warning cry'. Her poems recount definitive incidents in the lives of the chosen: the Apostles and 'The Unnamed Saints', St. Barnabas and St. Theodosius. Her heroes are 'truth-inebriated', 'God-intoxicated' disciples of Emerson and Channing; her Savonarola, her Giordano Bruno, her St. Francis trust the private vision. Her image of the thinker who, from unfathomed depths, seizes on the sublime truth is almost identical with the dominant figure in T. S. Eliot's numerous poems of 1911 and 1912.

Charlotte's strength is essentially that of a preacher. All the force of her poetry lies in passionate argument and dramatic illustration. She speaks particularly to those who 'by gift of genius' are set apart; her message is to endure with faith periods of religious despair:

> Ye who despair
> Of man's redemption, know, the light is there,
> Though hidden and obscured, again to shine . . .
> ('Saved!')

Charlotte's gift is didactic; she lacks the inventiveness and imaginative freshness of the great poet. Her son, using exactly the same traditional images, rescued them from triteness—the beatific light, the fires of lust and purgation, the pilgrimage across the 'desert waste ',[23] and the seasonal metaphor for spiritual drought that pervades Charlotte's poetry. In the extremity of 'the dying year' the boughs in her garden go stiff and dry, no flower blooms, while a new power awaits its birth.[24] 'April is the cruellest month,' T. S. Eliot was to write, 'breeding lilacs out of the dead land'. Mother and son used the same group of traditional images to register grace. In 'The Master's Welcome' Charlotte hears children's voices. Bells signal recovery of faith after a period of doubt. Water—the 'celestial fountain' and 'the healing flood'—promises relief after long ordeals.

* Saint-Gaudens's statue of Samuel Chapin was done in 1887. Thomas Stearns (1710–84) married Abigail Reed, great-granddaughter of Chapin.

Charlotte mapped out the states of being between loss and recovery of grace, a map her son redrew in his poetry with vivid, ingenious twentieth-century touches. The essential difference was Charlotte's optimism. She felt an assurance of grace which her son could not share. T. S. Eliot's faint-hearted character, J. Alfred Prufrock, feels obliged to frame an 'overwhelming' question but shirks it. In the context of his lack of nerve, it is curious to note the many serious but quite commonplace questions Charlotte poses in her poetry: How does one face 'blank annihilation'? Is life worth living since we know we must die? 'And is this all this life so incomplete?' 'What shall I do to be saved?' Eliot must have known all the crucial questions and answers before he left his mother's side, but it was to be many years before he made them his own.

In a talk, 'The Influence of Landscape upon the Poet', Eliot called himself a New England poet because he had been so deeply affected when, like Frost, he had come East as a child.[25] He was always happy near the sea and would remember with joy his boyhood summers at Cape Ann.[26]

In 1896 Eliot's father built a large, solid house for his family at Eastern Point, near Gloucester, on an uncultivated rough coast, surrounded by wild bush and slabs of rock going down to the sea's edge. The upper windows overlooked the granite shore, the white sails over the sea and, looking the other way, the harbour. Eliot remembered Gloucester harbour as one of the most beautiful on the New England coast.[27] A photograph by his brother Henry shows it at the turn of the century, the tall masts of what was then an all-sail fishing fleet dominating the village in the background with its clapboard houses and sloping roofs. From the beginning, fishing was the main preoccupation of Gloucester. When a divine came among the first settlers in the seventeenth century and said: 'Remember, brethren, that you journeyed here to save your souls', one of the brethren is reported to have remarked, 'And to ketch fish'.[28] In Eliot's day fishermen between trips lounged at the corner of Main Street and Duncan Street and told yarns of storms and shipwrecks on the half-hidden rocks offshore from Cape Ann. Working in hard winter gales, the deep-sea fisherman put out from the schooner in a tiny dory which often capsized or went astray in fog or snow.

And when a man lived through such an experience, he told the kind of yarn Eliot listened to as a boy, of human daring and tenacity beyond belief.

Admiration for the fishermen's casual acts of heroism and for their hardy self-reliance is reflected in Eliot's schoolboy compositions and sustained through his mature writings. In 'A Tale of a Whale', published in the *Smith Academy Record* in April 1905, and in 'The Man Who was King', published the following June, Eliot made proud use of sailing jargon. As a student Eliot imagined ancestors in the mould of the Cape Ann sea captains he admired. In an article called 'Gentlemen and Seamen' he extols as 'plebeian aristocrats'—men like his own ancestors, small-town patriarchs, seamen, small printers, and tradesmen, who established themselves in villages along the New England coast.[29] Eliot imagines their sombre faces, their compressed lips, their natures difficult and unyielding as a consequence of religious principle and endless struggle with the narrow resources of New England. This was the kind of man that impressed the young Eliot: an unworldly and inconspicuous pioneer, strenuous, resilient, and proud. Later, in sea scenes in his poems, Eliot again invoked the Gloucester hero. In a long section in the *Waste Land* manuscript he describes a fishing expedition to the Grand Banks, the gallant spirit of the men, and their destruction by an iceberg. Later yet, he reworked the perilous fishing expedition as a paradigm for his search for faith in 'Dry Salvages' in *Four Quartets*.

Eliot himself became a proficient sailor and the happiest moments of his youth were spent off the New England coast on expeditions, sometimes through fog and heavy seas, to Mount Desert Island or Rogue Island.[30] In 'Gerontion' (1919) and 'Marina' (1930) the dross of civilization is blown away by the sea wind, and in 'Marina' the slow lyrical awakening to redemptive love, with all its mystery and promise, is aligned with the perilous crossing of the Atlantic and slow approach to the New World, the dim New England shore with its woods and grey rocks. As a child Eliot explored the Cape Ann beaches for what the sea tossed up—starfish, a whale bone, a broken oar, a horseshoe crab.* The pools offered, for his curiosity, 'the more delicate algae and the sea anemone'. When he was ten, peering through water

---

* 'Dry Salvages', *CP*, p. 191. Eliot explained, in a letter to *NEW* (25 Jan. 1945) that he had used the term 'hermit crab' in error for 'horseshoe crab'.

in a rockpool, he saw the sea anemone for the first time, an experience, he remembered, 'not so simple, for an exceptional child, as it looks'.[31]

Eliot was to return again and again to the Cape Ann shore and sea for scenes of crisis and revelation in his poetry. To the Cape Ann summers of his youth he owed his model, drawn from the Gloucester fisherman, of a heroic quester living on the thin edge of mortality. His imagination fastened, too, on the still pool and the light-filled water that recurred in his poetry as a tantalizing memory of unspeakable bliss.

When Eliot was sixteen his mother published a biography of her father-in-law, William Greenleaf Eliot, and dedicated it to her children 'Lest They Forget'. 'I was brought up to be very much aware of him', Eliot said. 'The standard of conduct was that which my grandfather had set: our moral judgements, our decisions between duty and self-indulgence, were taken as if, like Moses, he had brought down the tables of the Law, any deviation from which would be sinful. . . .'[32]

William had a narrow frail body with large, calm, benign eyes. His son, Henry, recalled those magnificent eyes in his autobiography, and said that they seemed to read one's innermost thoughts. William's expression was sensitive and serene, the face of a man who looks on suffering from a citadel of moral assurance. He was not stern, but it would have been unthinkable, said his son, to argue with him or to attempt undue familiarity. 'How can one be familiar with the Day of Judgement?' said James Freeman Clark, a classmate at Divinity School. 'One feels rebuked in his presence. . . . Yet he is playful, fond of fun, and there is a sweet smile appearing on the corner of his mouth. But there is no *abandon*.'[33]

Charlotte revered her father-in-law and brought up her children to observe two of his laws in particular, those of self-denial and public service. T. S. Eliot acknowledged that his early training in self-denial left him permanently scarred by an inability to enjoy even harmless pleasures. He learnt, for instance, that it was self-indulgent to buy candy, and it was not until he was forced to stop smoking for health reasons in his sixties that he could bring himself to eat it as a substitute.[34] This kind of upbringing was, of course, not peculiar to the Eliot home. Henry

Adams, also constrained by the virtue of New England ancestors, recalled that he would eat only the less perfect peaches in his grandfather's garden.

As Eliot grew up he had to face the most important of his grandfather's laws, the subordination of selfish interests to the good of Community and Church. William Greenleaf Eliot perfectly exemplified the Eliot family's ideal of manhood, interfusing piety with public enterprise. In 1834 he moved from Harvard Divinity School to found the Unitarian Church on what was then the American frontier. A brilliant fund-raiser, he helped found both Washington University, where he served as unpaid professor of metaphysics, and the Academy of Science in St. Louis. He was an early advocate of women's suffrage and of prohibition. During the terrible typhoid epidemic of the 1840s he visited sick-beds indefatigably and during the Civil War organized the Western Sanitary Commission. In 1852, when Emerson visited St. Louis, he reported that the Unitarian minister had 'a sumptuous church and crowds to hear his really good sermons.'[35]

In a sense, William Greenleaf Eliot fulfilled Emerson's ideal of an individual with the power to remake his world. 'All history', said Emerson, 'resolves itself very easily into the biography of a few stout and earnest persons. . . . A man must be so much that he must make all circumstances indifferent. Every true man is a cause, a county, and an age.' T. S. Eliot once alluded to Emerson's dictum that 'an institution is the lengthened shadow of one man' in a poem which wryly examines the activities of the oblivious, pleasure-loving Sweeney in a brothel. The gambling and drinking habits of the French Catholics and American pioneers from Kentucky and Virginia (who first settled St. Louis) had called, said T. S. Eliot, for his grandfather's strong missionary hand.[36] Brought up to applaud William's reforming zeal, it is not surprising that his grandson should so boldly confront, a century later, the moral wilderness of post-war London. Even as a boy, said one cousin, 'Tom had a great sense of mission'.

In 'Animula' Eliot pictured a youth curled up on a window-seat with the *Encyclopaedia Britannica*, who feels the tug of idle dreams but feels too a call to act effectively in the busy world. Generations of Eliots before him had responded to the call to family and communal duties. Those Eliots who lived in the neighbourhood of Somerset, Wiltshire, and Gloucestershire in early

Tudor times made wills which did not forget the poor, and sent their sons to institutions of higher learning, and tended to marry rich widows of the landed gentry.[37] In 1937 T. S. Eliot visited East Coker, the village from which Andrew Eliot set out for New England, and imagined his sturdy Eliot ancestors, their furnished houses that rose and crumbled, their faces merry or solemn, their feet clogged with earth as they danced to time-honoured measures at folk festivals.[38] In a way he envied their unquestioning communal feeling, but he also bitterly resisted their endless activity. What did it come to? 'Dung and death.'

Nothing is known of the Andrew Eliot who emigrated to Salem, Massachusetts, except that he was a man of property and education and that he became a member of the First Church of Beverly in 1670 and in 1690 Beverly's first Town Clerk. He is also believed to have officiated at the Salem witch trials. By the next century the Eliots were flourishing as city people, conspicuous in the affairs of Boston. The first to distinguish himself was the Revd. Andrew Eliot (1718–78). Chubby-faced, with neat features and a double chin, he seldom gave controversial sermons from his pulpit in the New North Church. His Calvinism was moderate in temper but he practised it most earnestly. When Boston was blockaded during the Revolution, he was the only congregational minister, apart from Samuel Mather, to open his church every Lord's Day. When he was proposed as successor to President Holyoke at Harvard, and again after the resignation of Locke, he declined because of religious duties. One acquaintance used to call him 'Andrew Sly' because of his political prudence and circumspection. When he felt his temper rising he used to retire until he had controlled it.[39]

The Eliots were not heroes but they had a taste for one kind of daring, the moral challenge. T. S. Eliot was interested in Sir Thomas Elyot who risked reproving Henry VIII to his face on account of Anne Boleyn, and in *The Boke Named the Governour* (1531) attacked kings for their luxury and frivolity, and pleaded with them to rule for the common good. Two centuries later, in 1765, the Revd. Andrew Eliot preached a censorious election-day sermon before the colonial governor of Massachusetts. Both Eliots escaped charges of treason because their tones were sober. They felt strongly about morals, conduct, and the public good, but they did not resort to flaming rhetoric.

There was much in the model Eliot man to admire. Throughout his life, T. S. Eliot was to feel the disjunction between his poetic impulse and his compulsion to conform to the Eliot ideal. 'The primary channel of culture is the family', he wrote; 'no man wholly escapes from the kind, or wholly surpasses the degree, of culture which he acquired from his early environment.'[40] As a student in Boston, Eliot worried about the kind of practical career his family would applaud. But by the time he settled in England, he came to feel the claims of his poetic nature had priority over the claims of his family: 'The Arts insist that a man shall dispose of all he has, even of his family tree, and follow art alone. For they demand that a man be not a member of a family or a caste or of a party or of a coterie, but simply and solely himself.'[41] Eliot puzzled and alarmed his parents by staying in London in 1915 instead of finishing his doctorate at Harvard, and by spending years writing poetry that was published only sporadically and in little-known magazines. His father died in 1919 under the impression that his youngest child had made a mess of his life. Yet, although T. S. Eliot resisted the family pattern he also followed it, first as a poor clerk like his father in the early Mississippi days and, later, when he became a publisher, as a successful man of business. To the end of his life he faithfully performed the kind of responsible daily labour that had been, for generations, the self-affirming activity of the Eliot family.

Bred in a family which belongs at the very heart of Boston Unitarianism, Eliot's fervent nature found no nourishment there and, by the time he enrolled at Harvard, he had become completely indifferent to the Church.[42] The religion taught by William Greenleaf Eliot was morally strict rather than spiritual. He was not concerned with perfection, or doctrine, or theology, but with a code that would better the lot of humanity. He passed on to his children and grandchildren a religion which retained Puritan uprightness, social conscience, and self-restraint, but which had been transformed by the Enlightenment. T. S. Eliot was taught to be dutiful, benevolent, and cheerful. He was always acutely sensitive to the sinister power of evil, but was taught a practical common-sense code of conduct. Eliot once mentioned that his parents did not talk of good and evil but of what was 'done' and 'not done'.[43] In abandoning Unitarianism, Eliot

rebelled against those tepid, unemotional distinctions. 'So far as
we are human', he wrote, 'what we do must be either evil or
good.'[44] Like Jonathan Edwards, who had rebelled in the first
half of the eighteenth century against religion tamed into a
respectable code and had re-evoked the fervent religion of the
previous century, so T. S. Eliot in the first half of the twentieth
century sought out an older, stronger discipline, unmitigated by
nineteenth-century liberalism. Edwards and Eliot each seemed,
to his own time, an isolated reactionary.

Unitarianism arose in America in the mid-eighteenth century,
during the Great Awakening, in opposition to the old Puritan
conviction of man's innate sinfulness. The Unitarians were
confident of man's innate nobility (Channing spoke of man's
'likeness to God'). They rejected the Puritans' doctrine of
damnation, their tests of orthodoxy and heresy, and their undemo-
cratic distinctions between church members. They saw God as
benevolent not wrathful. The year before T. S. Eliot was born,
his mother was praising a benign, rational universe in her poem,
'Force and God':

> While worlds harmonious move in breathless awe
> We whisper 'God is here, and God is Law.'[45]

In view of the sincere piety of Eliot's mother and grandfather
and his father's lifelong support of the Unitarian Church, it may
seem odd that he should have come to think of himself as one
brought up 'outside the Christian Fold'.[46] But it is strictly true
in terms of the Unitarians' denial of the Trinity as against Eliot's
personal definition of Christianity as a belief in the Incarnation.[47]
In 1931 Eliot wrote to Middleton Murry that the perfection of
a Lord who was merely human did not seem to him perfection
at all.[48] He disliked 'the intellectual and puritanical rationalism'
of his early environment.[49] In his redefinition of the Christian
experience in terms of human need and desperate faith, in his
revival of ideas of depravity and damnation, in his craving for
orthodoxy, Eliot opposed his Unitarian background. Probably
the most important difference was his sense of man's unlikeness,
his distance from an unknowable deity.

Eliot said that to understand a modern writer it is necessary
to classify him according to the type of decayed Protestantism
which surrounded his childhood. Already in the 1830s Emerson

resigned his pulpit in protest against 'corpse-cold Unitarianism'. The Transcendentalists of the 1840s liberated themselves from formal Christianity and trusted, like Emerson, in the private light, but the next generation found themselves, as one historian puts it, 'in a chilling void. . . . The heir of Emerson was Henry Adams who turned away from the barren chaos of American life to the certitudes of Dante and St. Thomas; and after Henry Adams came T. S. Eliot who not only admired the lost traditions of Catholicism from a distance, but made a heroic attempt to recapture them.'[50]

For sensitive Unitarian children growing up in America in the nineteenth century, the bland surface presented by their religion must have seemed to resist too much of life. Eliot himself made only passing critical comments, but Henry Adams's analysis of the insufficiencies of Unitarianism suggests what Eliot reacted against:

Nothing quieted doubt so completely as the mental calm of the Unitarian clergy. . . . They proclaimed as their merit that they insisted on no doctrine, but taught . . . the means of leading a virtuous, useful, unselfish life, which they held to be sufficient for salvation. For them, difficulties might be ignored; doubts were a waste of thought . . . Boston had solved the universe . . . The religious instinct had vanished, and could not be revived, although one made in later life many efforts to recover it. . . . That the most intelligent society, led by the most intelligent clergy, in the most moral conditions he ever knew, should have . . . quite ceased making itself anxious about past and future'. . . . seemed to him the most curious social phenomenon he had to account for in a long life.[51]

The Unitarian code, with its optimistic notion of progress ('onward and upward forever' Eliot said as a graduate student[52]), glossed over unpleasant changes in American life, particularly after the Civil War. Walt Whitman, commenting on a widespread 'hollowness at heart', wrote: 'The great cities reek with respectable as much as non-respectable robbery and scoundrelism. . . . A sort of dry and flat Sahara appears, these cities, crowded with petty grotesques, malformations, phantoms . . .' with manners 'probably the meanest to be seen in the world.'[53] The authority of the class to which Adams and Eliot belonged, genteel responsible descendants of the Puritans, was superseded by the new power of the business moguls. In St. Louis the moral

law of William Greenleaf Eliot was ousted by the motive of
profit, and in 1902 the city's corruption was scandalously exposed.
Eliot was sensitive to the monotony that resulted from immense
industrial expansion at the end of the nineteenth century and to
the loss of native (New England) culture[54] to a new America in
which, as he put it, Theodore Roosevelt was a patron of the
arts. The muscular Virginian was the popular hero during Eliot's
adolescence, not Lambert Strether. Eliot belonged naturally to
an older America, before 1830 he said, when the country seemed
like 'a family extension'.[55]

Eliot had a remarkably happy childhood and during his
adolescence his mother was likely to have protected him as far
as possible from these jarring aspects of the new America. It is
necessary to look rather to the more trying years that followed
in Boston to explain why Eliot came to feel oppressed by the
American scene and sought to escape it.

2. *A New England Student*

ABOUT the same time that Eliot graduated from Harvard College, while walking one day in Boston, he saw the streets suddenly shrink and divide.* His everyday preoccupations, his past, all the claims of the future fell away and he was enfolded in a great silence. In June 1910 he wrote a poem he never published called 'Silence', his first and perhaps most lucid description of the timeless moment. Eliot's intuition in the noisy street is similar to Emerson's on the common when he felt 'glad to the brink of fear.'[1] At the age of twenty-one Eliot had one of those experiences which, he said, many have had once or twice in their lives and been unable to put into words.[2] 'You may call it communion with the Divine or you may call it temporary crystallization of the mind', he said on another occasion.[3] For some, such a moment is part of an orthodox religious life, for others—like Emerson—it is terminal, sufficient in itself, and gratefully received. For Eliot, however, the memory of bliss was to remain a kind of torment, a mocking reminder through the years that followed that there was an area of experience just beyond his grasp, which contemporary images of life could not compass.

In 'Silence' Eliot declared that this was the moment for which he had waited. Silence came to a prepared mind and, with the help of Eliot's Notebook, it is possible to trace the course of this preparation during the undergraduate years in Cambridge, Massachusetts. Through his mother, in particular, Eliot was steeped in Emersonian thinking which gave final authority to the individual's private light (there is nothing else beside, Eliot wrote in 'Silence'). During the formative years in New England this background was reinforced by Eliot's solitary habits, by his discovery of the alienated voice of nineteenth-century French poets, and by his growing distrust of family norms, Harvard clichés, and Boston manners. The Boston of Eliot's youth was no

---

* This is a paraphrase of an unpublished poem, dated June 1910, called 'Silence'. All the unpublished poems referred to in this and the following chapters are to be found in Eliot's Notebook and folder of miscellaneous manuscripts in the Berg Collection, New York Public Library. Eliot has dated most of these poems.

longer what Henry James termed the 'old Boston' governed
by Puritan conscience, but a society in decline.[4] Eliot deplored
turn-of-the-century Boston—as he would probably have deplored any city that he happened to be in at the time—but he was
not unaffected by its gentility, its high-mindedness, its provincial
avidity for culture, experience, and Europe.

Eliot was one of those rare beings who have a sense of their
own age when its images are yet incomplete and secret. He
salvaged from Boston's society and slums a certain sense of his
time and place which he projected in his juvenilia, in 'Prufrock',
in the 'Preludes', and even in *The Waste Land*. Eliot reacted against
an emotional inertia, a moral blight, and in *The Waste Land*
located it in England after the First World War. That war *did*
provide a 'waste land' experience, but its dramatic reality for
Eliot belonged to his youth in America at the beginning of the
century.

John Jay Chapman, a contemporary critic, located the blight
in the pervasiveness of the commercial mind in America, which
was, he said, indifferent to truth, to love, and to religion—all
things, in fact, Eliot tried to recover. 'I regret', wrote Chapman,
'the loss of the old cultivation; and yet I know that none of our
older cultivation was ever quite right. The American has never
lived from quite the right place in his bosom.'[5] This was not a
new idea. It had certainly perturbed Hawthorne, Mark Twain,
and James. But in Eliot's case it was to lead him to a new
imagined order, totally outside the American experience, based
on royalism, classicism, and Anglo-Catholicism.

Eliot first knew it as a mood that gradually engulfed Eastern
society after the Civil War. Richard Hofstadter defined it as a loss
of assertiveness. Eliot's class lost its moral leadership to men whose
energies were the greater, the less they wasted on thought. To
illustrate the demoralization of cultivated men, Hofstadter
quoted from *The Bostonians*: 'a nervous, hysterical, chattering,
canting age, an age of hollow phrases and false delicacy and
exaggerated solicitudes and coddled sensibilities which, if we
don't look out, will usher in the reign of mediocrity, of the
feeblest and flattest and most pretentious that has ever been.'[6]
Eliot knew this particular flatness first-hand, and suffered himself from the inertia of his class.

St. Louis had not much bothered Eliot. Its energetic vulgarity

1. William Greenleaf Eliot (1811–87). 'The standard of conduct was that which my grandfather had set'

2. Charlotte Champe Eliot in St. Louis, 1881. Her poetry mapped the states between loss and recovery of faith

did not pose to his particular temperament a serious threat or temptation. Boston, on the other hand, was unhealthy. 'I loathe mankind', said Henry Adams, and he blamed Boston. 'Indeed Boston cankers our hearts. I feel it in me. . . . I recognize the strange disease.'[7] Eliot lived during his most formative years in a city whose heart and life had become defective. The political and moral power of its oldest and most distinguished citizens, the descendents of the Puritans, had been displaced by great commercial corporations. The Brahmins' cultural life had been challenged by an invasion of immigrants. To Santayana the source of cultural deadness lay in the Brahmins' tenacious gentility: 'Serious poetry, profound religion (Calvinism, for instance), are the joys of an unhappiness that confesses itself; but when a genteel tradition forbids people to confess that they are unhappy, serious poetry and profound religion are closed to them by that.'[8] Their evil was vulgarity. Behaviour fascinated them. In Back Bay innumerable windows watched one another hopelessly for revelations and indiscretions which never disturbed the peace.[9] The smug righteousness and propriety of Beacon Street, of the Eliots, Millses, Bullards, Coolidges, and Parkmans was the triumph of a bourgeoisie without the shadow of an aristocracy to worry it. 'I yearn', said Henry Adams in 1906, 'for St. Simeon Stylites or sin.'[10]

Eliot was put immediately in personal touch with Boston society through his uncle, Christopher Rhodes Eliot, a prominent Unitarian minister, and the branch of the Eliot family which had remained in the city and flourished in its public affairs. He was related to Charles W. Eliot who was then president of Harvard and whose father had been mayor of Boston and a congressman. The latter, Samuel Atkins Eliot, was connected by marriage with the inner circle of Boston society, for his one sister married Andrews Norton and another, George Ticknor. Later, Eliot recalled his impressions of Bostonians in a few poems.[11] There is 'Cousin Nancy' who rebels rather awkwardly against her genteel aunts. It is not a passionate Puritan rebellion but a thinner kind, involving arid acts of will, smoking, drinking, riding the New England hills until she 'broke them'. On the library shelves favourite nineteenth-century authors, Emerson and Arnold, sanction the gentility of the aunts and the self-expression of the girl. There is, too, the rich spinster, 'Miss Helen Slingsby', who

lives in a fashionable area of the city and contrives all her life to
shut out the world by observing the secret codes of her milieu.
The important things are her four servants, her small house
(mansions are vulgar), her pets, her Dresden clock. Eliot, who
had been brought up to his grandfather's ideals of unselfish
service to the community, was struck by the absurdity of this
lady's oblivious, self-serving habits. Finally, there is 'Cousin
Harriet' to whom the young Eliot delivers the *Boston Evening
Transcript*, her substitute for life. The youth, parting mentally
from La Rochefoucauld, is rather worn, as though traversing
the Boston street were like wading through time.

A society 'quite uncivilized', Eliot called it, 'but refined beyond
the point of civilization'.[12] To some extent he mastered Boston by
understanding it; he felt aversion for it, but aversion did not
mean he was immune. He took upon himself, perhaps involun-
tarily, the character of late nineteenth-century Boston. He took
on its rigid manners, its loss of vigour, its estrangement from so
many areas of life, its painful self-consciousness. Adams said of
his generation, whose influence presided over Boston when Eliot
arrived there, that there existed only one mind and nature and that
the only differences lay in 'degrees of egotism'. 'We looked through
each other like microscopes. There was absolutely nothing in us
that we did not understand merely by looking in the eye. There
was hardly a difference in depth for Harvard College and Unitarianism kept us all shallow. We knew nothing—no! but really
nothing! of the world . . . God knows that we knew our want of
knowledge! the self-distrust became introspection—nervous self-
consciousness—irritable dislike of America, and antipathy to
Boston. . . . Improvised Europeans, we were, and—Lord God!
—how thin!'[13]

Failing to find life amongst his own class Eliot sought out the
slum areas. He later said that 'the contemplation of the horrid or
sordid or disgusting by an artist, is the necessary and negative
aspect of the impulse toward the pursuit of beauty. The negative
is the more importunate.'[14] In Roxbury, then, and North Cambridge,* Eliot deliberately courted squalour, but found that as
life-destroying as the well-to-do Boston squares. He was physically repelled by smells and depressed by slums. In St. Louis the

---

* Eliot's first three Preludes were originally called 'Preludes in Roxbury'. North
Cambridge was the scene of a series of 'Caprices'.

darker and grimmer aspects of the city had passed him by; in Boston, for the first time, he conceived a horror of the commercial city, its clutter and the sordid patience of its dwellers. In his unpublished 'Caprices in North Cambridge', a series rather like the 'Preludes', he described bottles, broken glass, dirty window panes, trampled mud mixed with grass, broken barrows, and tatty sparrows scratching in the gutter. His mind came to rest, with a curious sense of repose, on vacant lots filled with the city's debris, ashes, tins, bricks, and tiles. He was both horrified and, in a way, engaged. It seemed a far world from his studies, the neat definitions and laws he was piling up at college, but it touched him as Harvard did not. It was his first image of a waste land, a scene he was to make his own.

Although the transition from St. Louis to Boston changed Eliot, Harvard itself barely touched him, except to provide a secure cocoon. Only two teachers broke into his private world and touched a responsive growth: Irving Babbitt who helped him to become truly cultivated and Dean Briggs who used to read, with great persuasiveness and charm, the verse of Donne to freshmen.

Eliot did not ever comment on social life at Harvard, but other men who knew it during the presidency of Charles W. Eliot (1870–1909) seem to converge on a notion of coldness. To John Jay Chapman, President Eliot was the father of a 'glacial era' in Cambridge. Henry Adams, explaining his reasons for resigning his professorship, wrote that Cambridge was a social desert that would have starved a polar bear. Cambridge lacked the social idea. Professors were encouraged to make observations but not to converse. 'The liveliest and most agreeable men—James Russell Lowell, Louis Aggassiz, John Fiske, William James, who would have made the joy of London or Paris—tried their best to break out and be like other men . . . but society called them professors and professors they had to be. . . . Society was a faculty meeting without business.'[15]

When Bertrand Russell came to Harvard as a visiting professor (while Eliot was a graduate student) he found his colleagues impossibly pompous and laborious. Eliot satirized them and their relation to Russell in his poem, 'Mr. Apollinax'. The scene is a country house where he and Russell were guests of a snob

called Fuller whom Russell despised because he and his mother
aped the English manner. Eliot gleefully described Russell's
assault on the gentility of the professor's tea-party with his
passionate talk, his grinning foetus face, and easy laughter.
The dowager 'Mrs. Phlaccus' and the Professor and Mrs. 'Chan-
ning-Cheetah', bewildered but at all costs correct, concentrate
on lemon slices and bitten macaroons. Eliot immediately allied
himself with the alien. In his imagination the shy man among the
birch trees and the amorous gentleman were united in a frivolous
eighteenth-century pastoral by Fragonard. Russell quickly
recognized the allegiance. 'My pupil Eliot was there', he wrote
home afterwards, '—the only one who is civilized.'[16]

In Eliot's time students at Harvard did not live in dormitories,
and got together solely through clubs. Eliot conformed, he
lived in the approved affluent area of Cambridge called the 'Gold
Coast' and joined numerous clubs, but he experienced little of the
charms of enlightened companionship. He roomed with a
plump friend from Milton Academy, Howard Morris, who loved
to eat and drink, and had few literary interests.[17] 'Triflers' abounded,
young men who were satisfied with the 'gentleman's C' and took
four-day weekends in New York. The *Advocate*'s staff provided,
at best, 'hilarity', while the Southern Club seemed a 'drinking and
poker hell'. But he thought he had to discipline himself so as not
to miss experiences he did not naturally take to.[18] He dutifully
joined the Digamma, a social club, and went to a few initiations
and punch nights. Occasionally, tall, sybilline, and attractive,
but rather shy, he appeared at Buckingham and Brattle Hall
dances. More often he visited the Signet, a literary club, attended
editorial meetings with rum tea in the *Advocate*'s sanctum at the
top of the Union, and read in their small library to the perpetual
sound of Debussy on the piano. To most students, however,
Eliot was a bit of a recluse, studiously preoccupied in his room in
Russell Hall, Holyoke House, or Apley Court. And he always
immured himself behind a 'somewhat Lamian smile'.

It pleased Eliot to have been, as he saw it, an isolated cultural
phenomenon:

What the help and encouragement of men of an older generation may
be like, what it feels like, what useful stimulus or perhaps misdirection
it may give, I do not know. At a time which may be symbolized by the
figures 1910, there was literally no-one to whom one would have dreamt

of applying. One learnt something, no doubt, from Henry James, and might have learnt more. . . . As for other writers then rising to celebrity . . . they lived in another world altogether.*

In the *Paris Review* interview he recalled that he had read Yeats 'but it was the early Yeats. It was too much Celtic Twilight for me. There was really nothing except the people of the 90's who had all died of drink or suicide or one thing or another.' W. G. Tinckom-Fernandez, a fellow-editor of the *Advocate*, showed Eliot some verse by Pound, *Exultations* and *Personae*. Eliot was not impressed: 'It seemed to me rather fancy old-fashioned romantic stuff, cloak and dagger kind of stuff.'

Apart from two or three teachers and some brilliant instruction in reading Dante in Italian, Harvard was not particularly stimulating. The educational bias then was encouraging to scientists (Eliot took no science courses), while the humanities suffered from President Eliot's notion that cultivation was for women. 'Art is left to languish and die', wrote Eliot's brother, Henry Ware Eliot, Jr., in 1902.† 'The study of classics is practically dead at Harvard', wrote his cousin, Fred Eliot, in 1910—dead because they never helped build better bridges, or manipulate a market, or win battles. To the average undergraduate it was simply 'not a man's work'.[19] All that was necessary for cultivation, decreed President Eliot, could be found on a five-foot shelf.

In the English department Copeland, whose composition course Eliot took in 1908–9, taught histrionic effects and an entertaining, journalistic style. Eliot was one of a minority—which included Conrad Aiken, Dos Passos, Van Wyck Brooks, and Santayana—out of sympathy with his tastes. 'I never really hit it off with him', Eliot recalled. The feeling was mutual. Copeland regarded his pupil's literary fastidiousness with irritable incomprehension. 'Youthful rashness', Copeland told him, 'is not likely to be one of your attributes till you are middle-aged.'[20]

In the philosophy department Eliot remained impervious to William James's optimism, his faith in men's agency, his version of truth as relative rather than absolute. William James's *Pragmatism* was one of the important books published while Eliot was

* T. S. Eliot's 'Views and Reviews' column in *NEW* (12 Sept. 1935), pp. 351–2. The writers he referred to were Shaw, Wells, and Chesterton.

† The line is from a parody of Charles Eliot Norton, Professor of Fine Arts, now in the Eliot Collection, Harvard. Norton points feebly to Ruskin and Rossetti but a herd of collegiates rushes past him, entranced with 'brutal sports'.

at Harvard but Eliot remained unimpressed. In 1914 he said that the error of pragmatism was making man the measure of all things.[21] His courses with Palmer and Santayana were probably more useful to him. Palmer taught pre-Socratic philosophy, and introduced him to Heraclitus. Eliot noted the idea that the highest good was a combination of the greatest intellectual activity and the greatest receptivity to the divine around us.[22] Santayana was unusual with his supercivilized bearing and his classes so small and select that President Eliot inquired into their exclusiveness. Santayana had rejected the dogma of the Catholic Church, but he may have passed on to his student his admiration for rituals and forms he thought very beautiful.

At the same time as Eliot took an advanced course with Santayana in the autumn of 1909, he took a course in French literary criticism with Irving Babbitt. Babbitt used to make his class read widely in the classics of the past and he alerted them to the dangers of the modern secular world. Eliot later criticized Babbitt for not being a believer and deplored the inadequacy of his humanism, yet Eliot admitted that he had yet been an auxiliary to religion, for he had suggested to the students that the Catholic Church might perhaps be the only institution left in the West that might be counted on to preserve the treasures of the past. If one followed him to the end, said Eliot, one came to 'a Catholicism of despair'.[23]

In November 1909 Eliot produced a new batch of poems. They were the result of private reading and emotions, but perhaps the lonely cultivation and intellectual intransigence of his two great teachers fortified him. For a long time he remembered Babbitt as a man who had been 'very often right quite alone'.[24]

During his summer vacation in East Gloucester in 1910 Eliot decided to collect his unpublished poems. He bought a marbled notebook from the Old Corner Bookstore, inscribed his title in decorated capitals—INVENTIONS OF THE MARCH HARE—and copied in the more experimental poems he had been writing since November 1909.* (He did not include his earlier poems, those published in the *Advocate*.) He continued to use the Notebook

---

* The first poems in the Notebook were copied in at the same time i.e. in the same hand and blue ink. The latest is dated Aug. 1910. The poems were later revised in pencil and dates added.

during the following year in Paris, on his return to Harvard and, finally, on arrival in London in 1914. He also maintained a loose collection of rough drafts and of typescripts of poems composed after he acquired his own typewriter in about 1913–14. With extraordinary patience and self-restraint Eliot hoarded many poems—some very fine—without attempting publication. In 1914 Pound was amazed to come across a young American who had trained and modernized himself entirely on his own. Even in the first batch of poems, those that preceded his visit to Paris in 1910–11, his sense of the essential issues of his life is already clear-cut. Two great poems that followed in 1910–11, 'Portrait of a Lady', and 'The Love Song of J. Alfred Prufrock', give these issues a more mature formulation and a more sophisticated fictional setting.

From the first Eliot took up the task of recording the private habits of mind, the fears and the solitary impulses that led him to a religious position. That position became a serious alternative only in about 1914, but many of the earlier poems, particularly the unpublished pieces, record an underground phase of religious searching, a slow incubation and maturing of motives. 'Towards any profound conviction', said Eliot, 'one is borne gradually, perhaps insensibly over a long period of time, by what Newman called "powerful and concurrent reasons".'[25] At the end of his student years, in 'The Love Song of Saint Sebastian' and in 'The Death of Saint Narcissus' Eliot toyed with the role of martyr, emphasizing the martyr's abandonment of the ways of other men. The 'saint' as a person was ridiculous, but his impulse of worship was serious. Eliot was gradually formulating a choice all through his juvenilia. He set up the notion of an Absolute or Pure Idea or Soul over against ordinary experience. His strategy was to prove to himself that women, time, society were the Absolute's enemies (although he scrupulously acknowledged the pomposity of the project and always guarded himself with self-mocking humour). In 'Conversation Galante' (November 1909) he indicted the woman as 'the eternal enemy of the Absolute'. In 'Spleen' (January 1910) he turned his back on the tedious habits of Sunday church-going and waited impatiently 'on the doorstep of the Absolute.' In another confessional poem of the same month, 'The First Debate between Body and Soul', he called on the Absolute to rescue him from demeaning physical senses. He was rewarded, not immediately, but six months later, by his experience of Silence in the Boston street.

The debate shows Eliot's state of mind more clearly than any other poem of the undergraduate period. He feels the sanctuary of the soul is violated both by the insistent material facts about him —twenty leering houses in a shabby Boston square, the wheezing street piano, a blind old man who coughs and spits—and by the distractions of his own physical life—defecations, masturbations, and a useless supersubtle brain. He would like to dispose of a multiplicity of mundane observations with one pure Idea. His mother's high-minded appeals in her poems to 'loose the spirit from its mesh, / From the poor vesture of the flesh' provided Eliot with the unacknowledged standard against which, in poem after poem, he would list his quarrels with the world of sense.[26] Driven by an as yet vague and inherited notion of perfection, Eliot made body and soul enemies and set up the uncompromising dichotomy that ordered his early life.

In Eliot's mind perfection was only dimly conceived, while the enemies of perfection were quickly identified and reviled. For Eliot, time was the first enemy: at sixteen he wrote, 'For time is time, and runs away.' He started his poetic career with the smell of decay in his nostrils. Almost before he felt desire, he watched its bloom fade. In all three of the first poems he published in the *Advocate* blooming and withering flowers are the images of love, and the fragrance of decay interweaves with the fragrance of bloom.[27] Even before love's dawn, the young man notices that the leaves in the woman's wreath are already brown.[28] Lines he wrote many years later in 'Salutation', about the rose of love with its worm-eaten petals, suggest that to satisfy love was to spoil it forever.* Quite independently, without as yet the mediation of the French symbolists, he came upon Poe's fragile world poised on the brink of dissolution and upon grim nostalgia like Laforgue's, a youth writing as if youth were already reminiscent of itself, so conscious was he that time was passing. At the end of an unpublished poem, 'Opera', written in November 1909, he said that he felt like the ghost of youth at an undertakers' ball. It would be easy to dismiss Eliot's juvenile melancholy as no more than a *fin de siècle* routine. But for Eliot a horror of time and decay was real: it blew up later, in an unpublished section of 'Prufrock',

---

* *Criterion*, 7 (Jan. 1928), 31–2. This poem, revised, became part of AW.

into a prophetic vision of the world dissolving. Later yet it was the impulse behind 'Whispers of Immortality', and behind the falling towers of London, Jerusalem, Alexandria, Athens, and Vienna in *The Waste Land*. It was logical that he should come to feel, eventually, that the temporal world had to be transcended.

The next opponent of perfection was less abstract, more immediately formidable: women. In each of the poems written in 1908 and 1909 a woman manages to humble a man in a different way. First there is Circe who cultivates deadly flowers, very different from the delicate flowers he had previously imagined. Her flowers are fanged and red. Her fountain flows with the sound of men in pain. A snake lies sluggish along the garden stairs.[29] The sinister and emasculating witch who presides over this garden of experience gathers strength from Madeline Usher and Rappaccini's daughter, who radiate an energy that Poe and Hawthorne regard as dangerous, perverse, or abnormal. Male American writers (with the notable exception of James) do not readily conceive heroines with the depth and humanity they regularly accord to their great heroes.* Eliot's earliest heroines followed a tradition in which women exist as stereotypes of poison or saccharine, devouring energy or sickly pallor. His Circe appeared by November 1908. By January 1909 he had already created the traditional counterpoise: a pale white woman, thin as a sea-mist, fragile as a moonflower, elusive as a snowy owl.[30] Her escort, like poor Arthur Dimmesdale, has momentary regrets for the Circe spirit. 'Have you no brighter tropic flowers', he groans, 'with scarlet life for me?'

Turning irritably from one extreme possibility to another, Eliot studied women, it seems, from a literary distance. The distance was supported partly by his own inhibition, partly by a society in which the sexes were artificially separated. In the Long Island house of Theodore Roosevelt rooms full of horns, tusks, and other hunter's trophies alternated with rooms full of fragile tea cups and fussy upholstery. There was no overlap, no meeting ground. As a child Eliot knew girls (apart from his older sisters) as creatures on the other side of a wall that separated his parents'

* Fiedler, discussing the perfunctory and forced cataloguing of females according to stereotype, adds, 'Surely these are portrayals prompted by a secret hate!' *Love and Death in the American Novel* (1960; rpr. N.Y.: Dell, 1967, London: Secker, 1961), p. 292.

house from the Mary Institute. He used to sneak into the school-yard to play when they were gone. On one occasion he arrived too early and, when he saw some girls staring at him through a window, fled at once. He remained 'extremely shy' with girls.[31] Yet, of course, there were many spirited, humane, and active women around Eliot in his youth, not least his own mother, his clever eldest sister, Ada (who he often said was the Mycroft to his Sherlock Holmes), and his Boston cousins, Martha and Abigail. It is puzzling that the women closest to Eliot in no way shaped his judgement of their sex. In his early sonnet 'On A Portrait' (it was Manet's *La Femme au perroquet* which hung in a friend's drawingroom) Eliot chose to write about woman as a baffling and alien creature, frozen in an image, with exotic secrets but no ideas. 'Beyond the circle of our thought she stands', wrote Eliot in January 1909.[32]

Again and again in his student poems—in 'Conversation Galante', in 'Circe's Palace', in 'Portrait of a Lady', and in 'Prufrock'—Eliot caricatured his embarrassing friendship with an emotional older woman, Adeleine (or Madeleine) Moffat, who used to serve tea to Harvard men in a home crowded with bric-a-brac, behind Boston's State House. Conrad Aiken, who sometimes accompanied Eliot to these teas, recalled the 'oh so precious the oh so exquisite, Madeleine, the Jamesian lady of ladies, the enchantress of the Beacon Hill drawingroom—who, like another Circe, had made strange shapes of Wild Michael and the Tsetse (T. S. Eliot)'.[33] Adeleine is so elusive in Eliot's poems because he does not strive to elicit her character, in the manner say of James, but immediately fits her to a variety of female stereotypes—the gushy romantic, the dangerous enchantress, the languid socialite. The interest of these poems lies not in the woman but in her effect on the potential lover. He is uneasily aware that the woman points up his pallid appetite for what others might readily desire but is, at the same time, defensively scornful of her taste, conversation, and brains. Prufrock has fleeting erotic sensations—the perfume from the woman's dress or her arms moving to wrap her shawl or throw it off can whip his attention from his foggy self-absorption—but she is not capable of a real exchange and is therefore unworthy of his confession. In 'Portrait' the youth finds himself set to act in a darkened room with candles. He is ill at ease and bored (with the 'tom-tom' of a headache coming on), but it seems a reasonable reaction to absurd romantic clichés. When he saw *Tristan* in 1909 Eliot felt irritated by the lovers' passionate extravagance. It seemed to him so futile, that in the end life itself departs with a feeble smile.[34]

The characteristic irritability of Eliot's pieces on women was the rankling of inhibition compounded by a Jamesian fear of having dared too little. In 'Portrait of a Lady' the young man struggles to preserve his self-possession against the tide of an emotion that makes him queasy. Eliot's fastidiousness was not a sign of diminished sexuality, but the result of inhibitions caused, in the first place, by a distrust of women. Subtle and Jamesian in his analyses of gentlemen's consciousnesses, Eliot lacked insight when it came to women. There is no empirical interest here, as he deals out cultural and literary clichés. In 'Conversation Galante' (November 1909),[35] 'Humoresque' (November 1909),[36] and the unpublished 'Convictions' (January 1910) Eliot tries to demonstrate in dramatic scenes the shoddiness of women's minds and the poverty of their conversation. He places his women in sentimental situations, beneath a moon, surrounded by tissue-paper roses, exchanging the usual banalities, compliments, guesses, and promises—only the moon is bored and the conversation monotonous. He imagines in these poems a twittering, self-absorbed woman yearning to engulf a man in emotional claims and tells us in one of these early pieces that female readers drip tears of sentimental gratification at such scenes.

Another reason for Eliot's inhibition was possibly his father's view of sex as 'nastiness'. Henry Ware Sr. considered public instruction tantamount to giving children a letter of introduction to the Devil. Syphilis was God's punishment and he hoped a cure would never be found. Otherwise, he said, it might be necessary 'to emasculate our children to keep them clean'.[37] How far such an attitude affected his son is impossible to know, but later in life Eliot called the sex act evil though tempered this by saying that sex as evil was less boring than the natural cheery automatism of his contemporaries.[38]

The sexual instinct and associated sense of sin, flickering rather half-heartedly in Eliot's undergraduate years, came suddenly to life sometime during his graduate years at Harvard (from 1911 until 1914) when he wrote 'The Love Song of Saint Sebastian'.

A desperate and insecure lover fans his passions with fantasies of violent action which enforces the beloved's attention. In the first fantasy the lover flogs himself at the foot of the lady's stair until his blood flies. She is there watching in a white gown. His martyrdom attracts her attention and, in pity, she calls him to her bed where he dies between her breasts. In the second fantasy the lover's relation to the lady is reversed. This time he is a sexual menace, exerting brute power over the white-clad body he loves. He comes at her with a towel and bends her head beneath his knees, fingering the curve of her ear. When he strangles her— when he sins—she loves him more. As in the case of Browning's 'Porphyria's Lover', the strangler's love is liberated by the act of mutilation which is also a triumphant act of self-assertion and possession. For she will no longer be desirable to anyone else.

A traditional strategy for coping with woman, common in the literature and theology of the West, is to fix her image according to sinner and saint stereotypes, never allowing her full humanity. In *The Waste Land* manuscript Eliot blithely writes off women with their 'unreal emotions and real appetite'; in 'Ash Wednesday' he makes use of idealized figures he might revere, the Rose of memory, the Mother, the enchanted maytime when a girl's sweet brown hair was blown over her mouth, the veiled sister, above all the spotless object of Sebastian's distempered passions:

> The Lady is withdrawn
> In a white gown, to contemplation, in a white gown,
> Let the whiteness of bones atone to forgetfulness.
> There is no life in them.

In 'Ash Wednesday', when God wonders what to do with a penitent's bones, the Lady intercedes and her 'goodness' saves them. When Dante said of Beatrice 'imparadisa la mia mente' it is easy to believe a woman should have enlarged his spirit, for he sees her as a person. Eliot's divine Lady seems artificial because, from her first appearances in 'The Love Song of Saint Sebastian' and 'La Figlia che Piange', her true character is submerged in images of untouchable purity.

One day, in December 1908, Eliot went into the library of the Harvard Union and picked up the newly published second edition of Arthur Symons's *The Symbolist Movement in Literature*. He was immediately struck by Symons's call for a spiritual vision to eclipse the realistic tradition. Art which becomes religion, wrote Symons, may be an escape from time and mortality. He advised poets to wait on every symbol by which 'the soul of things can be made visible'. The sacred task of the poet is to shed the 'old bondage of exteriority' and become a prophet of the unknown, even if to shed externals is to come close to madness. The generation of Freud, Durkheim, Bergson, Croce, William James, and Weber gave prestige to half-glimpsed, half-articulated meaning, whose only logic lay in the emotions. Of that generation, Sir James Frazer, in particular, was to interest Eliot as an elucidator of the 'obscurities of the soul'. But this mood—the growing interest in consciousness—first came to Eliot through Symons who presented the artist in the role of privileged seer.

Arthur Symons's quotations from late nineteenth-century French poets had the effect of a mirror that flashed back to Eliot an image clearer, larger, and more dramatic than anything he had imagined. Particularly in the account of Jules Laforgue, he saw possibilities for himself. A poet, Symons revealed, could be 'eternally grown-up'; he did not have to be a Byronic *enfant terrible* to be a hero. There were others, Eliot discovered, who spoke with mature irony, others whose dreams dissolved in the grim business of the grown-up world. The crucial difference between the poems Eliot wrote before and after he read Symons is that the latter contain at their centre a wilfully defeatist identity.

Immediately Eliot ordered three volumes of Laforgue. The *Œuvres complètes* must have arrived in the spring of 1909, certainly in time for Eliot to read them over the summer, and late in the autumn he began to pour out new poems. From Laforgue, Eliot learnt to broadcast secrets, to confess through the defeatist persona his own despair and, at the same time, to shield himself by playing voices against one another—the wry voice of the sufferer, the scathing or flippant voice of a commentator, the banal voice of a woman. He learnt, too, another confessional strategy useful to a cautious and shy sensibility: to dramatize his most serious ideas as irrational, even ridiculous, emotions.

Laforgue's pierrot inspired Eliot's marionette and clown poems and his 'Conversation Galante' (modelled on 'Autre Complainte de Lord Pierrot', which Symons had quoted in full). They were exercises and not very good ones, but perhaps helped

Eliot to develop his central persona—a performer fixed in his silly role, unable to take command of his real self which is socially unacceptable, outcast, or elusive. Eliot discovered in Laforgue an alienation from the world and from women that accorded with his own feelings:

> Nous nous aimions comme deux fous,
> On s'est quitté sans en parler
> Un spleen me tenait exilé,
> Et ce spleen me tenait de tout. Bon.
>
> ('Solo de lune')

He read about an earth whirling inexplicably and lightly with its rotten cargo of war, suffering, and death and about a solitary loser who invites experience only to spurn it. He spurns especially the unclean couplings of brutes and at the same time suffers through all his nerves ('Souffrir par tous mes nerfs, minutieuse-ment'[39]). He yearns for a perfection which he knows is not to be found in the world in which he lives.

Yet while Eliot learnt from Laforgue, he also transformed that state of mind into something cooler, more relentless, that came from himself.[40] He shared with Laforgue and Baudelaire a power-ful sense of evil and a passionate antagonism towards society, but he did not share their tenderness. The pleasure of hating, said Henry Adams sourly, one's self if no better victim offered, was not the New Englander's rarest amusement. In his early work, at any rate, Eliot was unrelievedly cruel to his characters, and cruellest to himself. Laforgue and Eliot were both given to self-destructive introspection but Eliot's self-disgust was in a class of its own, quite uncompassionate, culminating in that sad joke, 'How unpleasant to meet Mr. Eliot!'*

Laforgue's public style also intrigued Eliot. He proceeded to cultivate the *dandysme* of his hero, the polished image described in Symons's book: 'fort correctes, de haut gibus, des cravates

---

* 'Lines for Cuscuscaraway and Mirza Ali Beg', *CP*, p. 137:

> How unpleasant to meet Mr. Eliot!
> With his features of clerical cut,
> And his brow so grim
> And his mouth so prim
> And his conversation, so nicely
> Restricted to What Precisely
> And If and Perhaps and But.

sobres, des vestons anglais, des pardessus clergyman, et de par les nécessités, un parapluie immuablement placé sous le bras.'[41] Eliot no doubt elaborated his polish in imitation of Laforgue but, as one critic noted, he probably did not have to alter himself that much: 'There was an element of Laforgue already in him: it was easy to progress to the pose from the urbane dandyism, the perfection of dress, manners, and accomplishments, which was the Harvard style of his time and in which he excelled.'[42] 'Manners', wrote Conrad Aiken, 'is an obsolete word nowadays, but he had them. He did things with an enviable grace.'[43]

This public image became, in various guises, Eliot's most useful literary persona. In an unpublished poem, 'Suite Clownesque', he calls himself the first born child of the Absolute, turned out neatly in a flannel suit. With 'Spleen', published in January 1910, he experimented with the image of a middle-aged gentleman whose absurd proprieties impede his advance on some final knowledge:

> And Life, a little bald and gray,
> Languid, fastidious, and bland,
> Waits, hat and gloves in hand,
> Punctilious of tie and suit
> (Somewhat impatient of delay)
> On the doorstep of the Absolute.[44]

The persona was finally perfected in the summer of 1911 when Eliot created the character of J. Alfred Prufrock. In 'Prufrock' the Laforgian split into mocking commentator and droll sufferer is reworked as a split into prophet and groomed conformist. Eliot's prophet-commentator evaluates experience from a withdrawn position, exhorts, mocks, and offers salvation; the conformist suffers the experience, doubts, despairs, and resigns himself to his absurd ties with society.

Although Eliot got his initial clue from Laforgue, he shaped his own persona with materials close at hand. His hero's speech was not the bitter, passionate speech of Laforgue but the understated, sour speech of New England. His *ennui*, associated with fear of action, was the neurosis of late nineteenth-century Boston. Eliot's impulse towards caricature was probably reinforced by a native tradition of burlesque. His comic repertoire—Prufrock wriggling and pinned to the salon wall, broadbottomed Sweeney, the hippo whose voice at mating time is hoarse and odd, the elephant who never forgets*—these versions of the actor-fool are not incompatible with the exaggerated stereotypes of American popular humour. As a student Eliot enjoyed the fad for comic strips, and admired Groucho Marx all his life, even wrote him fan letters. While at Harvard he used to frequent the vaudeville with his friend, Conrad Aiken. 'There was something of the actor in Tom,' wrote Aiken, 'and some of the clown too. For all his liturgical appearance . . . he was capable of real buffoonery.'[45]

Eliot's first batch of poems, written in November 1909, were modelled directly on French poems.[46] Then, in 1910, he suddenly dropped his newly-acquired façades for the autobiographical 'I'. Except for 'Spleen', the 1910 poems were all unpublishable because they fumbled with very strong feelings whose direction was not quite clear to the author. The year 1910, in fact, marked the beginning of a religious ferment and a rebellion against the world's dull conspiracy to tie him to its lifeless customs. These two tendencies moved along side by side but, at the time, the former was only dimly perceived in brief poems, while the latter was definite enough in his mind to lead him to the first radical act that separated him from his family and what they stood for: his decision to live in Paris.

In his last year at Harvard, Eliot badly wanted to get away from it all, from the set scenes of youth, dalliance with women, useless philosophical debates with other students, his family's insistent questions about his future career, his siblings and cousins—all those dutiful grandchildren of William Greenleaf Eliot who were settling into practical, public-spirited careers. His eldest sister, Ada, wrote case studies and worked in the Tombs in New York. Another sister, Marian, was enrolled at Miss Folsom's school for social service in Boston. Of his Boston cousins, Martha was to be a physician—she later specialized in child care and public health—and her sister, Abigail, was going into education—her school in Roxbury was to be the precursor of all 'head-start' programmes for underprivileged children. Their brother, Frederick, was destined for Harvard Divinity School. Another cousin, William Greenleaf Eliot II, was to be,

* Eliot used the elephant on his bookplates. It was also his identity in 'Noctes Binanianae'.

3. Eliot in St. Louis, 1892 or 1893, aged about four

4. Eliot with his father in 1898. Henry Ware Eliot, Sr. died in 1919 thinking that his son had spoilt his life

like his father, a minister in Portland's Unitarian church. In the context of these careers, Tom's decision to go to Paris appeared bizarre to his family. To him Paris might have meant a place where, as a poet, he might feel less at odds with society, and he probably dreamed, like any provincial, of belonging in a great centre of artistic and intellectual innovation. To the average American, however, Paris was for tourists and for female dilettantes to potter at art. American men simply did not go there seriously to live. 'Our people have forgotten', wrote Henry Adams, 'that any world exists outside America and their heads are excessively swelled. . . . One might as well talk about Babylon or Nineveh as about England or France.'[47] Predictably then, Eliot's mother wrote, on 3 April 1910, to her 'dear Boy' expressing her surprise that he had not settled for New York if he wished to write. To her France was incredibly remote and corrupt:

I suppose you will know better in June what you want to do next year. . . . I cannot bear to think of your being alone in Paris, the very words give me a chill. English-speaking countries seem so different from foreign. I do not admire the French nation, and have less confidence in individuals of that race than in English.[48]

Eliot hèld out against this opposition, but in May went down with a mysterious illness. He was hospitalized with suspected scarlet fever and his mother rushed to Boston. It was not serious, but it prevented him from taking his final examinations that spring in comparative literature, fine arts, and French. Nevertheless, on 24 June, he graduated from Harvard, attended the huge garden party in the Yard, sat in Sanders theatre amid the waving fans, and heard the Orator speak of the debt a Harvard man owed to the community and of efficiency as the quality to be cultivated above all others. He heard that he should strive to be a man of affairs like the two presidents of his time, Eliot and A. L. Lowell.[49]

Possibly it was during the next two months of idle summer at Cape Ann that he wrote a series of 'Goldfish' poems about the shifting scenes of family life and friends about him.[50] He was impatient with white flannels, with porcelain teacups at a window, the delicate, sharp outlines of women's gowns, the summer afternoons on the verandah, the waltzes turning on hot August

evenings, The Chocolate Soldier and The Merry Widow, the
sunlight on the sea, the salty days, and boys and girls together.
These pleasures seemed to him trivial, the essence of magazines,
but he thought he might try not to despise them, to make of them
the civilized outlines of a Chinese scene.[51] For himself, he longed
to turn impervious like a mandarin. The mandarin seemed so
enviably at ease in his obese repose. He had the world in his fist,
and could close in on himself. He was not haunted by perfection
nor by any urgent sense of missed experience.

The last of the 'Goldfish' poems describes a cleaning-up
session in October. Jumbled amongst the debris of the past
academic year, the old letters, bills, photos, programmes, and
tennis shoes in a bureau drawer, the poet comes upon a poem,
'Barcarolle', which haunts him with neurotic memories, rising
like waves, as he paces the shore. The following three leaves in the
Notebook which possibly contained 'Barcarolle' were excised.
The next poem transcribed into the Notebook is 'Portrait of a
Lady' and one wonders whether 'Barcarolle' could have been an
early version or, at any rate, also associated with the uneasy
attachment to Adeleine.*

Eliot's 1910 poems are mostly rejections of family and Boston
life, but he also recorded two experiences that struck a different
note. In 'Easter: Sensations of April' (April 1910), the smell of
some geraniums on a third floor sill calls up a long-forgotten
scene, perhaps in Missouri, a little black girl across the alley with
a red geranium in her hands that she has brought from church.
He imagines her obedient prayers and thinks wistfully—she was
very sure of God. Eliot's Easter poem is insignificant as poetry,
but it marks his growing distance from his family's religious
certainties—and his nostalgia for them. His mother wrote
numerous Easter/Spring poems promising the waking of the
spirit to 'the new life in its blessedness'. For her son the spring
only mocked his failures of faith.

Then in June there came the indescribable Silence in the midst
of the clatter of graduation, the exhortations of practical
men, the questions of parents, the frivolity of millinery and

---

* It was Eliot's habit to rework unsatisfactory fragments rather than discard them.
'Barcarolle' could have been the original of Part II of 'Portrait' (dated by Eliot,
Feb. 1910). The other two parts were written much later and the Notebook shows
that the present Part I was originally numbered 'II'.

strawberries in the Yard. Suddenly able to shed the world, he experienced a fugitive sensation of peace that he would try all his life to recapture. Eliot once said that his mind was naturally inclined to the metaphysical, and any mystical experience which put him in touch with another kind of existence would be treasured and made much of.[52] 'Silence' was the forerunner of later beatific moments in Eliot's work: in the hyacinth garden 'looking into the heart of light, the silence',[53] in the garden of Burnt Norton where the surface of the pool 'glittered out of the heart of light',[54] in the pulse in the arm 'less strong and stronger / . . . more distant than the stars and nearer than the eye'.[55] In each case it seems to him he has received some kind of message that disperses and obliterates ordinary reality, a message he badly needs to interpret. At first, Eliot did not conceive of the religious implications, simply that the Silence was antithetical to the world (perhaps reinforced by Laforgue's invective against the pitiful world and its wretched history: 'And thou, Silence, pardon the Earth; the little madcap hardly knows what she is doing'[56]). The revelation in the spring of 1910 had no immediate repercussions but yet remained the defining experience of his life. His immediate response was close, I think, to that of Hawthorne who distrusted it as a transient sensation, surrounded by the inescapable facts of the material world which could not be shed.*

Yet there was in the spring and summer of 1910 some critical intersection of Eliot's private problems—his social isolation, his uneasiness in Boston, his resentment against women, his fear of time and decay, the encounter with the French poets and Arthur Symons, and the secret wish to know the Absolute. From this intersection one might perhaps locate the beginning of Eliot's own religious journey. For a long time his caution and self-distrust kept him at a stage of religious intimation rather than of surrender and conviction. The latent interest remained balanced against the distractions of his immediate surroundings. During

* In *The Blithedale Romance* the hero suddenly sees through nature's mask and enjoys the novelty. 'But that was all', Hawthorne says. (For Emerson, of course, it would have been everything.) Melville, too, wrote in a letter to Hawthorne: 'This "all" feeling. . . . You must have felt it, lying in the grass on a warm summer's day. Your legs seem to send out shoots into the earth. . . . But what plays mischief with the truth is that men will insist upon the universal application of a temporary feeling or opinion.'

the next year in Paris the recurrence of the Silence provided only a brief escape from his insistent inspections of Parisian squalor and decadence. Yet although Eliot failed to find the truth he sought, his private sense of a special destiny gradually hardened and finally reached a point of articulation in the 'saint' poems at the end of his student years.

3. Beyond Philosophy

HENRY JAMES was intrigued by the fate of solitary Americans who would work out, like Columbus, a conception of the other side of the globe, the world 'imagined always in what one had read and dreamed'.[1] Eliot crossed the Atlantic to an imaginary Paris filled with the spiritual malaise and morbidness of the decadent late nineteenth-century poets he admired. ('La France représentait surtout, à mes yeux, la poésie', he declared many years later.[2]) He planned to 'scrape along' in Paris, and gradually give up English and write in French.[3] In the autumn of 1910 Eliot settled at 9 rue de l'Université, a pension on the Left Bank. Little is known about his personal contacts, except that he once visited Jacques Rivière, an editor of *Nouvelle revue française*. He practised French conversation with Rivière's brother-in-law, Alain-Fournier, and made one personal friend, a medical student called Jean Verdenal (both of whom were to die in the Great War). Eliot once suggested that the best way to know Paris as a place and a tradition would be to cut oneself off from it. 'When I was living there years ago', he added, 'I had only the genuine stimulus of the place, and not the artificial stimulus of the people, as I knew no-one whatever, in the literary and artistic world, as a companion—knew them rather as spectacles, listened to, at rare occasions, but never spoken to.'[4] Eliot made use of this spectatorial distance in his poems, rather like the young Emerson who wrote in his *Journal*, 'I am solitary in the vast society of beings; I consort with no species; I indulge no sympathies. I see the world, human, brute and inanimate nature; I am in the midst of them but not *of* them . . .' Still, Eliot must have expected to be nourished in Paris by the kind of intellectual ferment he had missed in America, and hoped that a poet's inevitable solitude would be, there, a very different thing from the isolation he had known in Boston. Yet the poetry he wrote during 1910 and 1911 suggests he was more isolated than ever.

Paris did not change Eliot very much. He simply imposed upon his observations of the city a point of view already manifest at Harvard, a mixture of horror at the monotonous drabness of the underprivileged and boredom with the smug formulas of academics. A poet in a gloomy garret gazes at the constellations and they do not enlighten him: the universe reverberates with empty abstractions, the Pure Idea and a Place in Life, the relation of life to matter, and the scheme of Vital Force.* From early January to 17 February 1911 Eliot attended seven lectures by the philosopher Henri Bergson at the College de France.[5] He found some of the philosophy suspect—the use Bergson made of biology and psychology, for instance, also his 'somewhat meretricious' promise of immortality—but Eliot drew on Bergson's methodology for new poems in which he cultivated indirect habits of mind. Discard solid intellectual supports, Bergson urged, admit only the fluid consciousness and intuitions in the making.[6]

By February 1911 Eliot was already disillusioned with Paris. Bored with the polite, proper gatherings he had known in Boston, the young traveller had looked forward to his initiation into a sophisticated society. He exhorted himself to have his fling but, as in Boston, the life he sought eluded him. In 'The smoke that gathers blue and sinks . . .' he describes a dinner in a Parisian nightclub which induces only torpor. A lady of indeterminate age, all breast and rings, singing 'Throw your arms around me —Aren't you glad you found me', does not enliven him. Why is he so hard to please, Eliot asks himself.[7] The French sauces, the smoke of rich cigars, the after-dinner liqueurs seem to blanket his perceptions.

When he paced the streets of Paris he saw a grey city, rows of blackened trees, rain dripping from slated roofs into a mess of mud. In 'Fourth Caprice in Montparnasse' he feels faintly amazed that the indifferent plastered houses should have such a resilient life of their own, should so insolently go on without fear of dissolution.

London, which Eliot probably visited briefly in about April, presented a similar drab aspect. He sees Londoners hibernating behind their bricks, shut in by sudden rains, and tied to their routines—tea and marmalade at six.[8] Whatever the city—Boston,

---

* 'Inside the gloom . . .', untitled first draft of holograph poem. All the manuscript poems mentioned in this chapter are amongst Eliot's 'Poems', Berg Coll.

Eliot's handwriting changed during the year he was in Paris. From about November 1910 his neat small hand became large and spiky, with few loops, tall capitals, and long tails. After November 1911 he reverted to a smaller, rounder hand. These changes make it possible to align the undated with the dated holographs.

Paris, London—he saw the same: people who were too apathetic
and inarticulate and undisciplined to hope to escape their dreary
fates.

The exaggerated hopelessness of Eliot's poems may be partially
a literary gesture, but there is always a genuine craving for experience and a fear that experience might so easily pass one by.
Neurotic love-fancies had risen like waves as he had paced the
Cape Ann shore the previous summer; now, in Paris, desires
curl upward again like a wave as he dreams of young Ariadne
abducted by Bacchus. At the same time he longs to escape these
agitating feelings and in his '2nd Debate between the Body and
Soul'* he tells of a ring of silence which closes round him and
seals him off, in a state of beatific security, from the floods of life
that threaten to break like a wave against his skull. There,
momentarily, he cherishes his chrysalis. His soul, he says, lies
still in its cell, sensing its wings, aching to be set free and fearful
it will miss its moment of birth through excessive caution. Contained there, he contemplates the power of some unverbalized,
elusive truth, taking command of it, and then bursting out,
ingenuous and pure.

Throughout his career, from the 'ring of silence' in the Parisian
attic to the 'heart of light' in the English garden of *Four Quartets*,
Eliot tried to understand this brief escape from a time-bound
world. But the wind from beyond the world evaporated too fast,
leaving no trace, and Time began again its remorseless work of
attrition. Ironically, for the brief spell Eliot enjoyed fresh visions
—in 1910 and 1911—he resisted a conventional religious interpretation. Given his sensitivity to human degradation in twentieth-
century cities he could not easily accept the benign enlightened
deity of his family. In his first blasphemous poem ('He said:
this universe is very clear . . .' dated March 1911) God appears to
be a sexual monster, a degenerate female who entraps her victims.
Here he contrasts the enlightened view of the universe, a scientific
ordered structure of atoms and geometric laws, with his own
comic fantasy of an Absolute with arbitrary powers sitting in the
middle of a geometric net like a syphilitic spider.

Eliot looked for the decadent Paris of *Bubu de Montparnasse* and
re-evoked it particularly in 'Interlude: in a Bar' (dated February

---

* I have used the second title which stresses the continuity of Eliot's thought.
The first is 'Bacchus and Ariadne'.

1911) where he observes scarred lives symbolized by dirty, broken fingernails tapping a bar and by floors that soak the dregs from broken glasses. It was not the sophisticated or innovative of Paris who interested him but the prostitutes and *maquereaux* of the Boulevard Sébastopol, the grave façades of the big black buildings which seemed to darken the sidewalks, the garish white arc lights among rows of trees, and the men who nosed after pleasure, especially men who had never known it. Slumming, for Eliot, was no pastime: he took it too seriously. He hunted down decadence, and allowed lust and drunkeness to circle round him, so that he might contemplate with horror a life bereft of morale or dignity.[9]

Eliot began to explore the streets during those hours of the night when they were deserted except for the occasional prostitute or scavenging cat.[10] He, too, was a kind of scavenger, turning over his observations to find some clue to the meaning of life—a rusty spring in a factory yard, the unfathomable eye of a soliciting prostitute, his own eyes peering through the lighted shutters of other people's houses. In 'Rhapsody on a Windy Night' Eliot experimented with Bergson's method of grasping truth not by means of analysis but by casting oneself on a current of immediate perception as it flowed through time. Bergson said:

> I perceive at first, as a crust solidified on the surface, all the perceptions which come to it from the material world. These perceptions are clear, distinct, juxtaposed . . . Next, I notice memories which more or less adhere to these perceptions and which serve to interpret them. These memories have been detached, as it were, from the depth of my personality, drawn to the surface by the perceptions which resemble them; they rest on the surface of my mind without being absolutely myself. Lastly, I feel the stir of tendencies and motor habits—a crowd of virtual actions, more or less firmly bound to these perceptions and memories. All these clearly defined elements appear more distinct from me, the more distinct they are from each other.[11]

Accordingly, in 'Rhapsody', the poet drifts from one hour to the next, while the moonlit street dissolves 'the floors of memory'. The twisted corner of a prostitute's eye reminds him of a twisted branch on a New England beach, the automatic lick of a cat's tongue recalls an old crab gripping the stick held out to him. Finally, the stir of habit takes the poet back to his garret at four in the morning—to his toothbrush on the wall and his shoes neatly at the door. Eliot thought the most important passage in Bergson's work had to do with the difference between 'the heterogeneous qualities which succeed each other in our concrete perception', perceptions which are discontinuous, and an underlying harmony which one should be able to deduce. In an essay on Bergson's philosophy Eliot asks whether reality is to be found in the observer's consciousness or in the material object. And where, he asks, is the one reality to subsume both of these, and can one know it?*

'Rhapsody' marvellously evokes a mood and a state of mind, the poet's almost painful sensitivity to his impressions of the deserted, vaguely sinister streets of Paris after midnight. But, from a philosophical point of view, Eliot's experiment failed: the impressions do not converge, there is no intuition to be seized. I think, behind the poem, lies an Emersonian premise that one might cultivate an angle of vision whereby diverse objects are penetrated and illumined as part of one design. 'What would we really know the meaning of?' Emerson asked. 'The meal in the firkin; the milk in the pan; the ballad in the street; the news of the boat; the glance of the eye; the form and the gait of the body;—show me the ultimate reason of these matters; show me the sublime presence of the highest spiritual cause lurking, as always it does lurk, in these suburbs and extremities of nature . . . and the world lies no longer a dull miscellany and lumber-room, but has form and order; there is no trifle, there is no puzzle, but one design unites and animates the farthest pinnacle and the lowest trench.'[12] Eliot saw the hidden atunement of the universe after his idyllic visit to Burnt Norton in 1935,[13] but in 1911 the sublime design refused to compose itself and the objects fell apart. He wished to find meaning, but could not say, with Emerson's blithe assurance, 'it always does lurk'.

Apart from the poet, there is only one other distinct character in the Paris poems. In 'The Little Passion: From "An Agony in a Garret" ' the poet meets a lost soul in a bar, a man of religious gifts, but damned for his inability to utilize them.† The drunk

---

* Holograph paper, perhaps a lecture, on Bergson, Eliot Coll., Houghton Library. It is not in Eliot's Paris hand and must have been written some time after Eliot's return to Harvard. My guess is 1913 or 1914 since he mentions F. H. Bradley and uses the same paper as that of an address to Harvard's Philosophical Society in 1913 or 1914.

† The first draft is undated, but is written in the spiky Paris hand. A later, more

is aware his soul has been dead a long time, yet continues to waste his energies in futile diving into dark retreats. He knows quite well that the lines of street lights lead inevitably to a cross on which souls are pinned and bleed but, instead of following the lights, he lets them spin round him meaninglessly like a wheel. This first draft of 'The Little Passion', really only fragmentary jottings, is nevertheless a reservoir of themes for some of Eliot's greatest poems. The lost soul in a Parisian bar is the predecessor of those wanderers of the city, those heroes of the wasted passions, J. Alfred Prufrock and Gerontion. The fragment also points to Eliot's martyr poems of 1914 and to the wastefulness of the turning world in the fourth Prelude. It is curious that the path, which in other poems of this period is so tortuous, should lead, in this one case, directly to a Christian terminus.

The '2nd Debate between the Body and Soul' and 'The Little Passion' show Eliot's mind edging beyond 'Silence' and 'The First Debate' towards a religious, even Christian, point of view. In one fragment, 'He said: this crucifixion was dramatic . . .', Eliot imagines for a moment an *imitatio Christi* and then falls back on his own paltry alternatives, on the one hand the Parisian garret, the seedy life of the would-be artist up six dingy flights of stairs or, on the other, the office chair, an equally unenticing inheritance from his businessman father.[14] Eliot posed God briefly as an alternative to an unwanted relationship in 'Entretien dans un parc' (Feb. 1911). He imagines strolling hand-in-hand with a woman up a blind alley, filled with nervous embarrassment in the face of her composure. Then, suddenly, with relief, he thinks how his dusty soul might expand to meet God.

Eliot's poems of 1911 seem to fall into two distinct groups. In the first half of the year, chiefly in February and March, his poems touch on local scenes: a glossy Parisian restaurant, an old man in a bar, the nocturnal life of the street. In the second half of the year and into 1912 Eliot's poems retreat into a private world of the mind, drawn there by some secret hovering on the edge of his consciousness. The hero of the most significant poem of this period, J. Alfred Prufrock, is driven by a secret just beyond his grasp which he terms 'the overwhelming question'.

compact version was written in about 1914 and is the last poem copied into Eliot's Notebook.

Eliot said several years later that a poet should state a vision which includes a coherent formulation of life outside the poem.[15] Eliot did not wish to create a rag-bag of moods, insights, and sensations; he wanted his poetry to terminate in a formulated philosophy and extend, ever further, into a way of life. He decided a poet should realize emotionally and dramatically 'that which constitutes the truth of his time, whatever that may be'. In Paris, in 1911, Eliot witnessed *la ferveur bergsonniene*, and took in the anti-democratic, anti-romantic notions of the *Action Française*, but these did not provide the larger philosophic view he needed. The latter was to come to him eventually from men outside his own time, from Dante and St. John of the Cross.

In the summer of 1911 Eliot told his friend, Aiken, over *sirop de fraises* at a sidewalk café, that he had to return to Harvard to study philosophy.[16] He had lived for a year in the most sophisticated centre of Western civilization but he had not found 'the truth of his time'. Eliot came to Paris to be a poet; he left a philosophy student.

In the summer of 1911, about the time Eliot made his decision to study philosophy, he began to write poems in which the nocturnal wanderer of the city is replaced by a new dominant figure, an almost demented philosopher, keeping all-night vigils in his room.* 'Thought ought to govern spiritual reality', Eliot had underlined in his copy of Hegel's *Philosophy of History*. In his new poems a philosopher makes his way along various mental paths, asking questions, but they seem to lead nowhere. It is a torture reserved for the intellectual, that nothing speaks to him but his own questionable logic. At dawn, the solitary meditations are curtailed by the damp breeze and rattling shutters, by new menacing shadows, stretching their tentacles, or by a 'vision of the street / As the street hardly understands.'[17] He thinks of broken lives in Roxbury, Massachusetts, or on the Left Bank. While the gas-jets flicker in the morning draught, the sound of a drunk

* Most of these poems Eliot left undated, but the change in handwriting makes it possible to group them. The third Prelude and most of 'Prufrock', dated July and August 1911, were copied into the Notebook in the spiky Paris hand. All the other poems in this batch, including a discarded section of 'Prufrock', were copied in the smaller, rounder hand Eliot developed after his return to Harvard. The rounder hand is very similar to the pre-Paris hand, but distinguishable by the capital 'I'—which gains a lower loop—and by a different flourish beneath the poems.

singing in the gutter reminds him of children whimpering in corners, women spilling out of their corsets in doorways, men in shirt sleeves leaning out of windows, and smoking boys drifting together in the fan of light from a corner drugstore. The outside world then seems so hateful that it dissolves, fades away.

Eliot once said that a narrow, unique, and horrible vision of life might come, as the result of a few or slender experiences, to a highly sensitive youth.[18] The young man's cynicism, his loathing and disgust of humanity of course exceed their object, they project from his own inner world of nightmare, 'some horror beyond words'. Yet Eliot believed that to know hatred of life in one's youth, to realize the true death-motive, was itself a triumph, something of a mystical experience. After he became a Christian he recognized that the religious life, for a certain temperament, began with a sense of 'the disorder, the futility, the meaningless-ness, the mystery of life and suffering'.[19] Particularly after his return to Boston, for the fall semester of 1911, he was greatly troubled to explain the twentieth-century world and wishes wildly in 'Do I know how I feel? Do I know what I think?' that just one person, say the porter on his stair, could acknowledge and share his despair.

This period of acute distress in Eliot's life was the result, I think, of a sense of prophetic power he could not quite grasp or express. He felt an overwhelming need to question an abhor-rent world based on attrition, poverty, and drabness, but he did not know in what direction to carry his questions or what exactly to do. Emerson had had similar intuitions and differed from Eliot only in the degree of self-reliance: 'I know that the world I converse with in the city', wrote Emerson, 'is not the world *I think*. . . . One day I shall know the value and law of this discrepance. . . . In the solitude to which every man is always returning, he has a sanity and revelations which in his passage into new worlds he will carry with him.'[20]

Eliot's mother gave him a blueprint he could only partially follow. She relied on private revelation, but insisted it be given a firm rational basis 'that superstition with inconstant light / May not allure my steps from Reason's way'.[21] One of Charlotte Eliot's most eloquent models, Giordano Bruno, spends sleepless nights in search of truth. His imagination is racked with a brood of loathsome shapes, yet he is able to say at last: 'The truth dawns on my vision . . .'[22] He realizes God is to be found 'upon the paths of knowledge everywhere / He dwelt in truth.' Eliot duly explored 'the paths of knowledge'—he speaks of them in 'Prufrock' and 'Oh little voices . . .'—but they led him into dark corners, wound him in question marks, finally abandoned him in an intellectual maze.

The first vigil poems, the third Prelude (dated July 1911) and 'Prufrock' (dated July–August 1911) were more dramatic and less obviously autobiographical than the others which were written after Eliot's return to Boston. In the third Prelude, Eliot describes the rather improbable thoughts of a grimy woman in curl papers. She lies on her back in a poor suburb of Boston, staring at the ceiling, where she projects 'a thousand sordid images' from her miserable mind—images, Eliot insists, the common man would not understand. Eliot is vague about the sordid images, but there are more explicit details in 'Prufrock's Pervigilium', a section of 'Prufrock' which Eliot cut on the advice of Conrad Aiken.*

I have allied 'The Love Song of J. Alfred Prufrock' with the vigil poems firstly because the unpublished section, originally at the centre of the poem, was about an all-night vigil; secondly because I support the view that Prufrock's visit to the fashionable lady was simply a possibility turning over in the mind of a nervous Bostonian who never, in fact, leaves his room. (Eliot wrote the poem just before his return to Boston, his thoughts turning to the social ordeals of the Beacon Hill drawingroom and solitary walks past Boston's sawdust restaurants with oyster shells.)

Eliot said J. Alfred Prufrock was in part a man of about forty and in part himself.† The demarcation between fiction and autobiography fits neatly along the lines of Prufrock's divided self. Prufrock the timid, ageing lover is a character out of the fiction of

* 'Prufrock's Pervigilium' is undated but it was probably copied into Eliot's Notebook in 1912. The rest of 'Prufrock' (i.e. the poem as it was eventually published) was copied into the Notebook, in his spiky hand, in July–August 1911. But Eliot deliberately left four pages in the middle of the poem blank which suggests he had a rough draft of the 'Pervigilium' which awaited completion. In a letter to *TLS* (3 June 1960) Aiken writes: 'Mr. Eliot maintains to this day that on my suggestion a certain passage—now presumably lost—had been dropped from the poem. I can only say that I have no recollection of this, but if so, what a pity!'

† Interview, *Grantite Review*, 24, No. 3 (1962), 16–20. Eliot used the notion of the split personality, which was first studied and widely popularized in his youth.

Henry James, especially the late tales of the unlived life.* Eliot
—with beauty, wit, and grace—had little in common with the
graceless lover, with his bald spot and his conspicuous lack of
muscle, who wishes to establish rapport with a rather overpower-
ing lady at a late-afternoon teaparty.

Elements of Eliot are transfused into the lover—his shyness, his
propriety of dress—but Eliot more obviously identifies with
Prufrock's other self, a solitary thinker who wishes to ask an
'overwhelming question' and assault the genteel surfaces of
Boston society with an apocalyptic truth. 'Do I dare / Disturb the
universe?' he wonders, and gropes in vain among New Testament
models—Lazarus and John the Baptist—for the appropriate
manner.† Prufrock's philosophic daring is continually checked
by his genteel scruples. At the same time, his imaginary social
drama is continually eroded by the emotions of a prophet who
may have 'a hundred visions', who can fast and pray, and who
wishes, like Emerson, to question and denounce the empty
diversions of his class. 'Let us affront and reprimand', said
Emerson, 'the smooth mediocrity and squalid contentment of
the times.' Yet Prufrock doubts his calling ('I am no prophet'),
for his visions evaporate in the fog that curls in questions.
Prufrock's natural arena, like Eliot's, is not the social gathering,
but the lonely winding streets that express his sentience, streets
that follow like his tedious arguments to their unnerving end in
dark retreats.

To what exactly did Prufrock's question point? In the Notebook draft a confession follows Prufrock's distraught query,
'How should I begin?' He recounts a night-long vigil which
climaxes in a terrifying vision of the end of the world. Prufrock's
overwhelming need is to ask not a lover's question but a metaphysical one, suggested by Bergson, about the point of man's
accumulated experience. 'To live', says Bergson, 'is to grow old.'

---

* Grover Smith notes that Prufrock's love-predicament almost exactly reproduces
that of a hesitant bachelor, White-Mason, in James's 'Crapy Cornelia' (1909). See
T. S. Eliot's Poetry and Plays (Univ. of Chicago Press—Phoenix, 1956), p. 15. Eliot
believed that initially he developed in the manner of James and, when he compared
the influence of James with that of Dostoevsky, he conceded that the spirit of James
'so much less violent with so much more reasonableness and so much more resignation than that of the Russian' was more useful to him personally. *Vanity Fair* (U.S.A.)
(Feb. 1924).

† Charlotte Eliot was devoted to these two figures. Her poem, 'The Raising of
Lazarus', dramatizes Lazarus's emergence from his tomb.

('I grow old . . . I grow old' Prufrock murmurs.) Life is a suc-
cession of psychological states, memories, and roles, 'a continual
rolling up, like that of a thread on a ball, for our past follows us,
it swells incessantly with the present that it picks up on its way . . .'[23]
Prufrock sees the world roll up into a ball and fall away—and he
hears the chatter of his own imminent madness. He longs to
confide in someone, an admired woman, but fears women only
want lovers' talk 'of you and me'.

Eliot learned from Dostoevsky (whom he read in Paris, in
French translation) to exploit personal problems in his writing.
He saw how Dostoevsky's epilepsy and hysteria 'cease to be
defects of an individual and become—as fundamental weakness
can, given the ability to face it and study it—the entrance to a
genuine and personal universe'.[24] Eliot exploited his inhibition in
his conception of Prufrock-the-lover and caricatured his visionary
moments in Prufrock-the-prophet's crazy fantasies: his head
brought in, like John the Baptist's, upon a platter. He imagines the
persecution. He sees his greatness flicker, and is afraid.

When, in 1912,[25] Conrad Aiken took 'Prufrock' to a 'poetry
squash' in London and showed it to Harold Monro, the editor of
Poetry and Drama, Monro flung it back saying it was 'absolutely
insane'. Those first readers of 'Prufrock' who thought it the
morbid ravings of a madman[26] were shamefully discredited, but
they may, in fact, have been closer to the poem's message than
Pound who applauded its contemporary satire. Despite the
poem's mannered surface, Eliot is looking beyond the Jamesian
scene and the obligation to cultivate human attachments—
towards a characteristic theme of his own, a prophet's obligation
to articulate what he alone knows.

At the end of the poem the sound of voices disturbs Prufrock
from his solitary ruminations, and the images of lover and prophet
die away. Neither are durable identities. Prufrock cannot be a
lover, a mindless body, seduced by mermaids he does not respect;
but neither can his mind pursue overwhelming issues without dis-
traction from his senses. The debate between would-be lover and
would-be prophet is a more dramatic and complicated version of
Eliot's earlier debates between body and soul. Eliot could forgo
human attachments, but the alternative—the Absolute in the
first debate, the ring of silence in the second, the prophetic figures
in 'Prufrock'—could not, at any point, compose a durable vision.

Eliot revived Prufrock's debate between two selves in a poem he wrote some time after his return to Harvard, 'Oh little voices . . .'* The shadowed abject self (sitting all night muffled in a shawl in an armchair) complains that he has searched all the by-ways, the dark retreats and twisty streets, but has ended in an intellectual maze. The philosophic self replies that what he has seen are appearances not realities, and exhorts him not to delay to take possession of some truth. Yet to the abject self the babbling men and women of this world *are* real, for they seem so comfortably at home while he feels so uneasy, consumed by his impulse to blow against the wind and spit against the rain.

Both in 'Oh little voices' and the fourth Prelude, also written after Eliot's return to Boston, Eliot is oppressed by multitudes of insistent, undirected feet of small-minded little men. (The same theme reappears in an early *Waste Land* fragment, 'So through the evening . . .' where a wanderer, bruised by ordinary jostling men, drifts away from the town.) In the fourth Prelude, Eliot assumes the prophetic role with more confidence.† He says boldly that he is the lone conscience of a blackened street, the only one who sees beyond the common knowledge of the evening rush-hour crowd who guards its oblivion with newspapers and stuffed pipes. His soul stretches, impatient to 'assume the world', yet still gropes for an idea. Curled round the insistent feet and mind-killing routines, lurks a 'notion', not an idea, but something less: a notion of suffering. Here Eliot begins to formulate a familiar motif, leaping from the vacancy of city scenes towards some intangible mood or emotion hovering nearby but strangely withdrawn. Characteristically, he relinquishes the intangible notion rather too fast and stubbornly resigns himself to watching the world go round.

Eliot's morale reached its lowest point in an acutely disturbed poem, 'Do I know how I feel? Do I know what I think?'‡ He

* 'Oh little voices . . .' is undated but is typed on the same paper as Eliot used for his 1914 poems. Thematically, it is an outgrowth of the vigil cluster, but the issues of appearance and reality associate it with the period when Eliot was reading F. H. Bradley, beginning in the summer of 1913.

† *CP*, pp. 14–15. Since the fourth Prelude is in the post-Paris hand it must be dated some time after November 1911.

‡ This rough draft was not completed. There is no date, but it is in the post-Paris hand.

5. The outer harbour and piazza of the Eliot house, Eastern Point, Gloucester, Mass. (1909): 'What seas what shores what grey rocks . . .'

6. Eliot aged nineteen (1907). A student at Harvard College, he was writing poems about the fragility of emotional experience

thinks, with horror, of the common plots of human fate, of beauty wasted in convenient marriages, or worn away in commuter trains, or stifled in dark rooms. He feels reverent love for an ethereal woman, but is crushed by knowledge of his own malaise. He imagines suicide, himself on the floor like a broken bottle. He will not have to care what happens after. A doctor with a pointed beard and black bag, chemicals and a knife, arrives to perform the post-mortem.

Years later Eliot told the Woolfs that he had had an upheaval after writing 'Prufrock' that had altered his rather Jamesian inclinations.[27] Eliot's poems of 1911 and 1912 document this upheaval, a period of nightly vigils, visions, and panic—'the nightly panic / Of dreaming dissolution'.[28] In his first draft of 'Little Gidding' Eliot's night-long watches as an air-raid warden during the Second World War revived memories of 'the dark night in the solitary bedroom' which he regarded as one of the essential experiences of his life:

> Remember rather the essential moments
> That were your times of death and birth and change
> The agony and the solitary vigil . . .*

Eliot returned to Harvard at a time when its prestigious philosophy department had just lost its leading figures—Santayana, Palmer, and James. While Eliot was an undergraduate the department had had an idealist bias, but in 1912 Ralph Barton Perry and five others inaugurated a doctrinal change with a book on the New Realism. Eliot admitted that the Realists might be refreshing, but he was put off by their subservience to mathematics and the exact sciences.[29] He could not accept that Bertrand Russell's course on symbolic logic, given in 1914, had 'anything to do with reality.'[30] Instead of joining the Realists, he turned first to Indian philosophy and, after two years, devoted himself to the work of an Oxford idealist, F. H. Bradley. With Bradley's help, Eliot was able to chart a way through the intellectual maze in which he found himself in 1912.

In June 1913 Eliot bought Bradley's *Appearance and Reality* (1893) and presumably read it over the summer vacation. He found an immediate acknowledgement of the disturbing gap that

---

* Helen Gardner's edition of the *FQ* manuscripts. (The line 'The agony and the solitary vigil' replaced 'The dark night in the solitary bedroom' in the typed draft.)

separates hints of Absolute truth from everyday experience. Bradley readily admitted that common knowledge does not go far enough, in other words the necessity of a religious point of view.[31] To Eliot, Bradley seemed to radiate 'the sweetness and light of the medieval schoolmen'.[32] His prose borrowed none of the persuasiveness of science or literature; it was 'pure' philosophy, yet throbbed, said Eliot, like the prose of James or Frazer 'with the agony of spiritual life'.[33]

Bradley followed the same paths Eliot explores in 'Oh little voices' but he admitted bafflement without Eliot's sense of defeat. Bradley's attraction for Eliot was not, I think, speculative bravery, but the graceful intellectual poise with which he accepted human failure to know final truth: 'We justify the natural wonder which delights to stray beyond our daylight world, and to follow paths that lead to half-known half-unknowable regions. Our conclusion . . . has confirmed the irresistible impression that all is beyond us.'[34] The sanity and range of Bradley's inquiries saved Eliot from a terrifying sense of intellectual isolation.

Bradley asked the same question as Eliot (in 'Rhapsody on a Windy Night'): 'whether the universe is concealed behind appearances'.[35] But where Eliot despairs of finding meaning in commonly observed objects—he complains, as early as February 1911, that these either pass right through or else clog his brain[36]— Bradley was more hopeful that through common objects 'we can discover the main nature of reality'. In 'Oh little voices' Eliot poses irreconcilable worlds of appearance and reality; Bradley insisted that the two worlds were linked. Admittedly appearances jarred one with a sense of discrepancy from the presumed underlying harmony, but the unifying harmony, Bradley asserted, was there. It simply inhered in appearances in different degrees: 'We can find no province of the world so low but the Absolute inhabits it. Nowhere is there even a single fact so fragmentary and so poor that to the universe it does not matter.'[37] Eliot, who had seen appearances dissolve, was perhaps comforted by Bradley's firm statement: 'We may keep a fast hold upon this, that appearances exist.'[38]

As in Eliot's debates between body and soul, Bradley felt the 'infection' of the material world and that the only perfection lay beyond it, with the Absolute.[39] But he was discouraging about the quality of possible contact, for his Absolute was remote and impervious and its nature inexplicable: 'As an object of contemplation it seems simply to *be*.'[40]

Bradley described a soul within a closed circle of consciousness. Eliot echoes this in his dissertation—'My mind . . . is a point of view from which I cannot possibly escape'[41]—and later reiterates it, by quoting Bradley, in one of his more serious notes to *The Waste Land*. Bradley said that private centres of consciousness are opaque to others which surround it, but he still asserted the private self's 'palpable community with the universe'.[42] Bradley warned against solipsistic interpretations of immediate experience: 'It would not follow . . . that all the world is merely a state of myself.'[43]

Two other issues, important to Eliot, Bradley deliberately avoided. He dismissed common notions of body and soul as too artificial: 'To comprehend them, while each is fixed in its own untrue character, is utterly impossible. But, if so, their way of connexion must remain unintelligible.'[44] Similarly, Bradley glided swiftly past evil and ugliness. In his harmonious universe they were 'subordinate aspects' in the Absolute's kingdom. For Eliot, on the other hand, evil and ugliness oppressed him as the most commanding of his experiences to which, for many years to come, even the ring of silence was subordinated.

Eliot wrote his doctoral dissertation, 'Experience and the Objects of Knowledge in the Philosophy of F. H. Bradley', between 1913 and 1916. Although it was based on *Appearance and Reality*, it strained beyond Bradley's bounds of inquiry. Eliot was less committed to a community of understanding, more willing to indulge in solipsistic speculation. He emphatically contradicts Bradley's dictum, 'my experience is not the whole world',[45] and asserts the primacy of subjective knowledge: 'What is subjective is the whole world.' 'All significant truths are private truths.'[46] When he tried to be objective, to adjust his private truths to accepted intellectual formulas, the connection seemed 'obscure'. His perceptions were 'shrunk' or 'impoverished' when personal feeling was cut loose.

Eliot's tortuous style obscures the content so that the dissertation is almost unreadable, but it becomes a significant document in the context of Eliot's manuscript poems of 1911 and 1912. The dissertation's concern with a maddeningly brief visionary moment and its contradictory interpretations may be seen as a continuation of Eliot's introspective vigils in his Parisian garret where he would mull over the elusive message contained in the ring of silence and fail to make sense of it. And the dissertation's denial of the substantiality of the material world fits neatly against poetic fantasies of a dissolving world. Neither the vigil poems nor the dissertation could formulate a coherent vision. All hinted at an extraordinary experience, an intuition of sublime truth, that was wretchedly curtailed. In *Knowledge and Experience* Eliot's trains of thought trailed, stopped, started in differing directions, like the streets Prufrock had followed. Eliot wrote like a restless sleeper, turning over and over, as he was tapped on the shoulder by new considerations. His long exercise in philosophy only taught him that that approach was futile. Whereas Bradley was willing to accept the incomplete truth gained by the calculations of 'mere intellect', Eliot strained towards a final truth contained in heightened moments of 'lived' experience— experience indeed so 'mad and strange' as to elude common understanding.[47]

By 'lived' experience Eliot meant something wholly mental. He found that if he cast his mind into the flux between different viewpoints, and held them momentarily together, he could sometimes envision a strange 'half-object', a composite of the viewpoints which yet transcended them.[48] When he made the necessary intuitive 'leap' he discovered his power to see 'the real future of an imaginary present'. The language, though vague and abstract, suggests a quasi-religious experience: there is a 'pilgrimage' into the space between two worlds; the prophetic power is the reward of an 'act of faith'. In his Harvard classes Eliot kept suggesting that 'illusion', 'hallucination', or 'superstition' might be more worthy of serious philosophical attention than social or material objects.[49] In February 1914 he complained of the failure to find an explanation for illusion that would not *diminish* the illusion. In March he asked, 'Can we do without superstitions as to causality?' In May, in a paper on the classification of different types of objects, he asserted the primacy of mental events like hallucinations, like God.

In his thesis Eliot insisted that the half-object appears only to a mind floating free, almost unconscious, from which all accidents of socially-conditioned personality are removed.* He said also

* *KE*, p. 148. In view of Eliot's famous rejection of personality in 'Tradition and

that the vision is timeless* and unlocalized and independent of social consequences: 'We are led to the conception of an all-inclusive experience outside of which nothing shall fall.'[50] It is only when the visionary power fails, said Eliot, that people resort to social custom and common knowledge. Eliot was unsure of his truth—his subjective self half-recognized it, his rational self half-resisted—but he was confident that it could be said to 'diverge' from common knowledge.[51]

Eliot looked upon the world as a precarious, artificial construction. Divergent images were rather arbitrarily drawn into a frame of common knowledge which was eroded at every moment by fresh subjective experience. Eliot's world was dangerously fragile—poised, like Poe's city on the sea, on the edge of dissolution. It had no permanent substance: it was 'essentially vague, unprecise, swarming with insoluble contradictions'.[52] Yet, it tugged. It insisted on acknowledgement. It made itself felt as a background to the heightened moments. And then, when he approached it, it fell apart.[53] Like Prufrock, owning to madness at the end of his vigil, Eliot watched the great world dissolve and fade.

Knowledge and Experience was written by a haunted young man, torn between the truth of his visions and his rational distrust of them. 'I have lived with shadows for my company', Eliot quotes.[54] The shadows point towards a higher reality which should suggest the meaning of the material world and confirm its lesser status. But he cannot be sure. The half-objects might be only 'figments of imagination' or, worse, terribly plausible hallucinations.[55] The dissertation resounds with confessions of suffering: the 'agony' when the vision refuses to be realized and the observer falls back into artificial life; the fatal persecution of an obsessional idea 'for one crazed by fear or passion'; the wrenching beginning and end of the vision—'annihilation and utter night'.[56]

The problem Eliot posed in his dissertation was his own. To live like a visionary in the dangerous space between two worlds was to court madness. But to fall back into the net of the material

the Individual Talent', it is important to note that in his thesis Eliot distinguishes between subjectivity, which he endorses, and personality, which he rejects. Note also that he rejects personality only in this special context of visionary experience.

* 'Immediate experience is a timeless unity', Eliot writes (p. 164). 'Any object which is wholly real is independent of time' (p. 110). It is curious to see, here, the development of an idea that came to fruition several decades later in *FQ*.

world, and to live enmeshed in its artificial customs and beliefs,
was to risk his gift for sublime knowledge.

Bradley, with his saving wisdom, his scepticism and air of
sophisticated disillusion, helped Eliot towards a sane academic
formulation—though not a solution—of the questions posed in
the vigil poems. But with Bradley, Eliot came to the end of the
philosophic path. He asked all Eliot's overwhelming questions
but was careful to abstain from pretensions beyond verifiable
knowledge. Together with him Eliot gazed on the vast territories
that stretched beyond philosophy on all sides while Bradley
planted flags marking the intellectual frontiers that should not be
crossed. 'His philosophy seems to give you everything that you
ask', said Eliot in despair, 'and yet to render it not worth wanting.'[57]

Eliot's thesis was essentially retrospective: a monument to
an earlier period in his life. But other developments during the
three Cambridge years—his political views, his falling in love,
his religious fantasies—look towards a later phase in his life and
found their monument in the great works of Eliot's maturity.
1911–14 has long been the most obscure period in Eliot's life,
yet the manuscripts suggest that his most characteristic ideas were
formulated at precisely this time.

Eliot returned to America with a polished European air. He
affected a malacca cane and hung a copy of Gauguin's 'Yellow
Christ', brought from Paris, on his wall. His friend, Aiken,
recalled a travelled, sophisticated young man rather at odds with
a New England college town still, in the early years of the twentieth century, a kind of village with white picket fences and horse-
drawn watering carts to lay the summer dust.[58] But Eliot's
personal documents suggest he was less of a lone figure than
during his undergraduate and Paris years, particularly in 1913 and
1914 when he went so far as to enrol for dancing and skating
lessons.[59] Photographs show him laughing with his older sisters
at Eastern Point or sprawled on the floor of the porch against the
whitewashed wall. He wrote ribald verses for the entertainment
of Harvard friends, 'Bullshit' and 'Ballad for Big Louise' and a
narrative about King Bolo and his hairy Big Black Kween who
'pulled her stocking off / With a frightful cry of Hauptbahnhof!'
He attended numerous concerts, Ravel, Dvořák, Wagner,

Sibelius, Chopin; heard violin recitals by Mischa Elman and Fritz Kreisler at Symphony Hall; saw Puccini operas and *Tristan*, once more, at the Boston Opera House. At Harvard, Eliot was well thought of by his teachers. For two years he taught under-graduate courses in philosophy in Emerson Hall, and in his last year was elected president of Harvard's Philosophical Society.

In an address to the Philosophical Society in 1913 or 1914 Eliot complained that no radical is so radical as to be a con-servative.[60] He scorned those optimists who offered glib solutions, economic or socialist, to human misery. Even more pernicious was a contemporary fear of dogma, which resulted in a light devotion to change as an end in itself. Instead of upholding absolute moral standards of goodness and evil, Eliot saw his contemporaries becoming subject to two fallacies, the idea of Progress (which he associated with Bergson) and the idea of Relativity (which he ascribed to William James's *Pragmatism*). Eliot saw what neither Bergson nor James acknowledged, that their absorption in a private psychological world of need and change was, in effect, a withdrawal from the great world and resulted from despair of a perfect political order. He was exasper-ated that neither philosopher followed his theory through to its pessimistic end.

On 17 February 1913 Eliot acted in a variety show in the Cam-bridge house of his aunt, Mrs. Holmes Hinkley.[61] Scenes from Dickens, Austen, and Maria Edgeworth were played by the parlour fireplace. The audience were relatives, friends, and neigh-bours. Eliot was Mr. Woodhouse in a scene from *Emma* and M. Marcel in a sketch 'M. Marcel and his latest Marvel', devised by his cousin, Eleanor Hinkley. Her friend, Emily Hale, played Mrs. Elton and sang songs called 'Ecstasy' and 'May Morning'. It is not yet known how deeply Eliot fell in love with Emily Hale, but Helen Gardner suggests that it was she who inspired Eliot's nostalgia, twenty years later in the rose-garden of Burnt Norton, for his youthful love and another life that might have been.[62] Emily Hale never married. She became a teacher of drama at various American colleges and over the course of her life ex-changed about two thousand letters with Eliot.[63]

This is little to go on, but it is worth noting that the rose-garden is the last of several similar garden pieces in which Eliot recalled a moment of romantic intoxication with a woman.

Eliot wrote the first two, 'Hidden under the heron's wing . . .'[64] and 'La Figlia che Piange',[65] soon after his return to Harvard. In the first the bird and the lotus (which reappear in 'Burnt Norton') celebrate a beloved gliding across the grass in the shadows or mist of the evening. In 'La Figlia che Piange' a lover and a girl holding flowers, her long hair irradiated by sunlight, part with artistic grace:

> Stand on the highest pavement of the stair—
> Lean on a garden urn—
> Weave, weave the sunlight in your hair—
> Clasp your flowers to you with pained surprise
> Fling them to the ground and turn
> With fugitive resentment in your eyes:
> But weave, weave the sunlight in your hair.

The poet wonders endlessly how they would have come together but enjoys, even more, the fantasy of the beautifully controlled, unmessy parting—'a gesture and a pose'—which he may enshrine forever in his memory and his art. The lover loses flesh and blood; the poet yet possesses her. There is more than a hint of triumph amidst his regret, like Henry James lamenting Minny Temple's death. (Minny would be 'a pure and eloquent vision' locked, incorruptibly, 'within the crystal walls of the past'.[66]) Ten years later Eliot worked this scene, or one very like it, into *The Waste Land* and, from that remote distance in mood and time, recalls a love almost holy in its intensity:

> . . . When we came back late, from the hyacinth garden,
> Your arms full, and your hair wet, I could not
> Speak, and my eyes failed, I was neither
> Living nor dead, and I knew nothing,
> Looking into the heart of light, the silence.   (*WL*: I)

Later in the poem the unlovable wife asks the disaffected husband, 'Do you remember / Nothing?' and, in an earlier draft, he gives his silent inexorable answer: 'I remember / The hyacinth garden.' He excludes his wife with that recollection of fertile love and its power to transform him: 'Those pearls that were his eyes, yes!'[67]

Eliot renewed contact with Emily Hale when he visited America in 1933, and she visited England for two successive summers, in 1934 and 1935, when the visit to Burnt Norton took place. 'Footfalls echo in the memory', wrote Eliot, 'Down the passage which we did not take / Towards the door we never opened / Into the rose-garden.' The light which had irradiated La Figlia's hair, the beatific light inspired by the hyacinth girl, re-appears as miraculous 'water out of sunlight' in the garden's dry concrete pool.

It is possible further to connect the idealized Figlia, on the highest pavement, with the pure and remote lady in the love-starved song of Saint Sebastian (1914) and with the divine lady in 'Ash Wednesday' (1930), both poised on the stair above. If so, La Figlia became a pervasive figure in Eliot's work.

Eliot's main objection to his department was its divorce of philosophy from religion.[68] He craved philosophy in an ampler sense—wisdom, insight, revelation. Immediately upon his return to Harvard he began to study Eastern philosophy: Sanskrit under Charles Lanman and Pantanjali's metaphysics under James Woods. He said he was glad to uncover in the *Bhagavadgita* philosophical and religious beliefs different from those of his family.[69] He acquired a catalogue of books on Vedanta and, in August and October 1913, bought two books by Paul Deussen, *Upanishads des Veda* and *Die Sûtras des Vedânta*. He also steeped himself in Dante's vision by memorizing long passages while lying in bed or on a railway journey.[70] Dante was to become the most profound and persistent influence in his life because, said Eliot, he helped him see the connection between the medieval Christian inferno and modern life.[71] The inscription over hell in-spired Eliot to write a prayer pleading the Lord's patience and promising to come to terms with accepted beliefs.*

There was one teacher at Harvard who might have helped Eliot effect a transition between philosophy and religion. Josiah Royce was Harvard's leading idealist philosopher. One of his books, *The Problem of Christianity*, was published in 1913, just before Eliot entered his advanced seminar in Comparative Metho-dology. Here Royce argued most eloquently that the Christian doctrine of life expresses 'universal human needs' and, in the twentieth century in particular, the need for community based on

* Although the prayer is undated, it is written on Boston paper (Carter Rice & Co.), therefore before Eliot left America. The leaf is in Eliot's folder of miscellaneous poems, Berg Coll.

worthy common traditions. As Eliot was to do later in *The Idea
of a Christian Society*, Royce put private experience to one side,
and stressed the social order, its dependence on religion for its
survival.[72]

Eliot picked up the notion of human need in a report on
primitive religions, which he read in Royce's class on 9 December
1913. He criticized the anthropologists—Frazer, Jane Harrison,
Durkheim, and Lévy-Bruhl—for giving no explanation of religious ritual 'in terms of need'.[73] He criticized their 'wanton
interpretation' based on uninvestigated assumptions, and suggested there was no adequate truth in the study of religion short
of an absolute truth. And that would be found, not through
methodological inquiry, only through intuitive sympathy. Again,
on 16 December, Eliot tried to bypass anthropologists' records
of behaviour with the question: 'What is he [the believer]
sincere about?' Behaviour is mere mechanism, Eliot added, unless
it has some sort of meaning. 'The question is, what is that meaning?'[74] Finally, on 24 February 1914, Eliot criticized all theories of
knowledge for their inability to 'treat illusion as real'.[75]

The turning-point in Eliot's life came not at the time of his
baptism in 1927, but in 1914 when he was circling, in moments of
agitation, on the edge of conversion. This supposition is based
on a group of intense religious poems Eliot never published.
He wrote four of these poems before he left Harvard, 'After the
turning . . .', 'I am the Resurrection . . .', 'So through the evening . . .',* and 'The Burnt Dancer' (dated June 1914). 'The Love
Song of Saint Sebastian' was written in Germany in July 1914
and 'The Death of Saint Narcissus' at the end of 1914 or beginning
of 1915, after Eliot's move to England. In the new cluster, a bold
convert, a passionate martyr or saint displaces the frustrated
philosopher of the 1910–12 poems. There is a confusing night
visitation and the poet's fear of divine commerce. There is a
monastic impulse to isolate himself from the crowd, to take off
for mountain or desert in search of initiation and purification.
There is, most persistently, fantasies of a martyr's passion. Eliot's
imaginary commitment to faith is both wild and tentative, cloudy
with unresolved, flitting perceptions and overburdened with
resolution.

---

* These *Waste Land* fragments are described in detail in Chapter 5. The evidence of
the paper and Eliot's hand suggest they were written before he left America.

There is a non-analytical breathlessness about the poems concerned with 'turning' or conversion. Eliot's comments both in Royce's class and in his Bradley dissertation showed his disillusion with logic. 'After the turning', 'I am the Resurrection', and 'So through the evening', the earliest visionary fragments of the *Waste Land* manuscript, signal Eliot's liberation from the studied paths of philosophy, his new willingness to give rein to strange intuitions and images:

> One tortured meditation dragged me on
> Concatenated words from which the sense was gone—
>
> .   .   .   .
>
> The This-do-ye-for-my-sake . . .
> The one essential word that frees
> The inspiration that delivers and expresses . . .
> A chain of reasoning whereof the thread was gone
> Gathered strange images through which I walked alone
> (facs. WL, p. [112])

'I am the Resurrection' acknowledges the unknowability of the divine force which decides our destiny but which cannot be judged in human terms. The implicit question, throughout this group, is how to behave in relation to the unknown. Eliot's answer in 'The Burnt Dancer' and the two 'saint' poems seems to be to attract attention by an extraordinary display of wilful physical self-abuse.

In 'The Burnt Dancer' an insomniac, listening all night to children whimper behind walls, suddenly observes a black moth dancing round a yellow ring of flame. The moth seems to symbolize himself hovering on the edge of a bright ring of illumination; its dance seems to invite him to some portentous fate beyond most human understanding. He watches curiously while the moth deliberately singes its wings on the flame as though he witnesses the expiation of a martyr. The extraordinary patience of the moth's passion exhilarates him, its superhuman endurance of pain. But he finds the end forbidding. For the moth, now broken, loses its passion and desires only the fatal end of its ordeal.

The poem has its sequel in the martyrdom of Saint Narcissus. The moth dances about a yellow flame; the saint dances to God on the hot sand while arrows pierce his flesh. In both cases there is a savage joy in pain.

The visionary period came to an end with the two 'saint' poems. Throughout his career Eliot was fascinated by the motives, the behaviour, the achievement of saints. Only saints can know 'a lifetime's death in love, / Ardour and selflessness and self-surrender', wrote Eliot in 1941, and seemed then to beg off personally in favour of a humbler life of prayer, observance, and self-discipline.[76] But the 1914 poems suggest that, for a time in his youth, Eliot's imagination toyed with the saint's ambitious task. Once more, Eliot's preoccupations can be traced to his mother— her numerous poems about 'Priests and prophets, saints and sages, / Martyred in successive ages'.[77] During Eliot's last years at Harvard he made a study of the lives of saints and mystics, St. Theresa, Dame Julian of Norwich, Mme Guyon, Walter Hilton, St. John of the Cross, Jacob Böhme, and St. Bernard.[78] He noted particular features of their visions: Dame Julian's steady gazing on the Crucifix, Böhme's at a dazzling light reflected from a tin vessel, and St. Theresa's assertion that she never saw visions with the eye of the body. Eliot made copious notes from Evelyn Underhill's book, *Mysticism* (1911), and copied in detail one passage which explains vision as a work of art created from real experience: 'If we would cease, once for all, to regard visions and voices as objective, and be content to see in them forms of symbolic expression, ways in which the subconscious activity of the spiritual self reach the surface-mind, many of the disharmonies noticeable in visionary experience which have teased the devout, and delighted the agnostic, would fade away. Visionary experience . . . is a picture which the mind constructs . . . from raw materials already at its disposal.'[79]

Eliot noted the dangers and the maladies of the religious life and also its disciplines and cures, St. Ignatius Loyola's *Spiritual Exercises* and St. John of the Cross's *Dark Night of the Soul*. At this time Eliot first came upon the disease of doubt, 'aboulie', by which term he was to describe his depression while writing *The Waste Land* in 1921. Reading of Mme Guyon, he noted that when the divine command is withheld it becomes impossible to act. (This is quite different from the deliberate withdrawal from sense, reason, and will of the Dark Night of the Soul which, as Eliot was to demonstrate in *Four Quartets*, is a period of construction not of negativity.) Jeffries's autobiography warned of another danger of the religious life, delusional insanity, which

Eliot described as mysticism turned upside down, become diabolical. He was more concerned, though, with what one of his sources termed 'la vie réligieuse normale', the traditional pattern of progress towards sainthood through phases of awakening, unworthiness, mortification of the senses, and illumination. As Underhill pointed out, the potential saint will naturally look to the historic life of Christ as 'an epitome . . . of the essentials of all spiritual life' with its pattern of birth and rebirth. Her three classic identities—pilgrim, lover, ascetic—were all to appear immediately in Eliot's poems and fragments of 1914.

'The Love Song of Saint Sebastian' represents Eliot's debates between body and soul carried beyond possibility of resolution. The poem is a ritualized attack on the flesh: in the first stanza, the body of the lover is whipped, in the second the body of the beloved is strangled. This violent, intentionally abhorrent annihilation of physical beauty is inspired only superficially by a sense of sin, more by an avidity for sensation. Both deaths are stylized and artistic. Saint Sebastian's story has only tenuous links with the real saint, a Roman martyr in the time of Diocletian who, the fable goes, was sentenced to be shot by archers. Although the arrows pierced his flesh, he did not die but was rescued by a woman and nursed in her lodgings. In the case of Eliot's saint, the martyrdom is not only self-inflicted, but is an exhibitionistic attempt to gain a woman's attention. He wants her to see him in a hairshirt and to watch while he flogs himself for an hour until his blood bespatters the lamp he carries. Only then does she accept him, hideous and dying, as her neophyte.*

---

* The immediate inspiration for the poem came from three fifteenth-century paintings which struck Eliot's fancy as he passed through the galleries of Italy and Belgium in the summer of 1914: the first by Mantegna in the Palazzo della Cà d'Oro in Venice; the second attributed to Antonello da Messina at Bergamo; the third by Hans Memling in the Brussels Museum. They show innocent, firm-fleshed youths exposed to penetrant arrows. In a letter to Aiken, Eliot noted the eroticism and emphasized that, for him, a female saint would have been more appropriate. (This and all subsequent references to Eliot–Aiken correspondence may be found in the Aiken Coll., Huntington Library.)

There are two typescripts of the poem, one in the McKeldin Library, University of Maryland, and one in the Berg Coll. Both are undated, but Eliot mentions in a letter to Aiken (Marburg, 19 July 1914) that he had recently written about fifty belaboured lines of a poem and, in the next letter (25 July) enclosed it together with 'Oh little voices'. Although the two poems now coalesced in Eliot's mind, he intimates that Aiken will have seen one part (presumably 'Oh little voices') some time ago. 'Oh little voices' remains untitled and 'The Love Song of Saint Sebastian',

In the second stanza there is a swift Jekyll–Hyde transformation from abject saint to instinctual man, while the world dissolves in heat or ice. Liberated from social constraints, the lover proceeds to strangle the beautiful lady with sinister fondness. From the instinctual side of Sebastian, wielding his towel, came Eliot's later characters, the brute Sweeney, playful with his razor in the brothel, and Harry, Lord Monchensey, with his murderous heart.

On the surface Eliot seems the antithesis of a Saint Sebastian or a Sweeney. He appeared particularly lacking in 'crude insistent passion', as Russell put it in a letter of May 1914, an exquisitely well-conducted student amidst a horde of 'vigorous intelligent barbarians'. Yet his poems' antithesis between extremes of body and soul genuinely expressed Eliot's private dilemma. Many years later he wrote of his sense of the void in the middle of all human happiness and all human relations: 'I am one whom this sense of the void tends to.drive towards asceticism or sensuality.'[80] Constrained in love, defeated in his search for religious identity, Eliot was able to submerge his private experience within the stylized, single-minded actions of allegorical characters.

The last of the visionary poems, 'The Death of Saint Narcissus', was based on T. E. Hulme's 'Conversion' which Eliot must have read, at Pound's direction, soon after arriving in England.[81] Hulme's 'conversion' takes place in a wooded valley, covered with hyacinths, when he is stunned by a revelation of beauty. Saint Narcissus is similarly rapt before his own beauty. Neither is enlarged by his sensations. Both in the end overreach themselves and suffer a psychic blow, some kind of ignominious death of the spirit. In Hulme's metaphor, the convert sinks silently in the 'final river' in a sack; Narcissus is burnt dry in the desert.

A large section of the poem is characteristically Eliot's and in no way derives from Hulme: the scene where the would-be saint chooses a solitary life of deprivation and worship. Narcissus sets out to win immediate experience of divinity by retiring from the world, like the desert fathers of the fourth century. It is a logical, if extreme, answer to the Prufrockian world of ridiculous conformity. Eliot demonstrated an ascetic's motives more plausibly in 1937 in *The Family Reunion*, where Harry seeks to subdue his

with its title, is on page '2'. I am indebted to Dr. Robert L. Beare of the McKeldin Library for useful information.

sickeningly murderous heart in 'the heat of the sun and the icy vigil'. Harry has willed his wife's death and his atonement is real. Narcissus, on the other hand, has nothing particular for which to atone; his solitariness is self-serving. He tries to win the glow of fervour through abuse of his body but whatever glow he achieves quickly subsides, leaving him exhausted and without grace.

Like Saint Sebastian, Saint Narcissus represents an idea. He is not a realistic character and, of course, Eliot cannot be identified with him. But take away the caricature of twisted motives and excessive egotism, and the poem reveals the consuming issues of Eliot's life—his longing for metamorphosis, his vision and loss of vision, and the avidity of his religious emotions. Eliot thought that imaginary characters should dramatize 'but in no obvious form, an action or struggle for harmony in the soul of the poet'.[82]

Why did Eliot not make any serious religious commitment in 1914? Among Eliot's student notes there is a warning from Evelyn Underhill that vision through the senses is imperfect, capricious, often a delusion.[83] One must await purely spiritual communication. Eliot refused to make more of feverish excitations and abasements than a kind of stunt. The wry, derisive note, entirely absent in 'The Burnt Dancer', undercuts the posturing of Saint Narcissus six months later. Eliot's heroes of the spirit genuinely experience the attractions of asceticism, they know dazzling glimpses of divine reality but these possess no decisive life-transforming power. There is awe in Eliot's 1914 cluster, but no enduring vocation; there is penance, but no real sense of sin.

Eliot himself said to Aiken that these poems were 'strained and intellectual'.[84] His models were traditional and literary, his scenes oddly unlocalized as though the mind that conceived them were floating free in space and time. What one misses most is the individual contemporary note of 'Prufrock'. Eliot failed to imagine saints in an appropriate contemporary guise as in the fourteenth century William Langland conceived of a Christlike ploughman, an appropriate curative figure in a time of disastrous famine, or as Malory's prosaic and quarrelsome knight, a fifteenth-century gentleman thug, can be converted without too much strain into *miles Christi*. It is difficult to pin-point the sensibility that moves through Eliot's poems. Perhaps, if Eliot's prowlers and flawed saints were merged, one might come up with one of Nathaniel Hawthorne's shadowed souls—say Arthur Dimmesdale, the saintly New England minister, who kept vigils night after night but could not purify his mind, who felt secret sympathies with the vilest of sinners, whose self-loathing drove him to punish himself with a scourge, and to whom the whole universe appeared so false and impalpable that it shrank to nothing.[85] The strain Eliot admired in the New England writers, Hawthorne and James, was their 'exceptional awareness of spiritual reality', their 'profound sensitiveness to good and evil', and their 'extraordinary power to convey horror'.[86]

In 1914 Eliot moved too fast, riding on intuitions and truncated visions without any real experience beyond his own self-absorbed fantasies. His poems did not satisfy him: 'I know the kind of verse I want, and I know this isn't it, and I know why', he wrote to Aiken in the letter quoted above. 'I shan't do anything that will satisfy me (as some of my old stuff *does* satisfy me . . .) for years.' A long period of poetic sterility followed, but by immersing himself in the metropolis of a foreign country and by marrying a terrifying, haunted woman he found, during this very period, the genuine trials against which he might refine his soul.

7. Emily Hale, at the age of twenty-three, as Eliot would have remembered her when he left for England in 1914

8. T. S. Eliot and Emily Hale in Vermont in the mid-1940s. He came to see her play in Noel Coward's *Blithe Spirit*

4. *Eliot's Ordeals*

ALL through his last semester Eliot was planning another journey abroad. In February 1914, or earlier, he decided to complete
his training in Europe as many leading American teachers of
philosophy had done. The Harvard authorities, who regarded
him as a future teacher in the philosophy department, awarded him
a Sheldon travelling fellowship.[1] Officially, he was to spend a
year at Merton College, Oxford, studying Aristotle under Harold
Joachim, a disciple of Bradley—Bradley himself was almost
inaccessible in his rooms overlooking Christ Church meadow.
Eliot also had a stint in Germany in mind. He planned to participate in Marburg University's summer programme for foreign
students in July and August 1914.

Eliot's first response to Europe was some distaste for the
'past-putridity' of old towns in Italy and Belgium, but Marburg,
built on the side of a steep hill, had beautiful, unkempt gardens
and he had the impression of great waves of roses. Each day he
walked in the woods, but not too far lest he be late for the five
excellent meals served by Frau Pfarrer. Lulled by a sudden tran-
quility, Eliot planned his first long work which, like the master-
works of later years, was to piece together poems written at
different times. A tentative title, he told Aiken, was the 'Descent
from the Cross'. The poem was to include first 'Oh little voices'
and the newly-composed 'Saint Sebastian'; to be followed by an
insane section; a love song of a happier sort with a refrain in
the manner of 'Portrait of a Lady'; a mystical section and, to
conclude, a Fool-House section in the manner of 'Prufrock' in
which the speaker attends not a teaparty but a masquerade. He
goes in his underwear as St. John the Divine. 'Descent from the
Cross' was never completed. Eliot had barely settled down in
Marburg when he realized that war was imminent. On 3 August
he moved, via Rotterdam, to London, and thence, in October, to
a new retreat, Oxford, where he remained till his marriage in
June 1915.

In London he was merely a tourist, politely curious about local
habits. He saw determined matrons in tailormade suits and ugly

hats advance on Assyrian art in the British Museum and then
fade beyond the Roman statuary.[2] He saw a vulgar shopgirl in a
department store, and her false teeth and the pencil stuck in her
hair spoke to him of heated nights in second storey dance halls.[3]
From his room in 28 Bedford Place he saw an old woman sing
'The Rosary' for pennies.[4] London itself seemed like a scene
from *Bleak House*: all brown waves of fog and trampled edges and
muddy skirts.

While London at least seemed to offer some promise of life
behind the iron railings and curtained windows, Oxford seemed
quite dead. He deplored the dons' smug domesticity, their preg-
nant wives, and the lack of female society. His senses felt numbed.
There were few men up in 1914–15, and these Eliot appraised, as
one fellow-student remembered, 'with feelings that were singu-
larly disengaged'.[5] His best friend, named Culpin, joined the
army and was killed on his first day in the trenches.[6] 'O Conversation, the staff of life, shall I get any at Oxford?' Eliot wrote
dejectedly to Conrad Aiken.[7]

Yet beneath this quiet life, Eliot was slowly moving, in 1914
and 1915, from a Jamesian position of retreat before experience
to make a resolute advance on experience. For Eliot this would
be the most difficult of tasks, to stab himself awake. And when he
failed to awaken to religious emotions, he abruptly tried an
alternative, to awaken himself through marriage. It was probably
this effort to bestir himself that lay at the root of *The Waste Land*,
the origins of which date back beyond this time.

Two compelling individuals made claims on Eliot during this
crucial year. The one was a young American poet, Ezra Pound,
with exuberant auburn hair and pince-nez, who flung himself
into chairs and emitted strange cries. He was interested in Eliot
as a poet. The other was the vivacious Vivienne (sometimes Vivien)
Haigh-Wood, who was to become his wife. Neither's claim was
unreasonable, but each distracted Eliot from his saint's dream.

In the summer of 1913 Pound had heard from Aiken that, as
he put it, 'there was a guy at Harvard doing funny stuff'.[8] Eliot
then invited Pound's attention by calling on him in September
1914. He showed Pound 'Prufrock' and Pound was immediately
captivated by Eliot's natural language and his uncanny grasp of 'an
extant milieu, and an extant state of comprehension'.[9] Pound
dashed off an excited letter to Harriet Monroe, editor of *Poetry*,

raving about his new find. 'Prufrock' was the best poem he had yet seen from an American.[10] To H. L. Mencken he wrote: 'I enclose a poem by the last intelligent man I've found—a young American, T. S. Eliot. . . . I think him worth watching.'[11] Eliot was stimulated and encouraged by Pound's enthusiasm. Pound energized Eliot at a time when he was more or less resigned to an academic career in philosophy and turned him firmly back to a career as a poet. They were drawn together as two young lapsed professors in exile from America. Eliot looked up to his older and better known contemporary as a teacher and campaigner, and was grateful for his truly generous attention and concern. 'He would cajole, and almost coerce, other men into writing well,' Eliot remembered, 'so that he often presents the appearance of a man trying to convey to a very deaf person the fact that the house is on fire.'[12] Pound gave Eliot entrée to his first artistic milieu in London, the group which included Miss Weaver, Wyndham Lewis, H. D., and Aldington. From mid-1915 Eliot attended their Thursday night gatherings in Soho and Regent Street restaurants where—tall, lean, and hollow-cheeked—he would listen to gossip of Amy Lowell's amazing descent on London, and Ford Madox Hueffer booming anecdotes of the great Victorians, and Arthur Waley on Chinese poetry, while overhead the air-raid sirens whined.

A common view of Pound is as a marvellous sponsor and teacher, wholeheartedly devoted to his disciples. Perhaps his sponsorship had its drawbacks too. Eliot recalled that he was so passionately concerned about works of art that he sometimes tended to regard his protégés 'almost impersonally, as art or literature machines' to be oiled for the sake of their potential output.[13] Pound said explicitly, in a letter to Quinn, that he was interested in Eliot's personal feelings only insofar as they affected his poetic productivity.[14] One observer said he treated Eliot as a kind of collector's piece. With his prize beneath his eye, he would recline in an American posture of aggressive ease, and squint sideways up at the visitor, over the rims of his pince-nez, to see how impressed he was with Eliot's apt answers.[15] Eliot allowed Pound to groom him as a sophisticated poet in some ways as Gurnemanz groomed Parzival as a knight. Parzival obediently polished his manners, Eliot his diction and versification.

The exact nature of Eliot's relationship to Pound is not clear, but he was not in those early years an admirer of Pound's poetry. 'His verse is touchingly incompetent', Eliot wrote to Aiken.* While Pound was impressed with Eliot's note of modernity, Eliot thought Pound's poems were old-fashioned.[16] In *After Strange Gods* he charged Pound with being attracted to the Middle Ages by everything except that which gives them their significance. 'I confess I am seldom interested in what Pound . . . is saying,' Eliot wrote in the *Dial* in 1928, 'but only in the way he says it.' He listened to Pound's pleas for exact objective presentation, hard reality, chiselled statement, and allowed himself to be turned from the exalted hazy impressions of his visionary poems. Composing reviews on the typewriter helped him slough off long sentences, an improvement in lucidity, he thought, at the expense of subtlety. An eight-line poem, 'Suppressed Complex', boasts a stereotyped image of a joyful young blade after a night of love. He jotted mocking character-sketches of Bostonians—the Channing-Cheetahs, Aunt Helen, Cousin Nancy.

Pound concerned himself with the material details of Eliot's life—his jobs, his poverty, his need for contacts and publication. It was as though Eliot were a precious plant to be watered and tended with care. 'Pray God', Pound wrote, ' "Prufrock" be not a single and unique success.'[17] Without Eliot's knowledge, Pound personally borrowed money to pay for the printing of *The Love Song of J. Alfred Prufrock and Other Observations*.[18] Eliot recalled that one might sometimes chafe against Pound's beneficence, though one never resented it. Once, when Eliot struck up an acquaintance with Roger Fry and Lowes Dickinson at the seaside in 1916, Pound behaved rather jealously and got Eliot to agree Fry was 'an ass'.[19] Eliot had to keep up an attitude of discipleship, but he felt that Pound deserved it.[20]

Pound reinforced Eliot's impulse at this time to cast off what they believed to be the thinness of American civilization. Pound saw a 'blood poison' in America, and Eliot, he said, had the disease. ' . . . Perhaps worse than I have—poor devil', he wrote, '. . . the thin milk of . . . New England from the pap.'[21] Disinherited together, they would float through other civilizations and ransack them for souvenirs. Henry James once spoke of the

---

* 6oth Birthday Coll., p. 23. Pound complained of Eliot's 1919 review of *Quia Pauper Amavi* that it was all 'granite wreaths' and 'leaden laurels, no sign of exhilaration'.

American appetite, 'morbid and monstrous, for colour and form, for the picturesque and romantic'.[22] Half a century before Pound and Eliot started to write, he had predicted American writers who would discover their freedom to pick and choose and synthesize the various tendencies of foreign civilizations with an unprecedented lightness and vigour 'and in short (aesthetically &c) claim our property wherever we find it'.[23]

One cannot say if Pound was aware of Eliot's religious appetite. Eliot himself retreated from the initial impulse, but he may have been further discouraged by Pound's disapproval of Western religions. 'Christianity has become a sort of Prussianism, and will have to go', Pound thought. 'It has its uses and is disarming, but it is too dangerous. Religion is the root of all evil, or damn near all.'[24] On another occasion he attacked monotheism: 'I consider the *Metamorphoses* a sacred book, and the Hebrew scriptures the record of a barbarian tribe, full of evil.'[25] In a 1917 issue of the *Little Review* (in which Eliot also appeared) Pound said: 'Organized religions have nearly always done more harm than good, and they have always constituted a danger.'[26] In 1918 he said Christianity should be taken lightly and sceptically, until it drifted back into a realm of fairy-lore and picturesque superstition.[27] Pound disapproved when Eliot eventually settled for Christianity as the cure for cultural despair. 'His diagnosis is wrong', he commented flatly. 'His remedy is an irrelevance.'[28]

Eliot was writing religious poems when he met Pound. Pound convinced him to return to the social satire of 'Prufrock' and, by 1918, Pound proudly announced 'new and diverting verses'.[29] They *were* diverting, but also bitter for, when Eliot focused on society, he saw only stupid men and fearful women—Sweeney copulating and Mrs. Porter's whores, the pimply youths at Sunday Service, Grishkin the female jaguar, and the threatening paw of Rachel née Rabinovitch. He fell into the habit of writing glib jibes at creatures so patently tarnished and futile as hardly to warrant the energy of his attack.

Yet while Eliot was writing his satiric verses and dining out with Pound's emancipated coterie, he continued to brood about Christianity, its dogma and institutions. Christian dogma, he realized, was not subject to logic, but could not be skipped over. 'Philosophy may show, if it can, the meaning of the statement that Jesus was the son of God. But Christianity—orthodox

Christianity—must base itself upon a unique fact: that Jesus was born of a virgin: a proposition which is either true or false, its terms having a fixed meaning', he wrote in 1917.[30] In 1916 and 1917 he reviewed a number of books about the relation of philosophy to religion, criticizing writers who tried to reformulate Christianity so as to make it more palatable to the enlightened bourgeoisie. He criticized specifically their removal of asceticism and radicalism from Christianity—it made it too tepid, too liberal, too much like the enlightened Unitarianism of his family. 'All that is anarchic, or unsafe or disconcerting in what Jesus said and did is either denied or boiled away,' he complained. He scorned one writer's suggestion that following Christ could be made easier. 'Certain saints', wrote Eliot crushingly, 'found the following of Christ very hard, but modern methods have facilitated everything.'[31]

His reviews also showed a concern for the religious emotions and for mystical experience. He read, with interest, the anthropologist Lévy-Bruhl's *Les Fonctions mentales dans les sociétés inférieures* and found there a recognition of the mystical side to the primitive mind which, he felt, Frazer had neglected. It struck him how much more mystical experience engrossed the daily life of the savage than that of civilized man.[32]

Eliot also worried about the Church as an institution. His resentment against the empty proprieties of Sunday church-going dated back to Boston days and must have been associated with the Unitarian churches attended by his family. In particular, he evidently resented Sunday morning services conducted by his cousin, Fred Eliot, who became a Unitarian minister. In 'Mr. Eliot's Sunday Morning Service' and 'The Hippopotamus' Eliot denounced empty idolatry of forms with the reforming zeal of his forebears. In the eighteenth century the Revd. Andrew Eliot had written: 'The greatest prodigies of wickedness have been those who have put on the guise of religion.'[33] In *Savonarola* Charlotte Eliot had written:

> The church of old
> Had chalices of wood, while all of gold
> Her prelates were. Now are her prelates wood,
> Her chalices of gold, and it is good
> For this to rob the poor.

T. S. Eliot's own comparison of modern congregants clutching 'piaculative pence' with the fervent asceticism of early Christians, stemmed from his desire for a revival. Ten years later, Eliot was campaigning to save churches from destruction, parading at the head of a protest march through City streets and chanting 'Onward Christian Soldiers'. During his first years in London he wrote blasphemous poems, but he explained later that genuine blasphemy stemmed from the 'partial belief' of a mind in a peculiar and unusual state of spiritual sickness. Blasphemy might even be 'a way of affirming belief'.[34]

Eliot's belief had its foundation, in 1914, in his sense of man's flawed nature and the necessity for drastic measures of purification. He cultivated a state of mind that was the very antithesis of the eclectic, tolerant, democratic mind that had surrounded his late-nineteenth-century Mid-Western childhood. In one of Eliot's Oxford University Extension lectures in 1916, 'The Reaction against Romanticism', he alluded to T. E. Hulme's theory: 'The classicist point of view has been defined as essentially a belief in Original Sin—the necessity for austere discipline.'[35]

As Eliot had sought depravity in Montparnasse in 1911, he sought it again in disreputable suburbs in South London. He found 'neighbourhoods of silence' which, he said, were more evil than neighbourhoods of noise. In 1917 he wrote about the secret life of a bank clerk called Eeldrop (Eliot himself was a bank clerk at the time and described by Pound as serpentine), who would indulge his taste for witch-hunts and smell out evil with the implacable curiosity of a master detective.* His passion is to surprise truth behind the masks and façades, and he prides himself on his moments of pure observation and insight that transcend the usual pigeon-holes. The clerk tries to grasp the uniqueness of each event, a sense of which, he feels, had vanished with the decline of the religious view. He is particularly fascinated by the medieval mind's identification of evil through the punishment— the eternal punishment—that followed. He himself is a sceptic 'with a taste for mysticism'.

Eliot's preoccupation with questions of Christianity, theology,

* 'Eeldrop and Appleplex', *Little Review*, 4 (May 1917), 7–11. Donald Gallup suggested that Eeldrop and Appleplex seem to have been Eliot and Pound. See *T. S. Eliot & Ezra Pound: Collaborators in Letters* (New Haven: Henry W. Wenning, 1970). The first Andrew Eliot is said to have been one of the jurors in the Salem witch trials and Eliot's Stearns grandmother, Charlotte Blood, was a descendant of the notorious 'hanging' Judge Blood.

and evil remained undercover because he remained in doubt. 'For people of intellect I think that doubt is inevitable', Eliot once told an interviewer. 'The doubter is a man who takes the problem of his faith seriously.'[36] In July 1917 he acknowledged life was poor without religion, but as yet he was unconvinced it was the greatest of all satisfactions and so worth the effort.[37] It was for Eliot a time of exile, when his own visions and impulses dried up, a time of 'silence from the sacred wood'.[38]

When Eliot failed to awaken his religious emotions in 1914, he had a sudden impulse 'to be a moment merry . . .'. He was ready for women to fall in love, he told Aiken, and naively expected shyness to vanish with virginity.

During the Trinity term of 1915 Eliot went punting with another American, Scofield Thayer. The party included Thayer's sister, Lucy, and an English girlfriend, Vivienne Haigh-Wood.* They met again at a lunch party in Thayer's rooms at Magdalen. Two months later they were married. Vivienne's excitable, eager nature combined with a fragile beauty stirred in Eliot a hope that she might supply the defining experience he so urgently needed. Marriage was Eliot's one memorable act of daring self-surrender and perhaps served as a compensation for the self-surrender he had failed to achieve during his religious crisis. A little more than a year after his marriage Eliot wrote of the attractions of passion after a practical, sensible, and emotionally undernourished upbringing:

> For the boy whose childhood has been empty of beauty, who has never known the *detached* curiosity for beauty, who's been brought up to see goodness as practical and to take the line of self-interest in a code of rewards and punishments, then the sexual instinct when it is aroused may mean the only possible escape from a prosaic world.[39]

He goes on to say that both sexual and religious passion offer possibilities of 'escape' into feeling, but already he recognizes—he was twenty-eight when he wrote these words—that religion promised a more durable satisfaction: 'We must learn to love always, to exercise those disinterested passions of the spirit which are inexhaustible and permanently satisfying.'

* Pound surmised that Vivienne was Thayer's best girl or that he was, at least, an admirer. Letter to Quinn (24 Mar. 1920), Quinn Coll.

Vivienne Haigh-Wood was a few months older than Eliot; when they met, both were twenty-six. She was, at the time, a governess with a Cambridge family, but was interested in the arts. Her father, whom she loved, was a painter; she herself painted and studied ballet and, later, wrote poetry and prose sketches.[40] To Russell, she seemed most like an actress. She liked original, dramatic clothes and bold colours—she owned a scarfdress in the postwar years and, in the thirties, got herself up in a cape and waistcoat and flourished a cigarette-holder. She was attractive to men, but evidently not the kind of woman a gentleman would like to introduce to his mother. Eliot, silent and shy, was touched by her free manner, her lavish temperament, and her downright opinions, frank to the point of what was then thought vulgar—but still charming. She was quite devoid of cultural snobbery, and would never say she liked Bach or Cézanne if she did not. Eliot was fascinated by a woman who could dispense so perfunctorily with masks and façades. He admired her daring, her lightness, her acute sensitivity, and her gift for speech. Later, the very qualities that attracted him—her emphatic rhetoric (she spoke with a 'strong Welsh shriek'), her unashamed behaviour, her frank eyes—accused him of his insufficiencies when their marriage failed.

Almost nothing is known about their relationship. There are a few anecdotes by friends, a few suggestive statements in their own writings, and the rest is guesswork.[41] Both had recently been in love with someone else, and were in need of consolation. Vivienne's love affair with a schoolmaster, Charles Buckle, had ended six months before she met Eliot. Her diary of that time is an ominous record of fluctuating moods. For nine months 'B' endured Vivienne's emotional scenes, screams and reproaches, 'heavenly' (but brief) reconciliations, frantic telegrams and phone-calls until in August 1914, with a relief evident even to Vivienne, he enlisted at the War Office, and so escaped. The diary does not do Vivienne credit: it exhibits a shallow and self-centred *prima donna*, preoccupied with her romance.

It seems that, for a brief spell, Vivienne Haigh-Wood liberated Eliot emotionally, but whatever oblivious emotion Eliot felt was soon replaced by a grim sense of responsibility. The momentum that carried them both to reckless consummation made Eliot think of Dante's Paolo and Francesca. He quoted the line 'ma solo un punto fu quel che ci vinse' (but one moment alone it was that overcame us), and Francesca's assertion that her lover shall never be divided from her. He recalled how their torment in hell was not to lose all recollected delight—that would have been a relief—but to continue to experience desires they could no longer gratify.[42]

Eliot married quickly on the crest of a moment of rapport, so abruptly that there was not time to inform his family. It was almost necessary for Eliot to act impulsively—to forestall habitual scruples—if he were to act at all. He once said that it was better to do wrong than to do nothing. 'At least we exist.'[43] He was impatient with the remote, stuffy atmosphere of universities, and Vivienne tempted him to fling himself inescapably into a 'real' world—where people made love and took care of each other and worried about money. That the adventure into the 'real' world did not turn out well, that Eliot was disillusioned with the marital relationship before it had fairly begun, should not distract from the important fact: Eliot, at one point in his life, took a plunge and chose a course where there would be no going back. 'There are always some choices', he said eighteen years later, 'which are irrevocable and, whether you make the right one or the wrong one, there is no going back on it. "Whatever you do," I wish someone had said to me then, "don't whimper, but take the consequences."'[44] His marriage was to be the grim underside of his life, the secret inferno to be traversed before he might be worthy of the genuine awakening only Christianity could supply.

I think Eliot's disillusion with his marriage was associated with sexual failures, and preceded his discovery of his wife's chronic illness. One Friday evening at dinner, about one month after their marriage, Vivienne Eliot told Bertrand Russell that she had married her husband to stimulate him, but found she could not do it. Russell's sympathies were, at this point, with the wife whom he saw as a spirited English girl tied to an over-refined New Englander. He thought she would soon tire of him.[45] I cannot help suspecting, however, that Vivienne misrepresented their relationship to Russell and that her nervous, hysterical, unsympathetic nature contributed substantially to their unhappiness. Eliot did not contradict his wife's complaint to Russell, but reclined listlessly across the table. He had already given up.

One wonders how Vivienne saw Eliot. She recalls in her diary his cleancut mouth, fine head, and keen, deep, hawklike eyes.[46]

'He was a very attractive fellow then', one acquaintance wrote, 'a sort of looks unusual this side of the Atlantic.'[47] At times he seemed like a Harvardian Rupert Brooke—with a Gioconda smile, dimples, and a graceful neck—and at times like a sleek cat, with an exactly articulated drawl that made a sleepy droning like 'some heavy hymenopter, emitting a honeyed buzz'. His charm, part of which was his reserve, and her faith in his artistic promise spurred Vivienne to save him from his cagey constraint. Both willed this awakening, but it failed.

There is no use denying that many of Eliot's early poems suggest sexual problems[48]—not lack of libido, but inhibition, distrust of women, and a certain physical queasiness. He was offended by blood on the marriage-bed,[49] and by French perfume that disguised 'the good old hearty female stench'.[50] Vivienne's slightly vulgar manner perhaps liberated him momentarily from his genteel constraint, but he was soon put off by it, and it was clear to friends who observed them early on that he felt ashamed of her. Years later, she wrote a sketch about a loudmouthed wife trying to energize her husband on the dance floor. 'Now *dance*, for a change', she says, exasperated. 'You never do dance, you know, you simply march about. . . . You've got no energy.'[51] The wife exhorts; the husband smiles feebly. (Someone remembered how Eliot and his wife used to foxtrot, very solemnly, in the twenties.) I think Vivienne never quite accepted their incompatibility, while Eliot accepted it too quickly. After a year, he said he had been through 'the most awful nightmare of anxiety that the mind of man could conceive', but at least it had not been dull.[52]

Eliot once wrote an Ode about an immature couple's disastrous first sexual intercourse. The inexperienced man, sailing expectantly towards a 'golden apocalypse', is frustrated by what appears to be a premature ejaculation. He is left, a good way below the stars, 'indignant / at the cheap extinction of his taking-off'. The Ode alludes to Whitman's lines about sexual exasperation:

> O Hymen! O Hymenee! why do you tantalize me thus?
> O why sting me for a swift moment only?

But while the bridegroom contrives to recompose his neat façade, he feels (probably exaggerated) guilt towards his partner who appears to him a 'succuba eviscerate', a sexual creature deprived of her force.* It is impossible to know how far the Ode recalls Eliot's own experience, but there actually was, according to Russell, a disastrous 'pseudo-honeymoon' at Eastbourne, with Vivienne not far from suicide.

Eliot's male characters suffer either from a sense of inadequacy, like Prufrock or Burbank, or automatic lust like Sweeney, or emotional barrenness in the case of the house agent's clerk. With the first the woman is unapproachable, with the second she is hysterical, with the third she remains indifferent. I am not suggesting Eliot should be identified with these lovers, for they are caricatures, but simply noting that all his accounts of sexuality in his early years, except one, show it to be joyless, forced, sporadic, and sordid. Eliot's main problem was his early distrust of women, reinforced by his unfortunate marriage to a moody *prima donna*. His early letters to Pound contain bitterly anti-feminist remarks and the women in his new poems were all rather frightening, barren, and parasitic: the feline Grishkin who plays the role of playful panther to the male's scampering marmoset, the sick Princess Volupine stretching a wasted hand, the hysteric in *The Waste Land* and, in the same poem, the fashionable, pampered Fresca. In this section (which Eliot cut on Pound's advice) he makes his final antifeminist statement:

> Fresca! in other time or place had been
> A meek and lowly weeping Magdalene;
> More sinned against than sinning, bruised and marred,
> The lazy laughing Jenny of the bard
> (The same eternal and consuming itch
> Can make a martyr or plain simple bitch);
> Or prudent sly domestic puss puss cat,
> Or autumn's favourite in a furnished flat,
> Or strolling slattern in a tawdry gown,
> A doorstep dunged by every dog in town.
> For varying forms, one definition's right:
> Unreal emotions, and real appetite.[53]

Eliot seems to have regarded a seductive woman not as a human being but as a man's ordeal, a figure of sin with whom the man had heroically to consort. I think that Eliot's view of women had much more to do with traditional and literary prejudices than

* The Latin 'succuba' (strumpet) came to mean, in the folklore, a female demon thought to have sexual intercourse with sleeping men.

with the reality of his marriage, however unsuitable. Vivienne's
1919 diary shows most frequently the mundane interests that
engaged most of her energies—a woman buying a hat or vege-
tables, making blackberry jam, enjoying a 'roaring time' amongst
her own friends. Yet, strangely, in her own sketches, her self-
image merges with the fictional stereotype of the alluring female
whose exceptional energy and intelligence becomes for the sensitive male monstrous and unnatural. The hyacinth blooms 'mis-
shapen'.[54]

Before the couple took over Russell's flat, in September 1915,
Vivienne Eliot became ill and, in January, nearly died. This
remained the pattern of the rest of her life: a pattern of illness,
crisis, convalescence, and relapse. In April 1919, when Virginia
Woolf met her, she saw a prematurely old and washed out little
woman.[55] Eliot said Vivienne made a heroic struggle against ill
health,[56] but one major or minor illness followed another, from
tuberculosis in infancy to an attack of colitis in 1923 when she
very nearly died. Eliot told Pound that Vivienne had all along
behaved very finely and even offered to live on her own so that
her illnesses should not interfere with his work.* But worse
than these physical ordeals was her perennial nervous self-
consciousness, amounting at times to panic and, in crowds, near-
delirium. There were frequent 'nervous collapses' associated with
severe headaches and heavy, dazed sleep all day and night for
weeks, sometimes months.[57] In one of Vivienne's sketches the
voices of guests drive an invalid mad as she lies in the dark.
Could her hysteria have been the side effect of drugs or sedatives
which she had started to take, quite innocently, under doctor's
orders, when she was sixteen?† (It has been suggested she
drank ether, which was, after opium, a common sedative in the

* Pound to Quinn (4–5 July 1922), Quinn Coll. In 1914 Vivienne mentions a liver
complaint, neuralgia, fainting. Eliot's letters in 1916 mention her stomach upsets,
exhaustion, a tendency to faint when not lying down. In 1919 she speaks of migraines
and a swollen face. In 1922 Eliot told Pound that her symptoms seemed to point to
pituitary trouble, a cramped *sella turcica*. In the spring of 1924 she nearly died again,
and in frightful pain, of what was tentatively (but obviously unsatisfactorily) diagnosed as rheumatism. There was pleurisy in 1929 and her diary of 1936 complains
of a permanent injury to the spine.

† Statement by Theresa Garrett Eliot (28 Mar. 1970), Eliot Coll., Houghton
Library. Russell considered that the difficulty between Vivienne and Eliot in the
first year of their marriage had a lot to do with her taking drugs and the consequent
hallucinations. (Letter to Robert Sencourt, 28 May 1968, Bertrand Russell Archive,
McMaster University, Hamilton, Ont.)

nineteenth century).[58] The Haigh-Woods, Vivienne's parents, were
not very helpful, and it was left almost entirely to Eliot to
care for her, which he did with devotion, as she deteriorated
year after year.

Both Eliot and his wife used the image of a couple in a cage.
Vivienne, in one of her sketches, pictured the cage as a deadly
isolation, where the confined woman beats herself against the
bars.[59] To Eliot the cage meant the opposite, the perennial lack of
privacy: 'It is terrible', he wrote, 'to be alone with another
person.'[60]

One of Eliot's friends said that posterity will probably judge
Vivienne Eliot harshly.[61] She could turn on her husband with
cruel accusations. She must have been, in her thwarted, insomniac moods, unpleasant company. Eliot had no notion
how to cope with her moods—during the first year of marriage and again, ten years later, he turned helplessly to Russell
for advice and aid.

It seems that, from Vivienne Eliot's angle too, the marriage
must have been a miserable trial. She mentions that her husband,
too, was often sick at night.[62] Vivienne's diary for 1919 (the only
year she kept a diary during her married life) shows a woman who
is self-sufficient and high-spirited, but only when her husband is
not there. Signs of neurotic complaining reappear on summer
weekends when, after a week or a fortnight's separation, she and
Eliot are reunited. When he leaves her in the country and returns
to town she becomes exhilarated by her natural surroundings.
On 10 July 1919 she has a 'wonderful impression of Bosham in
the evening, last thing. Full moon, and only half dark at 10, and a
mist. The water like glass.' On 19 September 1919 (at Wittering,
with Mary Hutchinson): 'Cold stormy day. Sat in the shed with
the wind roaring & the shed creaking like a ship.' By contrast
her references to her husband are laconic: Tom had a cold and
was cross. Tom went to France. Alone, in August, she enjoys
'the feeling of London in the still heat'. Her husband returns
'very nice at first, depressed in evening'. The diary suggests that,
quite possibly, she was not a parasite by nature (only when she
was ill), that she was a dutiful and devoted wife and at the same
time encouraged an unusual degree of personal freedom. Also,
although she never acknowledges this to herself, her husband's
company often dampened her spirits.

Vivienne's writings show an eager, emotional personality, with vague romantic yearnings, and a daring and nerve that could be easily daunted. Although she had only a flickering talent, she is not to be dismissed lightly. After her marriage, she soon receded into the background of her husband's life and remained there, a phantom of pain and reproach. Eliot's friends remembered a chic and literate woman who became, through illness, too hysterical and bothersome to be endured. One feels invited to dismiss her as a burden Eliot painstakingly upheld, beyond the call of duty, for many long years. She left no one to speak for her, and no evidence in her diaries that the marriage was disastrous from her point of view, but we know that her initial impulse towards Eliot was generous. 'She has been ready to sacrifice everything for me', Eliot wrote to his father soon after their wedding. 'She has everything to give that I want, and she gives it. I owe her everything.'[63] She wished to enliven the shy young American and help him to become a poet. She would offer her sea-hoard of curious oddments and trophies, gossip, and spars of knowledge, like the woman in Pound's 'Portrait d'une Femme'. She would make herself part of the poet's mind.* Eliot would not participate in her fantasy—he would not allow her the inspirational role—but remained flat, negative, and patently ashamed of her. And so she, in turn, retreated—into attention-getting illness. She ended tragically as the emblem of the material world against which Eliot's religious impulse tugged, to free itself.

In judging Vivienne, it is tempting to focus on unpleasant aspects of the thirties—her fascism, her empty-headed preoccupation with royalty, her letters, haughty or abject, demanding help from unlikely people, a bank manager, a doctor. But one really wants to know, not how she responded to disaster, but how she was during those seventeen years she spent with Eliot. For this reason most of her diaries are not very useful. There remains the 1919 diary, written in a more sensible vein, after four years of marriage, which shows a physically active woman, an enthusiastic bather and ballroom dancer. Yet, one must not play down two other aspects evident in her photographs. One shows a small timid woman, a visitor hesitating in the doorway at Garsington,

* 'As to Tom's *mind*, I am his mind': letter to 'Jack', inserted in Diary (8 Dec. 1935).

pretty and delicate in skirts drooping about her slender ankles, or
dwarfed by the confident stature of Philip Morrell in the garden.
She did not much care for literary gatherings. In her 1919 diary
she comments that Edith Sitwell's party was dull, a Hutchinson
dinner—with Nancy Cunard, Osbert Sitwell, and Duncan Grant
—was 'very drunken and rowdy but not fun'. Another, a later
image, shows her at home in Clarence Gate Gardens in 1922. Her
face is harder and her nose bolder beneath the severe haircut.
She stands in her own domain—next to a tea-kettle on a gas-ring
—her hands on her hips, her feet slightly apart. 'She is a person
who lives on a knife edge,' Russell wrote, 'and will end a criminal
or a saint. . . . She has a perfect capacity for both.'[64]

In 1933 Eliot left her, frenzied, in a flat decorated with pictures
of him. His friends sympathized for they considered her unbalanced. Eliot believed she was sane, but that she talked herself
into an unbalanced state.[65] Her diaries of 1934–6 resound with the
shock of Eliot's abandonment, which she could never quite
believe was voluntary. She made wild efforts to bring herself to his
attention. At the same time she joined numerous clubs and began
a career in music, but it became increasingly difficult to compose
herself to undertake even the most trivial daily chores. The lined
face that looked back at her from a portrait by a friend showed
'all the blank expression of one who has learned to keep out of
the way'.[66] 'My face is yellow like parchment,' she wrote in July
1934, 'no colour, dead eyes—am as thin as a rat. Too restless to
rest. Too tired to think constructively. *NO* hope, that I can see,
in any direction.' A creature of unblunted sensitivity, she continued to fight against nameless obstructions, bruised again and
again by the bafflingly evasive politeness of erstwhile friends
like Geoffrey Faber who had given their loyalty to Eliot and
screened him, at any cost to Vivienne, from contact with her. Her
sense of a nightmarish conspiracy sounds mad, but it is not un-
justified—for everyone she knew conspired to keep Eliot out of
sight. I find it admirable that she never blamed her husband for
his desertion. As the years went by, her passionate loyalty became
her sole claim to human dignity and the ideal which she intended
her diaries to publicize. She eventually entered a mental home
where she died in 1947.

Late in his life, in 1957, Eliot married again and, for the eight
years that remained to him, at last knew happiness. Vivienne

9. 'The Love Song of Saint Sebastian' (pp. 61–2) was inspired by Mantegna's *St. Sebastian* in the Palazzo della Cà d'Oro, Venice

10. In July 1914 Eliot was struck by this 'wonderful' *Crucifixion* by Antonello da Messina in Antwerp. At this time he was searching for a religious idiom

Haigh-Wood had been frail and helpless; his second wife, Valerie Fletcher, had sense and humour, and cared for him with all the generous love that he could have desired. His married happiness restored the self-confidence his turbulent years with Vivienne had undermined. 'Without the satisfaction of this happy marriage,' he wrote in triumph in the fiftieth anniversary report of Harvard's class of 1910, 'no achievement or honour could give me satisfaction at all.'

When Eliot was living in Russell's flat during the second year of the war, Russell confided strange observations which later found their way into *The Waste Land*. After watching the troop trains—full of patriotic Englishmen—depart from Waterloo, he would see London's bridges collapse and sink, and the whole great city vanish like a morning mist. 'Its inhabitants began to seem like hallucinations', he said. He would wonder whether the world in which he thought he lived was not merely a product of his own nightmares.[67]

In the autumn of 1915 Eliot came to settle in a city at war and saw it from the estranged angle of a non-participant. He saw a London from which almost all its energetic young were withdrawn, and only the sick and unfit, the elderly, the women, the workers, and a few outcast pacifist intellectuals remained. He knew the gloom, the privation, and the deadness of London in those war years. 'In the winter of 1915–16', wrote Lawrence, 'the spirit of the old London collapsed. The city, in some way, perished, perished from being the heart of the world, and became a vortex of broken passions, lusts, hopes, fears, and horrors. The integrity of London collapsed, and the genuine debasement began . . .'[68] Virginia Woolf recalled silent people huddled in omnibuses, looking cadaverous in the blue light (for the lights were all shrouded in blue paint) and the consenting mass of civilians whom one did not wish to join—'the strutting; the tiptoeing; the pasty; the ferret-eyed; the bowler-hatted, servile innumerable army of workers'.[69] Eliot shared in the horror of the English intellectual at the dehumanization of his countrymen, but I imagine that he felt less shocked, more resigned. The war bore out his dim view of civilization.

Although Eliot said he was not sure what he thought of the war, he was sure he was not a pacifist. After the U.S. entered the war, he made rather belated but feverish efforts to enlist in August and September 1918. There may have been conventional incentives—a sense of duty, the wish to belong, or the wish to escape—in his case, an unhappy marriage. He might have wished to please his mother who for years had been writing urgent newspaper appeals to Americans to fight and even wrote a war song for the *Boston Herald*. Pound, it is almost needless to say, opposed Eliot's enlistment, and he went so far as to go to the Embassy in person to point out that if this were a war for civilization, not merely for democracy, it was folly to shoot one of the six or seven Americans capable of understanding the word.[70] To Eliot's disappointment he was not accepted for active service in the U.S. navy on account of tachycardia and his old hernia, nor did he get a commission in the Quartermasters or Interpreters Corps despite the letters of recommendation from Arnold Bennett, Harold Joachim, Charles William Eliot, and George Herbert Palmer. The year after the war ended he recreated in one of his poems the emotions of a man who had not fought in rain or knee-deep in mud, nor fought bitten by flies—someone who had never ventured from his city retreats into heroic scenes.

Not only did Eliot miss the battles of his generation, he was also at a distance from civilians at home. His first encounters with Londoners—apart from his wife, Russell, and Pound's circle—were brief and unsatisfactory. For a year and a half, from September 1915 to the beginning of 1917, his days were spent with schoolboys to whom he was a foreigner, 'the American master'. He felt no interest in them, and looked upon his teaching not as a means of self-expression but as a barrier to it. 'After all,' he said, 'all I wanted to do was write poetry, and teaching seemed to take up less time than anything else, but that was a delusion.'[71] Teaching drained his energy so that he had no desire to write, even during vacations. 'To hold the class's attention you must project your personality on them, and some people enjoy doing that; I couldn't, it took too much out of me.'[72]

Eliot loathed schoolmastering but stuck to it, partly because he needed money for his wife's medical bills, partly for self-respect. Honest toil—regular employment, set hours, a full-scale commitment—had been for generations the self-affirming activity of the Eliot family. It would have been unlikely for Eliot to make a precarious living, like many English writers, by freelance or part-time work. He had to prove himself to his father who had decided, when Eliot made his rash marriage and deferred his prospects at Harvard, that he was making a mess of his life. He had to recover the approval of his mother who had always scorned 'the man without a hoe'. Rather bend beneath the strain of work, she urges in one of her poems, than lose your pride in action.[73] She pitied him—'it is like putting Pegasus into harness'—but she felt that he had, in the past, been overprotected and should now make his own future.[74]

In the summer of 1916 Russell asked Clive Bell to befriend Eliot and, through Bell, Eliot came in contact with Roger Fry, Virginia and Leonard Woolf, Lytton Strachey, and Lowes Dickinson. Eventually, he was gathered into Ottoline Morrell's circle where he met other members of the English literary scene like Aldous Huxley and Middleton Murry. He was treated kindly, invited to dinner at 46 Gordon Square, the home of Clive Bell, and to Garsington, the Morrells' place in Oxfordshire, but he remained an outsider. They did not feel at ease with him. His feeling for the conventional and his prim manners were not particularly endearing. His ostentatious learning (partly effrontery, he later admitted) did not impress. When Huxley met him, in December 1916, he wrote him off as 'just a Europeanized American, overwhelmingly cultured, talking about French literature in the most uninspired fashion imaginable'.[75] His studied reserve constrained the disciples of G. E. Moore, who observed frankness and truth as the highest good. Lytton Strachey found him nice at times, at other times 'rather ill and rather American; altogether not quite gay enough'. He added, though: 'But by no means to be sniffed at.'[76] Ottoline Morrell was more sympathetic. According to Vivienne, she knew how he was hurt and by whom. Vivienne mentions 'how often Ottoline used to say to me—and *how sadly*— "isn't Tom beautiful, Vivienne, such a *fine mind*, such a grand impression. Such a good *walk*." '[77]

Virginia Woolf rather liked him—his formidable air entertained her—but he remained peripheral to her life and, for a while in the early twenties, his self-pity became a bit tiresome. She did not look forward to his visits and used to sigh over him in her diary: O dear, Eliot on the phone again. The Woolfs and the Bells coped with Eliot's punctiliousness by treating him as a family joke. They found him deliciously comic.[78] 'Come to

dinner', Virginia would write to her brother-in-law. 'Eliot will
be there in a four-piece suit.'

That Eliot was not really accepted was not wholly his fault.
He had not been in any way fashioned by English life—neither
by a public school, nor a great university, nor by childhood or
family associations—and had only his manner to recommend him.
Henry James acknowledged ruefully when he was seventy that
he had cut himself off from where he belonged and had never
been wholly at home in England.

After the war, Pound left London. Eliot then became aware
that the only genuine literary milieu was the Bloomsbury Group,
and began to attach himself to its members and friends, in particular to Virginia Woolf and Mary Hutchinson, a daughter of
Winifred Strachey. Pound wrote scornfully from Paris that they
were an 'arse blasted lot' and urged Wyndham Lewis to 'get
Eliot out of England somehow'.[79] But Eliot remained, and
welcomed Virginia Woolf's invitations and her offer to publish
his latest poems.[80] She, on her side, tried to ignore Eliot's allegiance to Pound and challenged his façades that she might know
him better. One night at a dinner party she dared to laugh in
Eliot's white marble face and, to her surprise, was rewarded by an
answering twinkle. In March 1921, after a visit to the theatre, she
challenged him to confess his faults while they were cruising in
a taxi through the damp market gardens of Hammersmith. He
said that the worst thing in life for him was humiliation. From
that time he began to relax his formality and, by the end of 1921,
their friendship was firm. During the next twenty years of her
life he cherished her good opinion, and once said that whoever
else gave him approval, he only hoped 'that Mrs. Woolf'll.'

The turning point in Eliot's relations with English writers
came when the Egoist press published his first volume of poems
in 1917. Clive Bell took ten or twelve badly printed copies bound
in cheap yellow jackets to an Easter party at Garsington. They
were distributed; Katherine Mansfield read 'Prufrock' aloud and
Murry, Aldous Huxley, the Morrells, and Lytton Strachey applauded Eliot's talent.

By December 1917 Eliot was reading his poems under the
auspices of the Red Cross to fashionable society in the Mayfair
drawing-room of Lady Colefax. Also giving readings were troops
of nervous Sitwells, Aldous Huxley, a writer called Bob Nichols,

who hooted and moaned war poetry, and Viola Tree, who declaimed in a voice cloyed with syrup.[81] Gosse, who introduced the poets as 'bards', was rather shocked by one of Eliot's newest poems, the blasphemous 'Hippopotamus'. Eliot was also noticed for his polite manners. When Gosse rudely reproved him for being late, he listened quietly and did not protest, although he had come straight from his job at the bank. It occurred to Osbert Sitwell that he looked like an Aztec carving with his wide bone structure and 'yellow' eyes.[82]

When Eliot settled in London he had been an embryo professor; in 1917 he was born a poet. The critical time was probably March 1916 when he put off returning to America to defend his dissertation. It was then that he put all thought of America and academic prospects behind him. He decided to concentrate on becoming a poet. In April Eliot noted that he had fifteen to twenty publishable poems, and began to plan his first volume. After *The Love Song of J. Alfred Prufrock and Other Observations* had come out a year later, he began to put in order his more recent poems written under Pound's eye. Seven of these poems, including 'Mr. Eliot's Sunday Morning Service', 'Whispers of Immortality', and 'Sweeney Among the Nightingales', were printed by the Hogarth Press and bound in one of Fry's designs. Leonard and Virginia Woolf made about two hundred and fifty copies, to be sold at half a crown each. It was a gesture of faith which helped strengthen Eliot's position. When Aiken returned to London after the war he found Eliot 'so rootedly established, both socially and in the "politics" (as it were) of literature . . . as to have achieved what Emily Dickinson had called "overtakelessness" : he had built the splendid ramparts round that rare new domain of his, and behind them he had become all but invisible, all but intangible'.[83]

During this period of transformation Eliot was writing brief autobiographical fragments and poems which he kept separate from the quatrain poems he was writing for immediate publication. Between 1914 and 1919 the hoard consisted of three distinct batches, corresponding to Eliot's private trials: first the problems of religious awakening, then the problems of adaptation to a foreign city and to a demanding new wife. By 1919 Eliot had material for one long poem or series of poems. This was to emerge, three years later, as *The Waste Land*, the poem that fired the imagination of the 'lost' generation and made Eliot famous.

5. *The Waste Land Traversed*

ONE of Eliot's friends, Mary Hutchinson, who read *The Waste Land* soon after its completion, said it was 'Tom's autobiography'. Eliot himself said that it was only 'the relief of a personal . . . grouse against life'.[1] *The Waste Land* is clearly more than this— it may be read as a satiric critique on the postwar scene—but I should like to trace the confessional element which, though covert or deliberately muted in the poem itself, is more obvious in the manuscript. Over the course of seven and a half years, going back to Eliot's last years as a student, he slowly accumulated a hoard of fragments, the earliest of which show a different bias from the poem that emerged in the autumn and winter of 1921–2.

Eliot justified the necessity for autobiography as opposed to formal biography. The definitive experiences in the life are so private—'the awful daring of a moment's surrender'—that only the man himself can record them. To know the man, one must follow the poem which alone 'will give the pattern . . . of the personal emotion, the personal drama and struggle, which no biography, however full and intimate, could give us'.[2] There is no other hope of recovering this after death, Eliot is saying at the end of *The Waste Land*, neither in wills nor obituaries, nor in the memoirs of well-meaning friends and critics. 'Every poem is an epitaph', Eliot said in *Four Quartets*, suggesting that the poem is the last word on the life.

In the earliest fragments of the *Waste Land* manuscript Eliot works with what he once called 'some rude unknown psychic material'.[3] He speaks of impulses so inward that they are obscure even to himself. Such 'dark' experience must take its own unique form but, says Eliot, there is a 'shadowy' traditional form against which it shapes itself. From the beginning Eliot had in mind the traditional form of the spiritual journey from sin to salvation. 'So through the evening . . .', written in 1914 and the source of part V (according to Eliot the most important part) of *The Waste Land*, is a more sophisticated version of one of his mother's conventional poems, 'Ring Easter Bells', in which the soul tends nearer to God along an upward path and bells herald 'the faith that clearer vision brings'. Eliot was haunted by the model lives of the chosen, Dante and St. Augustine, against whom he matched the prosaic, sordid, and promising facts of his own existence. To climb the path towards salvation, to hear the bells and voices and thunder, differed from the beatific 'silences' Eliot experienced in 1910 and 1911 in that it is the culmination of a lengthy, earnest process of self-examination.

For several years, between the writing of the first visionary fragments in 1914 and the completion of the poem in 1921, Eliot, like Gerontion, was cut off from a 'sign', so that the exemplary life and the personal 'grouse' could not cohere as a unified statement. It was not until Eliot heard 'What the Thunder Said', during his illness in December 1921, that he was able to conceive, once more, of a special destiny, and so complete his long-unfinished poem.

The Waste Land goes back to Eliot's fantasies of religious extravagance in 1914. At the age of twenty-eight, when Eliot was living in the Ash Street attic in Cambridge, Massachusetts, he wrote three visionary fragments from which he later took lines, setting, and ideas for part V of *The Waste Land*.[4] All three fragments are concerned with revelation and its aftermath: the attractions and problems of 'turning' or conversion. Eliot seems struck, but without much conviction, let alone dedication. Two of the three fragments show a man suffering from the strain of living between two worlds. For Eliot, there was no sudden blinding certainty, but a long period of doubt. It was to be thirteen years before he was baptized and probably many more years before he knew grace. He had to endure a loneliness all the more terrible for his long hesitation. For thirteen years he was one of the 'straw men' poised to act but lacking, he felt, the stamina.

In 'After the turning . . .' Eliot tells of brief, elusive intimations which encourage him to spurn the everyday world. By night he faces another world—not quite accessible as yet, but hovering behind bristling spears and flickering lights. He wonders if, should he succeed in repudiating enough of the world, it will of itself fall away. And after his prayers and much painful soul-searching, the futile shows of this world do, at least momentarily, disappear. As the stars go out the poet sees himself on the brink of an Acheron-like river filled with tears and turbid and blackened by suffering. On the further bank, a pagan garrison threatens the oncoming sinners, suggesting an inferno and purgatorio yet to be traversed. A forbidding vision, apparently quite different from the beatific escape into the ring of silence of three years before, but there seems to be for Eliot, as for Dante, no other way.

Another fragment tries to put into words the substance of his vision. There is a strange infusion of power:

> I am the Resurrection and the Life
> I am the things that stay and those that flow.
> I am the husband and the wife
> And the victim and the sacrificial knife
> I am the fire, and the butter also.

This divine voice speaks to Eliot, as Emerson's Brahma, of an all-encompassing energy through which one transcends the vicissitudes of fortune.* Neither New Englander found truth in what William James called the 'professional philosophy shop'. James said that for certain minds truth would seem to exist for the express confusion of the machinery of philosophy and to reveal itself in whispers to the meek lovers of the good in their solitude. The repeated assertions in 'I am the Resurrection . . .', though derivative and perfunctory, confer on the poet a divine call in more familiar terms than the Sanskrit message of the thunder in *The Waste Land*.

The third fragment, 'So through the evening . . .', is a journey in search of enlightenment and a direct source for the journey in part V of *The Waste Land*. As the poet-pilgrim climbs the pathway of the mind at least two companions appear, dreamlike other selves. One is a crazy, gifted adventurer. He dares to turn him-

---

* Valerie Eliot noted (*facs. WL*, p. 130) the immediate source of both poems in the *Bhagavadgita*, ix. 16:

> I am the rite, the sacrifice
> The offering for the dead, the healing herb:
> I am the sacred formula, the sacred butter am I,
> I am the fire, and I the oblation [offered in the fire].

Michael Wood has noticed another likely source in Baudelaire's 'L'Héautontimo-rouménos':

> Je suis la plaie et le couteau!
> Je suis le soufflet et la joue!
> Je suis les membres et la roue,
> Et la victime et le bourreau!

self upside down to see a new world of reversed images;[5] he hears unexpected, miraculous voices:

> A man distorted by some mental blight
> Yet of abnormal powers
> I saw him creep head downward down a wall
> And upside down in air were towers
> Tolling reminiscent bells
> And there were chanting voices out of cisterns and of wells.

In his trance the poet witnesses a conversion scene and feels drawn to participate ('My feverish impulses gathered head'). But suddenly this dream is replaced by another in which a diver sinks through layers of water, deliberately discarding all ordinary faculties of perception and communication. He surrenders to an irrational impulse, swimming down rather than up, to the calm still deep where seaweed, purple and brown, crowns him. It is a reckless heroic quest, an act of faith. The sea is 'no place of habitation, but a passage to our habitations', Eliot later quoted from one of Donne's sermons.[6]

The last apparition represents a different type: a man lies on his back, passive and inert.* He gazes not on new worlds of experience, but on the old—'the established world'—from which he, too, is a renegade. He feels estranged from people he knows, even though, like Prufrock, Gerontion, and Tiresias, he chooses to remain among them. 'It seems to me I have been a long time dead', he confesses. 'Do not report me to the established world.' The seers in 'So through the evening' are not unalike: all despise the known world; all have, in their different ways, to 'die' that a new order may come into being. A clue to the complex nature of *The Waste Land*'s narrator perhaps lies in the fragmentation of personality in 'So through the evening'. Two seers are reckless explorers, transgressing the boundaries of normal experience; the last is a jaded and time-worn malingerer on the rim of the old world.

If Eliot had lived say in the time of Dante or, even more plausibly, in colonial New England, the sanity and relevance of

---

* A. Walton Litz has justly noted that 'it is a quintessentially Jamesian experience which lies at the heart of his work. The tragedy is that of one who can perceive but cannot act, who can understand and remember but cannot communicate.' '*The Waste Land*. Fifty Years After', *Eliot in His Time*, ed. A. Walton Litz (Princeton: Princeton Univ. Press, 1973), pp. 20–1.

visions would not have been the issue it was for a man coming to
adulthood in the second decade of the twentieth century. Eliot
had a capacity, rare in his time, to imagine living by visions. He
wrote that once there existed 'a psychological habit, the trick
of which we have forgotten, but as good as any of our own. We
have nothing but dreams, and we have forgotten that seeing
visions—a practice now relegated to the aberrant and uneducated
—was once a more significant, interesting, and disciplined kind
of dreaming. We take it for granted that our dreams spring
from below: possibly the quality of our dreams suffers in
consequence.'[7]

It is not possible to understand Eliot's visions and the associated confessional impulse outside the context of a native tradition.
It is true that Eliot's natural bonds were not with the America
of his own day, but perhaps he shared with earlier Americans a
deep, unacknowledged bond; with those who opposed spiritual
deadness through revivals like the Great Awakening and
Transcendentalism; with those New England saints who were
subject at all times to incursions from the unknown. Many New
Englanders kept private records of their religious adventures,
noting also their soul's health and their progress towards grace.
Spiritual autobiographies flourished in England after 1640 and then
declined towards the end of the century,[8] but in America they
never flagged and, in fact, the habit of self-examination never
really died out. In the journals of Emerson a Yankee is still taking
his pulse, as in *The Education of Henry Adams* and in the poems of
Dickinson and Eliot. In the early, more obviously personal fragments of the *Waste Land* manuscript Eliot climbed the twisting
path of his mind; he dived into his own deep waters; he kept an
account of his revelations and balanced them against his soul's
diseases. When religious life no longer existed chiefly in institutions, but was almost wholly internalized, the saint could prove
his existence only through personal testimony.

It is easy to dismiss the earliest fragments in the manuscript
as inelegant scraps Eliot sensibly discarded, but together they
announce a persistent mood. In 'Ash Wednesday' Eliot refers
again to his 'turning' towards the religious life. Other visionary,
introspective poems of the twenties—'Doris's Dream Songs',
'The Hollow Men'—seem to move so naturally out of the fragments of 1914 that, in retrospect, the witty, satiric poems Eliot

wrote between 1917 and 1919 seem like a digression from his poetic career. During his first years in England Eliot played half-heartedly at coming alive through emigration, marriage, and a new milieu. He told Aiken that it would be interesting to cut oneself into pieces and to watch, as if one's life were another's, and see if the fragments would sprout. His experiment was reinforced by Pound's urgent literary ambitions and Vivienne's equally urgent emotional claims. In 1914 Eliot, still a free spirit, had a vision of 'turning' from the material world—but Pound and Vivienne turned him back to face it.

Early in the history of the manuscript, in 1915,* there appears an arresting personality, a would-be saint, who was to become shadowy and diffuse in the long, more impersonal *Waste Land*. Eliot named the character after Narcissus, Bishop of Jerusalem who, towards the end of the second century, hid himself in the desert for many years.9 'The Death of Saint Narcissus' is a martyr's tale. 'Come,' Eliot says in the opening lines, 'I will show you . . . his bloody coat and limbs.' Of his actual career Eliot says virtually nothing; he concentrates on the inner life of a rather peculiar character who feels most intensely alive when God's arrows pierce and mar his flesh. Saint Narcissus wishes to become 'a dancer to God' and deliberately cuts himself off from his kind, but to his dismay sees no divine light, only his own flaws—his self-enthrallment, his indifference to others, his masochistic delight in the burning arrows.

In *The Waste Land* the Narcissus-figure reappears as the prophet in the desert in 'The Burial of the Dead', as the penitent who is 'burning, burning' at the end of 'The Fire Sermon', and as the solitary pilgrim in 'What the Thunder Said', who abandons civilization and its history in search of a new life. Where Narcissus differs from the *Waste Land* pilgrim is in his failure to receive a sign. And in Narcissus's failure lies the necessity for a biographic enterprise of larger scope. It is crucial to see *The Waste Land*,

---

* The paper of the first draft of 'The Death of Saint Narcissus' (*facs. WL*, p. [90]) is British, 'Excelsior Fine British Make', the same paper Eliot used for 'Mr. Apollinax'. On 2 February 1915 Eliot alluded to the two poems in a letter to Pound ('I understand that Priapism, Narcissism etc are not approved of . . .'), quoted in *Ezra Pound: Perspectives*, ed. Noel Stock (Chicago, 1965), pp. 110–11. Valerie Eliot reports (p. 129) that Eliot could not remember the date of 'Saint Narcissus', but it may have been early in 1915.

indeed all of Eliot's subsequent work, in the context of this early story of an aspiring saint.

Saint Narcissus fails the desert ordeal and succumbs to disappointment, but such setbacks are common, almost essential, to the plot of the spiritual autobiography. Bunyan set the pattern for the kind of religious quest that persists in an atmosphere of risk and frightful doubt. God's abandonment of Bunyan did not disqualify him from the pursuit of grace. On the contrary, it excited in him, as in Eliot, more rigorous self-analysis and self-condemnation. Behind both stands Augustine's exhibition of his life as a pathological development from the evil effects of which he was saved by a dramatic call.

Eliot's interest in 'Saint Narcissus' lies chiefly in diagnosing the man's failure. The well-known dangers of gazing into the mirror of election are pride and despair. Eliot was to face despair later; his concern here is with the consequences of self-regard. Eliot acknowledges how hard it will be for a 'Narcissus' to attain the selflessness and purity of motive requisite for sainthood. Narcissus's failure is summed up in the condemnatory line: '. . . he was struck mad by knowledge of his own beauty.' It gratifies his senses to think of himself as a tree tangling its roots together, or as a slippery fish, or as a smooth girl raped by an old man. He dares to court God with the same appetite for self-gratifying sensation. Narcissus has no moral impulse, only a masochistic one ('His flesh was in love with the penetrant arrows'). He wants to reform himself, to be more than himself, but instead of self-enhancement there is, at the end, the shock of self-loss. After the encounter he finds himself burnt out, abandoned on the hot sand, dry and stained, his beauty gone, his clothes bloody, and the taste of death in his mouth.

The strength of Eliot's analysis lies in the implied anti-Romantic need to curtail the self and its narcissism and to find a reliable external authority. (In 1917 Eliot told Russell that he would like to give new expression to Authority and Reverence.[10]) Between Narcissus and 'the Peace which passeth understanding' lay *The Waste Land*'s accumulation of texts from past and present, literature and history, and current circumstance. Narcissus had a genuine religious impulse, but was too ignorant of the ways of sin and redemption.

Although Eliot derides the passion of Narcissus, the details he selects are more penetrating than in the case of previous caricatures, Prufrock or Saint Sebastian. This is a case study of peculiar narrowness and moral intimacy. Eliot ignores the kind of physical and social detail with which he enlivened the portrait of Prufrock, and narrows in on the 'saint's' secret pretensions and strange obsession with pain. Narcissus went, Eliot says wryly, to the death *he* wanted. His death is not, as it purports to be, a religious drama, but a self-indulgence: the redness of his wounds 'satisfied him'. In his essay on Dante, Eliot distinguished between the pain of the damned which is almost natural to the sufferer and expresses his essence, and the pain of purgatory which is consciously and deliberately accepted in hope of salvation.* Eliot's saint is too grotesque to be fully human, but his emotional vices are real. His attitudinizing is deplorable, but his sense of God's abandonment is genuine:

> Now he is dry and stained
> With the shadow in his mouth.

This final picture of the failed saint, sealed in Eliot's matter-of-fact condemnation, has the unexpected effect of generating abrupt sympathy. The image of dryness came to dominate *The Waste Land*, but without this sympathetic feeling.

Associated with the condition of dryness is the desert setting which here and in *The Waste Land* figures as the proper place for a religious drama.[11] The mood of the solitary under his rock was the vantage point from which Eliot chose to reflect on modern civilization. In 'Saint Narcissus', *The Waste Land*, and 'The Hollow Men', he cultivated the state of mind of those early Christians who looked forward to the imminent ruin of a decadent civilization and wished to be alone. Precedents are to be found not only in the Bible and among the desert saints of the early middle ages but in the imagination of American Puritans who transported themselves 'into a *desert land* in America . . . in the way of *seeking first the Kingdom of God*'.[12] The renegade from civilization continues to retain imaginative vitality in America in the figures of Thoreau

---

* *SE*, pp. 216–17: 'In hell, the torment issues from the very nature of the damned themselves, expresses their essence; they writhe in the torment of their own perpetually perverted nature. In purgatory the torment of flame is deliberately and consciously accepted by the penitent.'

and Huck and the cowboy who rides out into the prairie's
horizon. 'So through the evening' ends with a decision to leave
town. Narcissus leaves because 'men's ways' interfere with self-
expression:

> He could not live men's ways, but became a dancer to God.
> If he walked in the city streets, in the streets of Carthage
> He seemed to tread on faces, on convulsive thighs and knees,
> So he came to live under the rock.

The city evokes images of hell and sin, Dante walking over bodies
beaten down on the ground[13] and Augustine's cauldron of unholy
loves during his youth in Carthage.[14] Narcissus sets up an antithesis that persists in *The Waste Land* between damned city and
the desert. Here is the hot sand and rock, glimpsed in 'The Burial
of the Dead', and developed at length in 'What the Thunder Said'.

Eliot's imaginary desert has a parallel in the grail romances
where a knight customarily traverses a waste land in his quest for
grace. Eliot's desert has a parallel too in the way the Puritans
conceived of New England—as a howling desert—because they
associated their Migration with the Israelite exodus. They saw
themselves marching across a wilderness to create a new ideal for
mankind. For Eliot's mother the wilderness was also charged
with moral meaning. In 'The Man Without the Hoe' Charlotte
Eliot hails America as the place where pilgrims came, not out
of greed, but to try themselves morally in a wilderness, to
face 'the rocky shore' and 'a churlish climate'. This notion of
pilgrimage from imperfection to perfection was deeply rooted
in Eliot's family and their Puritan past. For him to experience the
world as a waste land was a prerequisite to experiencing it in faith.

The first three pieces of *The Waste Land* manuscript were
obviously fragments, but 'The Death of Saint Narcissus' was a
complete poem. Pound submitted Eliot's second draft to Harriet
Monroe's *Poetry* in August 1915, while Eliot was briefly in
America. Evidently, this was against Eliot's wishes—he might
have considered the poem too confessional—for, when he returned to London, he withdrew it from publication. There is
another possible explanation. As the conditions of Eliot's own
life in London, bound up as he was in 1915 with Pound and
Vivienne, made a religious commitment improbable, he began
to play down the issue in his poetry. By the time Eliot produced

the final draft of *The Waste Land* the dream of sainthood had almost wholly disappeared.

For a year and a half after Eliot's disastrous marriage he felt as if he had dried up.[15] Yet within six months, in January 1916, he confided to Aiken that although he was not actually writing he had '*lived* through material for a score of long poems in the last six months'.[16] It was during this period of financial hardship and disillusionment with his marriage when, as Eliot told his father, the war belittled private suffering,[17] that he accumulated in their first sharpness the impressions of London and the distraught wife that formed the basis of the urban sections of *The Waste Land*. In new manuscript fragments written between 1916 and 1919* Eliot turned from his earlier preoccupation with the philosophic model of the ideal life to see what could be learnt, more empirically, from ordinary lives around him—the wife, the merchant, the fishermen lounging on the banks of the Thames. In a sense the two enterprises are complementary and remained so throughout *The Waste Land*: one way of proclaiming sainthood is by abandoning civilization for the solitary vigil; another is by discerning in one's civilization the moral contours of a waste land—lust and avarice, mindless workers bound upon the wheel of fortune, and betrayed and wretched women.

Eliot's most autobiographical fragments have to do with a mismatched couple. In 'The Death of the Duchess', which was rewritten in 1921 for part II of *The Waste Land*, the wife is playing a scene in a love-drama while the husband is absorbed in a quite

---

* My supposition is that 'The Death of the Duchess' and a collection of fragments written on small 'Hieratica Bond' sheets from a notepad—'Elegy', 'Dirge', 'O City City', 'London', and 'The river sweats . . .'—were written between 1916 and 1919. This cannot yet be conclusively proved and I have doubts about the date of 'The river sweats . . .'. The fact that fragments were written on the same paper is no guarantee that they were written at the same time. Valerie Eliot tells me there is a letter to Eliot, written in 1919, in which the correspondent refers to 'The Death of the Duchess' and Mr. Bleistein (in 'Dirge'). The theme of death by water and the name Bleistein appear in poems written in 1918 and 1919. The idea for 'Dirge' and its first line came from the Proteus episode of *Ulysses*, published by the *Little Review* in May 1918 and republished by Eliot in the *Egoist* in March–April 1919. The form of 'Elegy', on the verso of 'Dirge', suggests it was written during Eliot's quatrain period (1917–19). The two City fragments would have been written after the spring of 1917 when Eliot began his career as a bank clerk in the City. Taking in all the evidence, 1918 seems a reasonable date for the Hieratica fragments.

different, more sinister plot of life and death.* The husband is a solitary who finds the continual physical proximity of his wife unendurable. His only hope of life is to escape from the marriage, but to do so would mean death—psychological death—for his mate. The title suggests a sequel to 'The Death of Saint Narcissus': God denies the saint his chosen role, as the husband shuns the wife. 'The Death of the Duchess' describes a couple trapped in a hotel bedroom and unable to communicate their separate needs. (Eliot called the 1921 version 'In the Cage'.) The wife silently urges her claims as she determinedly brushes her hair in the fire-light, her bare arms poised above her head. The husband silently longs to escape through the door. There is no respite from their differences, not even sleep, only barren diversions, a game of chess, an afternoon drive. (In one of his January 1916 health-bulletins to Russell, while Vivienne recuperated at the Torbay Hotel, Torquay, Eliot mentioned an afternoon drive in a hired car after one of Vivienne's bad nights.[18])

Eliot's Duchess is identified with Webster's Duchess of Malfi, a proud, self-assertive woman whose reckless marriage to her steward leads to her ruin. But this allusion, like most of Eliot's, is so coloured by personal circumstance that to pursue it is rather pointless. Eliot shapes his marital scene ostensibly in terms of drama, but there is no dialogue and the husband shuns his role, craves solitude and anonymity. Within the privacy of his mind he

---

* *facs. WL*, pp. [104–6]. It might be possible to be more specific about the date by matching the paper with that of non-*Waste Land* manuscripts but, in the absence of other clues, the paper evidence is inconclusive. The paper matches that of an unpublished review (1916) of H. D.'s translation of choruses from *Iphigenia in Aulis* (Berg Coll.). It also matches a draft of 'Gerontion', which Eliot sent to John Rodker in the summer of 1919 (David Schwab Coll., Alderman Library, Univ. of Virginia at Charlottesville). In a letter to Rodker (9 July 1919) Eliot mentioned the prospect of another poem, about the same length as 'Gerontion'; this might be 'The Death of the Duchess'. I think it is most likely Eliot wrote the fragment before 1918. There is a joking reference among Pound's comments on 'Whispers of Immortality' to a Duchess who is outraged by Grishkin's animality. Pound may have been alluding to 'The Death of the Duchess' in his *Egoist* review of Eliot's poetry, June 1917, when he says that a great deal of the poetry is personal and in no way derives from Webster and others.

The poem is the first of *The Waste Land* fragments in typescript: Eliot used his own typewriter which he had brought with him from Harvard. According to Eliot there were never any handwritten drafts of the sections in typescript, only scattered lines (letter to Quinn, 21 Sept. 1922, Quinn Coll.). Eliot composed some *Waste Land* fragments on his Harvard typewriter, others on an alternative typewriter to which he had free access. This was probably his office typewriter.

11. Vivienne Eliot in London. 'I owe her everything', Eliot wrote to his father soon after their marriage in 1915

12. 1921—Vivienne at Garsington: 'My nerves are bad . . . Yes, bad. Stay with me.' (*The Waste Land*)

dwells on memories and dreams of metamorphosis, but he cannot act or speak in relation to his mate. Eliot's later comments about the dead wife in *The Family Reunion* are suggestive of the Duchess: 'She has sometimes talked of suicide', Eliot wrote. 'She is trying to play one of her comedies with him [the husband]—to arouse *any* emotion in him is better than to feel that he is not noticing her.' Her effect on the husband is to fill him with 'a horror of women as of unclean creatures'.[19] In 1917 Eliot was generalizing crassly from his private misfortune: his letters to Pound repeatedly dismiss women as unworthy of attention, lower beings. In one of the drafts of 'Whispers of Immortality', in May–June 1918, he deplores the social framework that demeans sons of God to entertaining the wives of men.[20]

'Elegy' is another manuscript poem about a mismatched couple.[21] Although it was not retained in any form in *The Waste Land*, it is interesting for the husband's heightened psychological terror and the same play of two irreconcilable plots. The wife belongs in a story by Poe and her determination to possess her mate beyond death conflicts with Eliot's old plot of sin and redemption. The 'Poe-bride' haunts her husband's mind with an energy that becomes more perverse, overwrought, and malevolent in proportion to his evasiveness. Again the wife is a complex of victim and demon, and again the husband would be rid of her. Her revenge for having been emotionally dismissed is to refuse to go away. She will not allow the man to retire, but follows him tenaciously with her reproaches and consuming emotional claims. She appears no longer lovely, but filled with avenging poison. Scorpions hiss about her head.

In Eliot's fantasy the wife is followed by God. Both make fearful claims, both are avengers, both are associated with his sense of failure—yet they act not in conjunction but in competition. And the wife loses. Her presence intrudes upon the husband's welcome of God, and interferes with his receptivity. In the end she is forced to recede before a more compelling claim. Pursued by God, obsessed, the man's mind has no place for her. The poem ends:

> God in a rolling ball of fire
> Pursues by day my errant feet.
> His flames of anger and desire
> Approach me with consuming heat.

From the man's angle 'Elegy' is about an awakening sense of sin
in which a woman plays a crucial part. He regrets having wronged
her, but wishes he might dispose of her and, after sanctimonious
mourning, get on with his own destiny. In his scenario remorse
is followed by expiation and then, hopefully, bliss.

Like 'Elegy', 'The river sweats . . .', which was to become the
finale of part III of *The Waste Land*, associates religious emotions
with remorse for a sexual wrong.[22] In each, guilt for violation or
abandonment precedes purgatorial pain. Eliot believed one might
hold to the visionary power promised in 'I am the Resurrection'
only if the flesh were purged. The raining arrows of 'The Death
of Saint Narcissus' are one attempt to punish the flesh. They are
followed by the consuming flames of 'Elegy' and by the burning
agony which follows scenes of promiscuity on the River Thames,
at Moorgate, and on Margate sands:

> To Carthage then I came
>
> Burning burning burning burning
> O Lord thou pluckest me out
> O Lord thou pluckest
>
> burning

Again sexual guilt precedes religious fervour. The penitent
confesses, in the manner of Augustine, to his idle lusts, and his
sense of sin propels him smoothly into the burning routine. There
is no concern for the abused London women, only for his own
purification. Over the course of his career Eliot repeatedly alluded
to the refining fire, the cure for lust, on the highest terrace of
Dante's *Purgatorio*.* There is also the allusion to the Buddha's Fire

---

* *Purgatorio*, XXVI:

> '. . . consiros vei la passada folor;
>   e vei jausen lo joi qu'esper, denan.
> Ara vos prec, per aquella valor
>   que vos guida al som de l'escalina,
>   sovenha vos a temps de ma dolor!'
> Poi s'ascose nel foco che li affina.

('I see with grief past follies and see, rejoicing, the day I hope for before me. Now
I beg you, by the goodness which guides you to the summit of the stairway, to take
thought in due time for my pain.' Then he hid himself in the fire that refines them.)
The last line was the original epigraph to 'Prufrock' and was one of the fragments
to be shored for future use in *WL*: V. 'Ara vos prec' was the title of Eliot's second
collection of poems. 'Som de l'escalina' was the title of one section of AW. Lines 1
and 5 were quoted in 'Exequy', a *Waste Land* fragment Pound persuaded Eliot to
cut.

Sermon, in which the Buddha directs his followers to the holy life through the cultivation of aversion for all the impressions of the senses.[23] But Eliot's own asceticism can possibly be traced back, past his own miserable marriage and the spiritual biographies of Augustine and Dante, to his mother who wrote:

> Purge from thy heart all sensual desire,
> Let low ambitions perish in the fire
> Of higher aims. Then, as the transient dies,
> The eternal shall unfold before thine eyes
> The fleeting hours will grant thee thy request:
> Take thou immortal gifts and leave the rest.[24]

The pattern of spiritual biography is to move from a dead world to a new life. Eliot associated the dead world with the City of London, where he went to work as a bank clerk in 1917, and two new manuscript fragments are associated with that experience.[25] 'O City City', which was inserted into part III of *The Waste Land*, is a series of epiphanies, suggesting one or two ways of transcending the sordid city: the fishermen lounging near Billingsgate fish market, the splendour of Anglican churches nearby. Since his Gloucester childhood Eliot idolized fishermen whom he saw as unworldly gallant adventurers. During his lunch hours at Lloyd's Bank he used to wander along Lower Thames Street to a fishermen's wharf, perhaps the oldest on the Thames, in use from Saxon times. Seeing fishermen always at rest at midday, he imagined they 'spat time out' and spurned conventional habits. The fishermen suggest something much more natural than Narcissus's willed search for grace, and recall Bunyan's impression of the natural grace of three or four poor women in a doorway lit by sunlight.[26] From there he moved on to view the 'inviolable splendour' of Magnus Martyr, a church near the fish market. At other times, when he walked across London Bridge amidst horse-drawn carts, open-topped buses, canvas-topped lorries, street vendors, and dark-suited busy hordes, he saw in the distance St. Magnus the Martyr rise out of the dingy mass of London buildings, its white tower and fine Wren steeple surmounting the brown ratty buildings near a quayside edged with rusty machinery. A circle of windows stood out beneath the dome and spire.* In Eliot's

---

* Eliot owned an album of *London Views* containing a photograph of this scene, *c.* 1924. He took his brother to see this view in 1921 and Henry Ware Eliot took a photograph, preserved in the Eliot Coll., Houghton Library. Henry Ware Eliot

London, Wren's lovely empty churches soared above the city as a splendid counterpoise to the crowded hideous banks and vulgar commercial houses, somehow enduring against all those 'flying feet'. In the evening after work he would observe the tower of St. Michael, Paternoster Royal, its red windows lit up in the dark sky, a marvellous antidote to the 'ghastly hill of Cannon Street'.[27] Or on winter mornings, as he emerged from Bank Station, buried in the mass of hurrying workers, he would look up and see the church of Saint Mary Woolnoth (built by one of Wren's pupils) and hear it strike nine from its oblong tower with unusual square turrets. At lunch hour a tower down a grimy lane would strike his eye and empty naves would receive him, a solitary visitor, from the dust and tumult of Lombard Street.[28]

The second fragment, 'London', was eventually cut, but it contains the germ of the Unreal City scenes in *The Waste Land*. Briefly, Eliot contrasts the city of men, swarming and dead, with the City of God.[29] Eliot's approach here is still general and philosophic rather than individual and dramatic. He sees ghostly gnomes burrow in brick and steel, huddled between concrete and sky, with bodies mechanical as toys. But he perceives, also, that around this meaningless wheel of fortune there curls an 'ideal meaning' which his 'penumbral consciousness' may yet decipher. As yet it appears 'indistinctly', 'vaguely', 'doubtfully'. All he can grasp are the tarnished creatures, blindly gratifying immediate needs and unconscious of a 'formal destiny'. At this time Eliot wrote to Lytton Strachey that he could not endure being ground down to the level of the City's workers: 'I am sojourning among the termites'.[30] All the violent fragments written during Eliot's early years in London—the dramatic deaths and purifications of the flesh by fire and water—foretell the need, eventually realized at the end of *The Waste Land*, to declare civilization 'unreal' and so escape.

By 1919 Eliot had amassed a little collection of poetic fantasies and ordeals. 'Gerontion', written in May–June 1919,[31] marks the imaginative turning-point between these fragments and a unified poem. Although Eliot submitted to Pound's advice to exclude 'Gerontion' from *The Waste Land* and did not even include it in the *Waste Land* manuscript, 'Gerontion' nevertheless contains all

also photographed City men hurrying outside Bank Station with Saint Mary Woolnoth on the right.

its crucial organizing ideas. In the figure of Gerontion, Eliot brought back the disappointed religious candidate but made him into a contemporary, postwar character. The major innovation was the historical perspective. From the narrow biographic formula of the early fragments Eliot expanded his subject to take in contemporary lives, and now after the war he extended his judgement further, into history. Six months after Eliot finished 'Gerontion' he confided to his mother and to John Quinn that he was about to write a long poem he had had in mind for some time.[32]

With the case study of Gerontion, Eliot came back to the question of failure. Reviewing his life, Gerontion deplores its lack of action or commitment and the unenlightened death he faces. His self-absorption and his anxiety for experience recall Henry James's late tales of the unlived life: middle-aged gentlemen who crave and shrink from a tremendous experience, like the leap of a beast in the jungle. 'Came Christ the tiger', Gerontion muses—necessarily a 'tiger' to the loner unsupported by an institutionalized tradition of mysticism. Gerontion's theological position recalls that of the American Puritan who sees himself without spiritual agency, abject, wholly at the mercy of divine omnipotence.

At the same time as Eliot wrote 'Gerontion' he analysed the New England temperament in a review of *The Education of Henry Adams*.[33] 'A Sceptical Patrician' is clearly a bit of self-analysis and suggests links between Eliot, Gerontion, and Adams (to whom Eliot was distantly related). This refined type of American, Eliot said, had a strong Puritan conscience which laid upon him 'the heavy burden of self-improvement' and an obligation to experience more than liberal Unitarianism, an imperfect education at Harvard, and a narrow Boston horizon might have provided. His native curiosity was balanced by a scepticism which Eliot called 'the Boston doubt'. The Boston variety was not a solid scepticism but quirky, dissolvent rather than destructive, a kind of vulnerability 'to all suggestions which dampen enthusiasm or dispel conviction'. Eliot contemplated the respectfully attentive New England congregation who would have heard Emerson announce that he would not administer the Communion because it did not interest him. Wherever the well-bred American steps, said Eliot, the moral ground does not simply give way, it fragments. Gerontion's ground, too, flies into 'fractured atoms'.

Gerontion's last thought is of a traveller blown about by winds like the white feathers of birds in a snowstorm.

Later in 1919 Eliot wrote of his sense of the artist as an Eye curiously, patiently watching himself as a man.[34] Gerontion's distinction derives partially from Eliot's own peculiar circumstances: he was a lodger in an alien place, he had failed to fight the battles of his generation, he had not subscribed to its outdated values—romantic heroism, physical courage, and sentimental nostalgia. The poem is a private statement—Eliot tried to formulate a personal position by measuring his distance from his generation—yet at the same time a public exhortation, an attempt to alert a blighted society.

Eliot placed Gerontion outside community, among other drifters and petty individualists, in a lodging-house in a dingy city after the Great War. To the collector of porcelain or to the frivolous lady of fashion Gerontion's ranting monologue must seem pathetic; but from a historical distance this lone man's impulse to think and question seems sensible and brave. Gerontion asks some curious questions:

> What will the spider do
> Suspend its operations, will the weevil
> Delay?
>
> After such knowledge, what forgiveness?
>
> I have lost my sight, smell, hearing, taste and touch:
> How should I use them for your closer contact?

Gerontion asks here what one can do about the horror of mortality. And he asks how humanity may atone for its vacant present, its stupid pastimes, and its unforgivable history. And, finally, he asks how he personally may revive a decayed religious appetite. These were not new questions for Eliot, but he brought them together in Gerontion's monologue with renewed urgency.*

Gerontion tries to give his religious impulse a clearer intellectual basis by defining it against the backdrop of history. He thinks of history as a mistress, and secular leaders as her dupes. She

---

* He had raised the issue of mortality in the first poem he published in the *Harvard Advocate* ('For time is time and runs away'). He had questioned the purpose of social diversions and the banal pleasures of youth in a batch of poems written in 1910. And he had speculated on the nature of God's contact and demands in the first fragments of the *Waste Land* manuscript.

panders to men's vanities and deludes them with bogus favours, sometimes indeed granting them more than they expect, but in the end leaving them graceless and baffled. Through the ages she toys with and betrays the human race. Most immediately, through the Great War she betrays Western pride in progress, knowledge, and civilization. History induces men to forsake the salvation plot for her own tortuous plots. In this passage Gerontion denounces secular ambition as a reasonable alternative to faith.

During 1919 Eliot read the sermons of John Donne, Hugh Latimer, and Lancelot Andrewes, and became interested in the sermon as 'a form of literary art'.[35] It is a form that merges readily with Eliot's confessional–instructive mode.[36] Gerontion, in making his personal statement, uses preacher's terms of 'forgiveness', 'vanities', 'unnatural vices', 'virtues', 'our impudent crimes', and 'the backward devils'. While most of the postwar generation liberated itself from faith, Eliot moved in the opposite direction. The moderns rebelled against a Victorian version of faith, full of cant and hypocrisy. Eliot held on to an older faith—devouring, passionate, and mystical. From his earliest juvenilia Eliot consistently deplored contemporary life and secular history, not with the helpless voice of his generation, but with the authoritative voice of Old Testament prophet or New England divine. He speaks most like Emerson who said 'the centuries are conspirators against the sanity and authority of the soul. . . . History is an impertinence and an injury if it be anything more than a . . . parable of my being and becoming.'[37]

Gerontion and, later, the nameless pilgrim in *The Waste Land*, is poised at the extremity of a dry season, waiting for rain, the traditional symbol of grace or fertility. Gerontion asks for a miracle: 'We would see a sign!' he says in the words of Lancelot Andrewes, and his wish is fulfilled by the thunder's message and its promise of rain at the end of *The Waste Land*. Gerontion knows he may yet be saved from withering and decay if only he can recover some passion.* But his senses have atrophied and all that is left to him are fearful premonitions of savage experience, analogous to fighting in the warm rain or heaving a cutlass in a salt marsh or

* 'I have lost my passion . . . I have lost my sight, smell, hearing, taste and touch' is an allusion to Newman's sermon on Divine Calls, quoted in the *Apologia Pro Vita Sua*, ed. M. J. Svaglic (Oxford: Clarendon, 1967), p. 111: 'Let us beg and pray Him day by day to reveal Himself to our souls more fully, to quicken our senses, to give us sight and hearing, taste and touch of the world to come.'

drowning, like a seagull, off some distant shore. The warm rain, the marsh, the Gulf Stream are the mirages of a man dying for want of water.

It is not easy to follow the sequence of *The Waste Land*'s composition during 1921, but some details are clear. After resolving to write the poem at the end of 1919 Eliot did nothing about it during 1920. That year he busied himself with a volume of criticism, *The Sacred Wood*. The reviews were disappointing and he went about looking pale and ill.[38] Then, in the autumn of 1920, Vivienne's father became dangerously ill and she and Eliot sat up night after night nursing him. The anxiety was too much for Vivienne who broke down. In March and April 1921 she was in bed but in May went away to the seaside, and Eliot was suddenly free to think about his long-delayed poem. There were probably two periods of composition in 1921: first, in the spring, a brief effort to get something on paper[39]—but Eliot was exhausted from the strain of the previous six months and may well have done no more than scattered lines; then, in the autumn, from October to December, a sustained stretch of writing. For, finally, Eliot himself broke down and during his recuperation at Margate and Lausanne had, at last, the continuous privacy and leisure he needed to write his poem.

The event that immediately preceded Eliot's illness was a long-awaited visit from his mother, accompanied by his sister, Marian, and brother, Henry. He had not seen his mother for six years. He feared that Charlotte, now seventy-seven, would be old and weak, but when they met he was taken aback by her formidable energy. The real strain was having to keep his marital problems out of sight and Vivienne quietly in the country. At the end of the summer, after his mother left, he collapsed. When overstrained, he said, he used to suffer from a vague but acute sense of horror and apprehension.[40] In late September he went to see a nerve specialist. 'I really feel very shaky,' he wrote to his friend, Richard Aldington, 'and seem to have gone down rapidly since my family left.'[41]

On 12 October, Eliot was given three months' sick-leave from the bank. Vivienne bought him a mandolin and accompanied him to Margate where she left him to follow the rest-cure his doctor prescribed. It now became clear to him that he was suffering neither from 'nerves' nor insanity, but from 'psychological troubles' which, he complained, English doctors at that time simply did not acknowledge. He decided to seek help abroad, and Julian Huxley and Ottoline Morrell recommended Dr. Vittoz in Lausanne.

In the meantime, on 22 October, he moved to the Albemarle Hotel, Cliftonville, Margate. It is likely that it was during his three weeks there that a good deal of *The Waste Land*—almost certainly 'The Fire Sermon'—was written. Eliot ironically attached his hotel bill to the manuscript: the work he did in Margate cost him about £16 in all. The first week he indulged himself in the 'white room' and took all his meals. The next two weeks were spent rather more frugally in a modest room *en pension*. Vivienne, reporting to Russell, said that he seemed to like Margate.[42] He was in a precarious state, but the purposeful letters he wrote at this time suggest that he was convalescing rather than declining.[43] Pound, briefly in England in early October, found him enlivened by the prospect of leisure.[44] There was evidently no discussion of Eliot's poem, and I doubt that Eliot had completed any section before he went to Margate.

During the final stages of *The Waste Land*'s composition Eliot put himself, for what was to be the last time, under Pound's direction. On 18 November, on his way to Switzerland, Eliot passed through Paris and left his wife with the Pounds who were then living there. It seems likely that Eliot showed Pound what he had done in Margate. Pound called Eliot's Lausanne draft 'the 19 page version' which implies that he had previously seen another. He marked certain sheets on two occasions: once in pencil, probably on 18 November, once in ink, on Eliot's return from Lausanne early in January.* Pound undoubtedly improved particular passages: his excisions of the anti-Semitic portrait of Bleistein and the misogynist portrait of Fresca curtailed Eliot's excessive animus, and his feel for the right word improved odd lines throughout.†

---

* 'Exequy' and 'The Fire Sermon' are typed with Eliot's office typewriter on yellowish sheets with a 'Verona' watermark. The carbon of 'The Fire Sermon', with Pound's marginalia in pencil, was clearly shown first. Eliot then revised the top copy in accordance with Pound's suggestions before submitting it for further consideration on his return from Lausanne.

† Pound changed 'When Lil's husband was coming out of the Transport Corps' to 'When Lil's husband was demobbed', and suggested that Mr. Eugenides should not issue his invitation to lunch in 'abominable' but in 'demotic French'.

Pound was proud of his hand in *The Waste Land* and wrote:

> If you must needs enquire
> Know diligent Reader
> That on each Occasion
> Ezra performed the caesarian Operation.[45]

I think that Pound's influence went deeper than his comment during the winter of 1921-2, going back rather to 1918, 1919, and 1920 when he and Eliot were engaged in a common effort to improve their poetry. Pound's *Hugh Selwyn Mauberley* (1920) is a covert dialogue with Eliot, a composite biography of two great unappreciated poets whose flaws are frankly aired.[46] Pound criticizes a Prufrock-like poet too given to hesitation, drifting, 'maudlin confession', and aerial fantasy—the phantasmal sea-surge and the precipitation of 'insubstantial manna' from heaven. As though in answer, Eliot put aside his most confessional fragments, 'Saint Narcissus' and 'Elegy', and in 1921 overlaid private meditation with documentary sketches of contemporary characters—a pampered literary woman, Fresca (like Pound's Lady Valentine), Venus Anadyomene (another *Mauberley* character), Cockneys, a typist with dirty camisoles, and a scurfy clerk. The Pound colouring in these sketches did not quite suit Eliot. Where Pound is exuberant in his disgust, Eliot becomes callow or vitriolic—and Pound himself recognized this in his comments on typist and clerk: 'too easy' and 'probably over the mark'. Eliot's characters are not as realistic as Pound's. They are projections of Eliot's haunted consciousness—they could be termed humours.* Unlike the satirist, Eliot does not criticize an actual world but creates a unique 'phantasmal' world of lust, cowardice, boredom, and malice on which he gazes in fascinated horror. *The Waste Land* is about a psychological hell in which someone is quite alone, 'the other figures in it / Merely projections'.[47]

In 1921 Eliot deliberately played down the meditative voice of someone out of line with ordinary people and transferred the weight of his poem to the Voices of Society. A temporary title,

---

* See Eliot on the comedy of humours, *SW*, pp. 112, 116. In the essay on Ben Jonson, Eliot writes of characters that conform to the logic of their creator's emotions. Each character is 'a simplified and somewhat distorted individual with a typical mania'.

'He do the Police in Different Voices', refers to the experimental method of *Our Mutual Friend*, Dickens's apparently disconnected anecdotes and panoramic reportings which gradually cohere as the hard manipulative tone of society.* In *The Waste Land* there is no longer a central figure, like Narcissus or Gerontion, hovering between the remote role of religious candidate and a more immediate despair, but a medley of voices which represent the weak human mass with its modest potential and meagre opportunities. Yet the tones of the different voices are frankly contrived, even mocking, for the meditative voice is never truly submerged. Stripped of divine love in 'The Death of Saint Narcissus', stripped of marital love in 'The Death of the Duchess', stripped of misplaced fame in 'Exequy' it is the voice of a ghost, without visible shape or identity, but his need for forgiveness, attention, and sympathy is real. In the shape of St. Augustine he is purged of all sensuality. In the shape of a New England fisherman about to go under he asks that his life be remembered for its boldness and endurance even if he never knew God's will.† And in the shape of a fake poet who has misused his gift and buried himself in suburbia he pleads pity for his pain: 'SOVENHA VOS A TEMPS DE MA DOLOR.'[48]

One difficulty of attempting to speak from the centre of a common culture was its variety. Eliot had a more ordering mind than Pound; the collage of representative characters to be found in *Hugh Selwyn Mauberley* would not have satisfied him. In 'Rhapsody on a Windy Night' and in his doctoral thesis on Experience, Eliot had despaired of a philosophic principle that would master multiple, disparate perceptions. But in the mid-summer of 1921, while *The Waste Land* gestated in his mind, Eliot found an answer, oddly enough, in the Russian ballet.[49]

It was a time when Diaghilev's ballets represented a collaboration of the greatest innovators in music, art, and choreography, and London's intelligentsia went night after night to Covent Garden. Eliot was struck by the strange effect of 'a simplification of current life' in *La Boutique fantasque* and *The Three-Cornered Hat*.[50] The phenomenon was particularly striking in the strange, harsh

* Eliot used this title on his typescripts of parts I and II. He refers to the orphan, Sloppy, who would read the newspaper statements of London policemen 'in different voices'.

† *facs. WL*, p. [60]: 'Remember me. / And if *Another* knows, I know I know not.' Eliot aligns this shipwreck with that of Ulysses in the *Inferno*—'as pleased Another'.

music of Stravinsky's *Le Sacre du Printemps*. Eliot was so infuriated with the audience for laughing that he poked his neighbours with the point of his umbrella. The music seemed to him to 'transform the rhythm of the steppes into the scream of the motor-horn, the rattle of machinery, the grind of wheels, the beating of iron and steel, the roar of the underground railway, and the other barbaric noises of modern life.' Stravinsky, like *Ulysses* and *The Golden Bough*, provided a revelation of a vanished mind of which the modern mind was a continuation. Primitive man on the dolorous steppes, modern man in the city with its noises: there is an unchanging predicament, said Eliot. He saw that one might strip brute experience of its contexts and explanations, leaving the abrupt fact exposed, and simplify it further by showing the repetition of the same experience along the continuum of history. (As far back as 1914, in Josiah Royce's seminar, Eliot had insisted that 'there is no importance *at one time* historically'.)[51] Eliot uses real men and women and real historical events but reduces them to emblems of vice, lust, weakness, mediocrity. The typist awaiting the clerk, Elizabeth flirting with Leicester, Cleopatra in her barge: 'all the women are one woman', said Eliot in his notes. The woman, then, becomes an emblem of the decadent natural world which should be abandoned or dismissed. Eliot was puzzled when, later, people said *The Waste Land* was a difficult poem. 'My poetry is simple and straightforward', Eliot told Vassar girls in 1933, and looked pained when the audience laughed.

The Waste Land was to differ from its manuscript sources in its novelistic attempts at a cultural document and in its curtailment of a central figure and his wild, atemporal dreaming. Eliot decided that a long poem had to be more impersonal, more prosaic.* Still, in its fundamental conception, *The Waste Land* remained true to its sources. Throughout his career Eliot framed a choice between the sordid city street and the transcendental silence, between shuttling to no purpose on London's commuter trains and communing with God on Little Gidding's holy ground. On the one hand, the speaker of 'Song' (published in April 1921)† is

---

* In 'The Music of Poetry', Eliot said that a poet must master the prosaic in order to write a long poem. In 'Blake' (*SW*, p. 156) he said: 'You cannot create a very large poem without introducing a more impersonal point of view, or splitting it up into various personalities.'

† *facs. WL*, p. [98]. Eliot published 'Song' in Wyndham Lewis's *Tyro* under the pseudonym, Gus Krutzsch, which appears in the original opening scene of

tantalized by an intangible golden vision, on the other alarmed by his proximity to human suffering, his wife's face that 'sweats with tears'.* The hero of this poem, swinging 'between two lives', confesses the autobiographic basis for Eliot's debate between the claims of society and the claims of the soul. Eliot's fertility in devising a variety of dramatic scenes disguised the repetitiveness and simplicity of this philosophic debate, a favourite theme of Eliot's mother. 'Ring out the world's temptation and illusion!' cried Charlotte in one of her sermon-poems. 'Ring in immortal hopes that shall endure!'[52] For her son hope was less easy but there was no more question of choice. The abandonment of civilization at the end of *The Waste Land* is as inevitable as it had been for Saint Narcissus. The only difference is that Narcissus acts instinctively whereas the *Waste Land* pilgrim acts rationally—before he escapes he accumulates evidence against civilization and makes his categoric judgement: 'Unreal'.

If civilization is 'unreal' and if Christ sends no 'sign', where then was Eliot to find a reliable authority? First of all, like other modern writers, he could rely on the authenticity of his private life. He took his epigraph from Conrad's *Heart of Darkness*:

Did he live his life again in every detail of desire, temptation, and surrender during the supreme moment of complete knowledge? He cried in a whisper at some image, at some vision,—he cried out twice, a cry that was no more than a breath—

'The horror! the horror!'†

Here is the heart of Eliot's depression in the autumn of 1921: a horrifying discovery of innate depravity and the associated fear that few have the stature to transcend it. Pound should not have dismissed this epigraph for, as Eliot modestly protested, it is 'somewhat elucidative'.[53] It certifies the authority of the shocked, knowing heart stripped of cultural superstructures.[54]

WL: I. The name suggests someone deformed or maimed. It also sounds a bit like Kurtz, the hero of *Heart of Darkness* by Conrad. Eliot referred to Kurtz again in the original epigraph to *The Waste Land* ('The horror! the horror!') and in the epigraph to 'The Hollow Men' ('Mr. Kurtz—he dead').

* Eliot told Pound in January 1922 that 'sweats with tears' would fit the hysterical wife in *WL*: II (*Selected Letters of Ezra Pound*, p. 171).

† The epigraph is typed under the title 'The Waste Land' on the same Verona paper that Eliot used for 'The Fire Sermon' and 'Exequy'.

'To live his life again', to master the facts of his autobiography, could not alone release Eliot from his depression. His sense of 'horror' was not a symptom of derangement but a fair judgement, and his only hope of patching up his 'ruin' was by following the pattern of certain authoritative lives. In the lives Eliot invokes— Dante, Christ, Augustine, the grail knight, Ezekiel—there is always a dark period of trial, whether in a desert, a slough of despond, or a hell, followed by initiation, conversion, or the divine light itself. The external biographic events that form part of this plot do not have to cover the lifespan from birth to death, for time has nothing to do with redemption. Augustine's life story ends at thirty-three with the voices in the garden. In Switzerland Eliot concludes his own record with a journey into the mountains and three thunderous calls.

The traditional schema of the exemplary life usually opens with the kind of confession of youthful vanities with which Eliot originally opened *The Waste Land*. The young Bostonian, humming tunes of the early nineteen-hundreds, seeks out the clichés of wine, women, and song, but soon finds his appetite jaded. The painful awakening to sin is the substance of Eliot's 'Fire Sermon' which concludes with his recognition of the necessity for punishment. There follows a stage of committed action and purification in 'Death by Water' and then, at last, enlightenment in 'What the Thunder Said'. While Eliot could safely expose the heart of darkness to a modern audience, this traditional blueprint had to be subdued. To the intellectuals of Eliot's generation it would have seemed an anachronism.

The Waste Land is about the trials of a life in the process of becoming exemplary. In the first two parts Eliot puts forward the prosaic facts. Here is autobiographic material of a different order from the introspective manuscript fragments, an external chronicle of action and conduct (recognizably Eliot's life to his mother and Mary Hutchinson).[55] The worldly young man in Boston having a drink at the Opera Exchange, the intoxicating moment of love for the hyacinth girl, the religious crisis—the saint in the desert, the sage advice of a bogus clairvoyant (Eliot's friends would have recognized Bertrand Russell),* the routines of a suburban husband

---

* Grover Smith in 'The Making of *The Waste Land*', *Mosaic*, 6 (Fall 1972), 136, noted that Mr. Scogan who impersonates Sesostris the Sorceress in *Crome Yellow* is modelled on Bertrand Russell.

in the City, and finally the failed marriage. Although this story tells of a decline in fortune, Eliot is taking command of the facts and composing them as a series of instructive ordeals. In 'The Burial of the Dead' the demeaning routines of suburban corpses are aligned with Dante's abject neutrals on the outskirts of hell. 'A Game of Chess' is hell itself, the diabolical routines of marital powerplay.

In the first three sections of *The Waste Land* sanity or detachment is maintained by the exercise of wit. But with the growing sense of contamination in 'The Fire Sermon' wit is no longer possible. The manuscript shows Pound levelling off Eliot's revulsion for the clerk who urinates and spits on street corners and for the clerk's and typist's automatic coupling: 'these crawling bugs'. The only hope of sanity is now physical escape. It is obvious why Eliot had to leave London to recuperate, and the poem seems to follow the course of his sickness and recovery. From the close of 'The Fire Sermon' the sordid city is blotted out by exemplary characters who escape contamination either by the practice of asceticism—like the Buddha or St. Augustine—or by dreams of a voyage, a journey, a pilgrimage, the metaphoric clichés of spiritual biography. Eliot gives over urban realism for dreams of a bold sailor, washed clean and refashioned by the ocean, and the hooded figure of the resurrected Christ on the road to Emmaus.

'Death by Water', which Eliot completed at Lausanne, is an account of a fishing expedition from Cape Ann to the Grand Banks, off Nova Scotia.* In the London of 'The Fire Sermon' someone fishes futilely in the polluted canal; here, in the North-Atlantic, the New England fishermen lead purposeful, honest lives, far from the contamination of cities. They are constantly in danger of death off some remote shore, but to Eliot this is healthier than some death-in-life, like Gerontion's, in a soiled corner of familiar trade-routes.[56]

The transition from the Babylon of 'The Fire Sermon' to the New England of 'Death by Water' re-enacts, as it were, the Puritans' sense of release from the sinfulness and stale clutter of the Old World. Eliot's treacherous North-Atlantic is new unexplored

---

* *facs. WL*, pp. [54–60]. Eliot did his handwritten drafts at Lausanne on quadruled paper (which he did not use at any other time). These were 'What the Thunder Said', fair copies of 'Death by Water' and 'Dirge', and a rough draft of 'Venus Anadyomene' (which was soon discarded along with the Fresca episode for which it was designed). Eliot used the same black ink for the two fair copies.

territory, a testing-ground. Eliot thinks of the fisherman as a concentrated will confronting the sea, 'something inhuman, clean and dignified'. As the vessel flies north, far off course, the voyage becomes an allegorical dream. As the stars become invisible the fisherman sees three crosses and, in front of them, three women with foaming hair, singing a siren's song. Prufrock longs for mermaids to sing to him; Londoners are charmed by the Thames daughters' 'la la' to their senses; but the fisherman coolly rejects them. He sees how their siren's song blends with the 'illimitable scream' of the whole natural world. At the height of the storm, he leaps to the notion that the shrill world with its provocative women is simply an illusion:

> . . . while I was
> Frightened beyond fear, horrified past horror, calm
> (Nothing was real) for, I thought, now when
> I like, I can wake up and end the dream.

Yet no sooner does he reject the natural world as a dream than he knocks up against it. Literally, the vessel drives against an iceberg. One moment the fisherman looks into infinity, a meeting of sea and sky; the next, a long white line breaks into it like 'a wall, a barrier'.

This journey is thwarted by the recurrence of Eliot's philosophical debate about the reality of natural world versus dream. But the drowning at the end of 'Death by Water' reinforces the authority of the dream even while it falls short of enlightenment. For the death that follows a life of honest endeavour is not conceived as a disaster but as a stage of purification and metamorphosis.

Eliot found no real answer to his *aboulie* in modern psychiatry with its Romantic ideal of self-expression. He favoured the sterner medieval view that one should 'look to *death* for what life cannot give'. In this view the death of the flawed natural self is preliminary to a new purified life. In 'The Death of Saint Narcissus', 'The Death of the Duchess', 'Elegy', and 'Dirge', and finally, at the end of 1921, in 'Death by Water' Eliot imagines rather violent and abhorrent annihilations of flawed characters. Only later in Eliot's life, when he returned to the Catholic mystics, St. John of the Cross and *The Cloud of Unknowing*, did he contemplate a more gradual and complex process of self-abandonment.

13. 1921—The spire of St. Magnus the Martyr, whose 'inexplicable splendour' provides momentary relief in *The Waste Land*. Photographed from London Bridge by Eliot's brother, Henry Ware Eliot, Jr.

14. Eliot with his mother, who visited England in the summer of 1921

At the same time as Eliot made his fair copy of the New England voyage, he suddenly found the pilgrim's journey of 1914 reviving in his imagination—the sunbaked road winding among the mountains, the bells and chanting voices, the reversed point of view of the saint. Very swiftly, almost automatically, Eliot related another journey, this time one that is completed. Eliot thought this the only part of *The Waste Land* 'that justifies the whole at all'.[57] Unfortunately here, in 'What the Thunder Said', the visionary element, so forthright in the earliest manuscript fragments, is now depersonalized and even disguised. In place of the man with extraordinary powers there is now a 'form' and, in a later revision, merely a bat. And instead of a voice saying plainly 'I am the Resurrection', the thunder now rumbles obscure Sanskrit words.

The pilgrim, with two companions, journeys away from the cities, across a sandy desert, where the rock will not yield miraculous water, as it did for the Israelites in Sinai. It is a wasted, barren land dotted with empty, exhausted wells. The pilgrim's quest in a desert recalls Saint Narcissus's passion; his thirst fever recalls Gerontion's parched body and his plea for rain. Both Narcissus and Gerontion lived in a state of feverish anticipation, awaiting an experience that would shape and define them; both were left unrewarded. But the nameless wanderer, his commitment now entire, is finally initiated and, at the same time, the healing waters break overhead.

As soon as he abandons the city he hears it explode and dissolve—the fate of all great cities in the course of time, Jerusalem, Athens, Alexandria, Vienna. For him the fate of such cities is of no importance. When he walks over London Bridge he knows London to be an 'unreal city' and he lets his conviction extend back in time to encompass all secular history. He moves out of 'unreal' or dead history into a bracing atmosphere of stirring grass and gusts of wind. For a man caught up in the grandeur of the triple thunderbolt that follows, the distant fall of London must seem justifiably insignificant, as insignificant as the fall of the Roman Empire for Saint Augustine. For both, the real plot of one's life is an inward adventure: its climax is to hear a supernatural message. The dialectic of 'Gerontion' and *The Waste Land* sanctioned the dismissal of temporal history so as to concentrate on timeless moments of truth; of course later, in *Four Quartets*, Eliot made a *rapprochement* with time.

The pilgrim comes to the truth in a cave in the mountain wall, like the best of knights in search of the holy grail. ('Than sir Galahad com to a mountayne where he founde a chapell passynge olde, and found therein nobody, for all was desolate. And there he . . . harde a voyce . . .')[58] The thunder's first law is 'datta', to give. The pilgrim understands it by recalling the one moment in his life when he knew self-surrender, when he was in love and the blood raced in his veins.

The thunder's next law is to sympathise: 'dayadvam'. The pilgrim has been imprisoned, like Narcissus, in the circle of self-consciousness. But now he realizes the prison is an illusion, for he has an escape-route through his nocturnal intimations. 'Aetherial rumours' are breaking through and revive his hopes. By 'sympathy' the thunder means not so much human sympathy as a kind of receptivity to intimations and signs. 'I carry the keys of my castle in my hand,' wrote Emerson, 'ready to throw them at the feet of my lord, whenever and in what disguise soever he shall appear.' And then, quite suddenly, the 'angel-whispering' comes to him.[59]

Thunder is spelling out the old rigid formula for conversion:* self-surrender; hope—of aetherial rumours; and then, finally, 'damyata' or control. Spiritual biography always ends with a gesture of obedience towards a superior power which has directed one's life to this moment. His lyrical emotions at last reawakened, the pilgrim has the sense of 'beating obedient to controlling hands'.

I am sure that before Eliot could have written this section he must himself have had some 'sign'. He said that religious poetry is so difficult to write because it demands actual experience, those moments of clarification and crystallization which come but seldom.[60] He explained the extraordinary facility with which he wrote 'What the Thunder Said' in terms of the illness from which he was, at this time, recuperating. 'It is a commonplace that some forms of illness are extremely favourable, not only to religious illumination, but to artistic and literary composition. A piece of writing meditated without progress for months or years, may

* Shea, *Spiritual Autobiography in Early America*, pp. 90, 100–1, shows that the settlers of New England had 'an early reputation as English Protestantism's most sophisticated students of the process, the signs and stages of conversion'. Edward Taylor in his 'Spiritual Relation' divides the process into conviction or illumination and repentance. In turn, repentance divides into aversion to sin and conversion which expresses itself in Love, Hope, Joy, and Obedience.

suddenly take shape and word, and in this state long passages may be produced which require little or no touch.'[61]

The pilgrim is now in command of his life and its circumstances. Behind him lies the arid land: a psychological waste has been traversed. He thinks tentatively of 'order', and believes he might shore up the 'ruin' through his biographic sense for the instructive moment. He should remember Arnaut Daniel suffering for lust in the flames of purgatory. He should be warned by the fate of Hieronymo, driven by a righteous, vengeful rage into madness.* And, finally, he should remember Nerval's disinherited prince who dreamt in the siren's cave, who experienced hell and returned to life, and conceived his *mélancolie* to be the sign of a saint.[62] There is, at last, mental peace: 'Shantih'. Eliot again uses Sanskrit for its novelty, but his explanatory note shows that he thinks in traditional Christian terms: 'And the peace of God, which passeth all understanding, shall keep your hearts and minds through Christ Jesus.'

One might ask, if this is a religious poem, where is the deity? Unlike other religious poets, Eliot never speculated on the face God showed. Even in 'Little Gidding', when he experiences the 'unimaginable zero summer', he fastens rather on his own sensations. Why was God 'unimaginable'? Was he too distant to be conceived? Other religious poets tend to beat against something alien to themselves. Herbert, Donne, Dickinson, and Hopkins conduct dramas of submission and rebellion. Eliot, on the other hand, was curiously unrebellious. His drama was contained within himself and was, essentially, a choice between two kinds of passivity. One alternative was to submit to the demands of the actual world; the other was to submit to the will of God. He made out of his native passivity a dramatic conflict: it was the only way he could achieve and command experience.

A perceptive early reviewer of *The Waste Land* suggested that 'some unsympathetic tug has sent Mr. Eliot's gift awry'.[63] When, early in January 1922, Eliot stopped again in Paris on his way

---

* Thomas Kyd, 'The Spanish Tragedy'. In the first draft, the allusion to Hieronymo's madness comes after the allusion to Arnaut Daniel and is therefore one of the fragments the wanderer shores against his ruins. In the next draft Eliot exchanges it for the line 'Quando fiam . . .' and moves Hieronymo further on. In its transposed position the line has a different effect. It suggests not recovery but the babblings of encroaching madness.

home, Pound thought badly of 'Death by Water'. He drew a thick line through the focal 'London' fragment in 'The Fire Sermon' and cancelled references to churches, St. Mary Woolnoth and Michael Paternoster. What excited Pound's enthusiasm was not Eliot's private hallucinations and hopes but the helpless sense of submission ('deploring action') to the stings of fortune, to London's odour of putrefaction and dull routines.[64] He congratulated Eliot on the outline he had found for their 'deformative secretions'. Eliot's despair was no longer oddly isolated but measured against 'common woes'.

Eliot's submissiveness to Pound's idea of the poem was due, perhaps, to the timidity with which he had gazed into the mirror of election. Pound was often ruthless about lines or passages that suggest an imaginative control of the waste. He refused Eliot the authority of St. John the Divine when he bears witness to his generation's muddled efforts to communicate with spirits: 'I John saw these things, and heard them.'[65] Pound also scratched the prophecy of metamorphosis: '(Those are pearls that were his eyes. Look!)'.[66] He persuaded Eliot to omit his most penitential fragment, 'Exequy', in which a poet confesses having abused his gifts in order to court immediate fame and resolves to carry through the Dantean schema. Silly devotees wantonly admire the fake-pastoral love poetry and celebrate the poet with fireworks; but he is warmed by a 'constant fire' within, a purgatorial fire. Pound, who for years had helped Eliot to fame, could not see the reason for Eliot's great cry of 'DOLOR'.[67] Another fragment, 'Song', also rejected by Pound, demonstrates Eliot's recovery of religious aspirations. It describes a nocturnal vigil for the divine 'touch' and is slightly more explicit about Eliot's private objective than other random moments of 'inexplicable splendour' in *The Waste Land*.

When Eliot offered *The Waste Land* to the *Dial* on 20 January, he said it had been three times through the sieve by Pound and himself and should soon be in its final form.[68] Eliot probably left the Lausanne manuscript, or part of it, in Paris so that Pound might consider it a third time. With the last sieving of the manuscript Eliot cut the whole of the fisherman's voyage in response to Pound's numerous cancellations on the typescript copy, though vague doubts lingered as to the effect of this on the poem as a whole.[69] Pound wrote that the Conrad epigraph was not 'weighty enough', and Eliot dropped it. But the main force of Pound's attack in his late-January letters was directed against the three closing lyrics of the Lausanne draft: 'Song', 'Dirge', and 'Exequy'. On 24 January Pound advised Eliot repeatedly 'to abolish 'em altogether'. Eliot replied that he accepted criticism 'so far as understood'. They were not impressive pieces, aesthetically, but essential facets of Eliot's emotional ensemble. What Pound called the 'superfluities' were cut.

When Quinn saw the original manuscript he wrote to Eliot that he would not have cut as Pound advised.[70] In the Lausanne draft the cultural statement in the first half of the poem is more or less evenly balanced by the visionary speculation in the second half. The effect of Pound's last suggestions is to curtail the second half so that cultural statement comes to dominate the poem. From the point of view of Eliot's well-being, Pound effectively blocked, at several points, Eliot's impulse to exhibit the whole truth—the strength as well as the sickness of a suffering soul. When Eliot left Lausanne he was master of his autobiography, but from the time Pound revised the manuscript in Paris there was a recrudescence of Eliot's depression. He began to doubt his grasp of the facts of his life and in Paris wrote his last, most emotional fragment, a lament for an improper marriage. In 'The river's tent is broken . . .' a man weeps for his bondage.[71] Eliot's troubles were, of course, domestic as well as literary. He took his commitment to Vivienne seriously and could not condone Pound's view that a poet should be exempted from earning his living.

Back in London, Eliot complained to Pound that he was sick, miserable, and 'excessively depressed'.[72] He wrote to America: 'I have been led to contemplate, for many moments, the nature of the particular torpor or deadness which strikes a denizen of London on his return.'[73] He saw everywhere a cowardly fear of independent thinking. That winter he used to meet Conrad Aiken regularly for lunch, and would confess to him—over rump steak at a pub in Cannon Street—how he would come home from work, sharpen his pencil, and then be unable to write. Yet it seemed to him there was material there, waiting.[74] He told his mother he planned another poem. She understood that it was to be a sequel to *The Waste Land*, a more optimistic poem about the coming of the grail.[75] More than anything he wanted to give the religious ordeal back to his generation, and the dimensions of a universe in which such an ordeal belonged. At the time he was finishing *The Waste Land* he carried Dante everywhere with him in his pocket—Dante who had surveyed that universe and then written his autobiography in colossal cipher.

Eliot published *The Waste Land* in the *Criterion* and *Dial* in mid-October 1922, but he remained uneasy. He said *The Waste Land* seemed like something he had written as far back as 'Prufrock' and could no longer speak for him.* His uneasiness was confirmed when he came to be hailed as spokesman for a disillusioned post-war generation.† They fastened hungrily on his despair and erudition and ignored the fact that these were subsidiary to an exemplary life. In 1933 Eliot told Virginia Woolf that he was no longer sure there was a science of criticism. He felt the critics had mistakenly fastened on the erudition of his poetry, and got things very wrong.[76] When I. A. Richards stated that the poem was devoid of belief, Eliot published a personal statement: 'As for the poem of my own in question, I cannot for the life of me see the "complete separation" from all belief—or it is something no more complete than the separation of Christina Rossetti from Dante. A "sense of desolation", etc. (if it is there) is not a separation from belief; it is nothing so pleasant. In fact, doubt, uncertainty, futility, etc., would seem to me to prove anything except this agreeable partition; for doubt and uncertainty are merely a variety of belief.'[77]

The manuscript of *The Waste Land* shows that at first Eliot made the divine 'touch' an unmistakable priority, but that he played this down in 1921-2. The poem originated in the purely personal record of a man who saw himself as a potential candidate for the religious life but was constrained by his own nature and distracted by domestic claims. Eliot began writing a kind of spiritual autobiography in an age that was not cordial to the genre. He decided he could reach his audience only by indirection. Like

* In November 1922 Eliot wrote to Richard Aldington that, for him personally, *The Waste Land* was a thing of the past. 'My present ideas are very different', he told Gilbert Seldes, a *Dial* editor (letter, 12 Nov. 1922, rpr. Casebook Series on *WL*, p. 85). In 1930, still disappointed with the poem, he told McKnight Kauffer, the illustrator, that he did not want anything he wrote to have *The Waste Land* stamped on it.

† See 'Thoughts After Lambeth', *SE*, p. 324: 'I dislike the word "generation", which has been a talisman for the last ten years; when I wrote a poem called *The Waste Land* some of the more approving critics said I had expressed the "disillusionment of a generation", which is nonsense. I may have expressed for them their own illusion of being disillusioned, but that did not form part of my intention.'

many autobiographers, he compelled attention by presenting himself as a child of the times, but that gambit proved so catchy that readers ignored the would-be saint. Eliot's strategy failed by its success, for the strategy took over the poem, and he was forced to rewrite his saint's life in more explicit terms in 'Ash Wednesday' and *Four Quartets*.

6. Conversion

WHEN Eliot visited Rome in 1926 he suddenly fell on his knees before Michelangelo's *Pietà*, to the surprise of his brother and sister-in-law who were with him. His entry into the Church of England the following year astonished many friends and readers, but for Eliot there was no dramatic change, only 'an expansion or development of interests.'[1] Eliot did not turn from atheism to belief but from spiritual self-reliance to the support of a Church. Eliot in his youth had trusted the inner light, but came to perceive the danger of untempered individualism. The visions of Blake and Yeats, he said, are based 'on the wonders of their own existence'. They enjoy 'a shortcut to the strangeness'[2] without the reality that a Catholic tradition would have ensured. In an essay on the church, which Eliot published in the *Criterion* in 1929, P. E. More grants that private intuition is the essence of religion but finds that insufficient.[3] He admires Whittier's poem, 'The Meeting', which celebrates the holiness of 'naked' experience, without trappings of sacrament or creed, but the experience of the New Englander is too fragile; the private deity fades into 'the flimsiest aura of transcendentalism':

> No, for our growth and sanity in religion we must have something to supply what the inner light will not afford to the isolated souls of men, something to make us conscious of our citizenship in the communion of saints, to supplement our limited intuition with the accumulated wisdom of the race, and in our moral perplexities to fortify the individual conscience with the authority of ancient command.[4]

Eliot's intuition was based on solitude. In his early poetry he repeatedly gives assent to an impulse to withdraw from the world, but at the age of thirty-eight he found a way back through the Church of England whose latitude and tolerance for ordinary sinners provided a corrective to the fanatic edge of his temper. Eliot's youthful imagination came down on the reckless, solitary vigil of Saint Narcissus in the desert; now, in middle age, the Church of England suggested possibilities for saintliness within the parish. The layman must do his saint's work unobtrusively

among ordinary people in the home, the bank, the factory or field.*
The heroes Eliot created after his conversion—the martyred
Thomas, the missionary, Harry, his own reminiscing self in *Four
Quartets*—work out their salvation at home, among mostly pre-
dictable people and familiar English scenes.

Churchmen who knew Eliot in later life deny that he was in
any way distinguishable from an Englishman born into the
Anglican Church. There is no question of superficiality about
Eliot's submission to the Church's authority. His confessor,
Father Hillier, stressed his unmistakable humility and called him
'a thoroughly converted man'.⁵ It is impossible to measure the
extraordinary success of Eliot's adaptation to the Anglican community without understanding something of the stubborn self-
reliance which he relinquished or controlled.

Eliot's early poetry revives the attitude of the Desert Fathers
who, during the century before Rome fell to the barbarians, felt
little hope of civilization and retreated into the silence of the
desert. For the young Eliot too the highest good depended on
an imaginative escape from a corrupt civilization into that haven
of silence he first experienced as a student in 1910. The desert
idea emerges in 1914 in the figure of Saint Narcissus who is
oppressed by a multitude of faces, thighs, and knees, and goes to
the desert to become a dancer to God. It recurs in the visionary
who persists on his way out of town at the end of 'So through the
evening . . .' and in *The Waste Land*'s rejection of the different
Voices of society for the sandy road winding among mountains
of rock. There is the dead cactus-land of 'The Hollow Men', bleak
and threatening, but in 'Ash Wednesday', in a state of genuine
penitence, the poet discovers at last 'the blessing of the sand'. He
identifies with the prophet, Elijah, who fled to the desert in fear
of Jezebel, the avenging queen. Elijah prayed for death under
a juniper tree, but was roused by an angel to continue to the
mountain where God once made a covenant with the chosen. In
'Ash Wednesday' the exile under the juniper tree wonders if his
bones have a right to live, but at that most abject moment he is

---

* See Keble's hymn, 'New every morning is the love':

> The trivial round, the common task,
> Will furnish all we need to ask,—
> Room to deny ourselves, a road
> To bring us daily nearer God.

granted a vision of the promised land: 'This is the land which
ye / Shall divide by lot. . . . This is the land. We have our
inheritance.'[6]

Despite his solitary nature, Eliot did not find it easy to reject
society. There was always the side, distilled in Prufrock, that felt
keenly its attractions. In a poem 'Necesse est Perstare?' Vivienne
Eliot describes a moment after a literary luncheon when the guests
have departed.[7] The wife is thankful for an end to the inane
gossip about Clive Bell and Aldous Huxley. She longs to win her
husband from his resolve to master London's cultural scene. But
he stretches his arms above his head with the weary air of a very
old monkey, impervious to her silent plea. In another of Vivienne's
sketches she accounts for Eliot's block during 1923 and 1924[8]
by his distracting urge to possess all the kingdoms of this world:

'Isn't he wonderful?' whispered Felice. 'He is the most marvellous
poet in the *whole world*.'
'He might be if he wrote anything,' said Sybilla dryly.
'Yes, why *doesn't* he write more?'
'Because he wants to be everything at once, I expect. Perhaps the
devil took him up into a high mountain and showed him all the king-
doms of the world—unfortunately for him!'
'And so, I suppose,' asked Felice naggingly, 'that he doesn't know
which kingdom to choose?'
'He's still up on the mountain so far as I know. . . .'[9]

Vivienne pounced on the omnivorousness but she did not understand it—that American hunger for experience, knowledge,
people, Europe that Henry James presented so sympathetically
in a similar image of Milly Theale, poised on a mountain in Europe
'in a state of uplifted and unlimited possession. . . . She was looking down on the kingdoms of the earth. . . . Was she choosing
among them, or did she want them all? . . . It would be a question
of taking full in the face the whole assault of life, to the general
muster of which indeed her face might have directly presented
as she sat there on her rock.'[10] But Eliot differed from Milly in
his suspicion of the world as a snare. What Vivienne *did* understand was her husband's vulnerability to the devil's temptations.

In some way Eliot was quite alien to the secular mind of his
century, as alien as the Desert Fathers had been to the eighteenth-
century civic conscience of Gibbon to whom solitaries were
deserters from civilization. The monk, Thomas Merton, tried to

explain their point of view. Solitaries, he said, regard the world as a wreck and are helpless to do good so long as they flounder among the wreckage. Their first obligation is to find a solid foothold and then to pull others to safety after them.[11] Eliot found his own theological justification in the words of St. John of the Cross which he used as the epigraph to 'Sweeney Agonistes': 'Hence the soul cannot be possessed by the divine union, until it has divested itself of the love of created beings.' It is easy to misunderstand this denial of human love as a sickness of the egotistic imagination but it must be seen in terms of monastic rather than humanitarian or romantic values. Eliot took up a position opposite to the humanitarian attitude of his mother and grandfather that it is through love of one's kind that one approaches love of God. 'I don't think that ordinary human affections are capable of leading us to the love of God', Eliot said, 'but rather that the love of God is capable of informing, intensifying, and elevating our human affections, which otherwise have little to distinguish them from the "natural" affections of animals.'[12] Eliot's early misfortune in his experience of human love perhaps lay behind this monastic conception of divine love as utterly different in kind.

Fantasies of a man's escape from a constraining tie persist in Eliot's works—in 'Elegy', in 'The Death of the Duchess', in 'Sweeney Agonistes' ('Any man might do a girl in'), and in 'The Family Reunion'. Eliot's marital and religious crises were inextricably mixed: through his impulsive love of Vivienne, Eliot made 'that frightful discovery of morality' when 'the not naturally bad but irresponsible and undeveloped nature [is] caught in the consequences of its own action' and 'becomes moral only by becoming damned'.[13] The sense of damnation, the remorse and guilt that Vivienne evoked were essential to Eliot's long purgatorial journey that continued long after his formal conversion and their separation six years later. He could escape her, morally, only by embracing the ascetic Way of the Catholic mystics.

People who met Eliot casually were charmed by his fine manners and modest silence, but those on whose friendship he relied saw a man constantly on the verge of a breakdown, peevish and complaining, oppressed by self-pity, weakened by weariness, and preoccupied with fears of poverty.[14] During 1923 Virginia Woolf was baffled by Eliot's sudden withdrawals from friendship, by his refusal to respond when his shell was prodded, by the laboured perplexities of his rhetoric in which he would enshroud private feelings. One day she, her sister, and husband found him in a state of collapse in his flat. His eyes were blurred, his face ashen, and he could barely stand up to see them out. Eliot wrote to John Quinn: 'I have not even time to go to a dentist or to have my hair cut. . . . I am worn out. I cannot go on.'[15]

Eliot's complaints of poverty—of long hours at the bank that left him exhausted, or huge doctors' bills during Vivienne's bouts of illness—had some foundation, but chiefly they provided a front for other personal problems, moral and domestic, which I think disturbed him more profoundly. Not the grandest stipend, not the pleasantest part-time job could have assuaged Eliot's misery during 1923, 1924, and 1925. Pound and Ottoline Morrell set up separate funds to rescue Eliot for poetry,* Virginia Woolf schemed to appoint him a literary editor for the *Nation*, and then all were baffled when he turned their offers down.

The problem, briefly, was Eliot's moral obligation to secure the future for a wife whose health, Eliot told Russell, was now a thousand times worse than when he had married her.[16] For a whole year she had lain in an 'abyss' at 9 Clarence Gate Gardens, 'a helpless and unspeakable wreck of drugs, fear and semi-paralysis'.[17] There was no chance that she would ever manage to shift for herself or endure any privation. And at the very time that Vivienne's needs became so desperate, Eliot first tasted fame and began to feel more strongly than ever the claims of his poetic career. Eliot's friends urged him to leave the bank, but he had to think of Vivienne. He had $2,000 from the *Dial* prize for *The Waste Land*, and could rely on Quinn for substantial gifts. He also had a substantial inheritance from his father, but Henry Ware Eliot, Sr. had disapproved of his son's marriage and had not left the money outright, as to his other children. On Eliot's death the money was to revert to the Eliot family. Until 1923 (when Charlotte Eliot provided for Vivienne in her Will) Vivienne's sole security was Lloyd's Bank, which meant an annual income of £500 and provision for employees' widows, and she insisted that her husband should not leave his job. 'Indeed, if he did take such steps

---

* Pound set up the 'Bel Esprit' scheme. Ottoline Morrell set up the 'Eliot Fellowship Fund'. Eliot told Pound that he would need at least £600 a year, a flat in London, and six months abroad (letter, about 1922, Beinecke Library, Yale).

I should bear him a considerable grudge', she wrote to Mary Hutchinson on 4 March 1923. Although she had been one of the first to believe in Eliot as a poet, she refused the traditional demand that a wife sacrifice herself in the cause of genius. She owned to the quite defensible view that it is *not* picturesque to die in a humble cot.

Early in April the crisis broke when Eliot considered leaving the bank without an alternative position[18] and, at the same time, tried to settle Vivienne alone in a cottage near Chichester. Vivienne's colitis took a dangerous turn. Within three weeks she wasted away to a skeleton. She was at the point of death seven or eight times. Eliot, shaken, gave up his plan to leave the bank and fretted over the expense of two specialists from London, the local doctor twice a day, not to speak of the year's rent on a cottage that had proved rather uncomfortable. In a despairing cable and letter to Quinn on 25 and 26 April Eliot said that his affairs were in complete chaos.

The first serious impetus towards the Church of England seems to coincide with the crisis in 1923. It was then that Richard Cobden-Sanderson introduced Eliot to a fellow-American, William Force Stead, who had had himself ordained in the Church of England. Stead drew Eliot's attention to the writings of seventeenth-century Anglicans, in particular those of the Bishop of Winchester, Lancelot Andrewes. Eliot read the sermons on the Incarnation (a notion his Unitarian family would not have stressed). He saturated himself in Andrewes's prose ('but sure there is no joy in the world to the joy of a man saved') and found his examination of the words 'terminating in the ecstasy of assent'.[19] When Eliot first read sermons in 1919 he had been attracted by Donne's spellbinding personality. He now came to prefer the 'pure', 'medieval' temper of Andrewes,[20] who did not stir the emotions so much as stress a settled and resolute will to holiness.

Eliot's entry into the Church was not brought about by a ferment that mounted naturally to a point of action. He said that the thought of the intelligent believer 'proceeds by rejection and elimination' until he finds a satisfactory explanation both for the disordered world without and the moral world within. Eliot stressed rational progress rather than emotional states.[21] He accepted the morality of damnation and could not save himself without help. It seems that at this time he felt no religious excitement, and was driven to the Church almost as a last resort.

Eliot first visited an Anglican chapel at Merton College in 1914. (He kept a picture postcard of its interior.) He began to frequent Anglican Churches in the City of London, some time between 1917 and 1921, in search of a quiet spot to think during his lunch hours. At first, he enjoyed the high Anglo-Catholic St. Magnus the Martyr aesthetically, for its 'splendour'; later he appreciated its 'utility' when he came there as a sinner. He was struck, once, by the sight of a number of people on their knees, a posture he had never seen before.[22] Eliot's family was not accustomed to kneel. An aunt, Mrs. Charles W. Eliot, wrote censoriously to a friend who had joined the Episcopalian Church: 'Do you kneel down in church and call yourself a miserable sinner? Neither I nor my family will ever do that!'[23] But Eliot admired this gesture of abasement and worship. Some time during the early 1920s he began to think of the Church not simply as a place where he could find, now and then, some private consolation, but as a way to a new life.

Eliot craved a stronger, more dogmatic theological structure than was to be found in his purely ethical background. Associating his parents' injunctions about 'what is done and not done' with Puritanism, he scribbled on the back of an envelope in about 1923 or 1924: 'There are only 2 things—Puritanism and Catholicism. You are one or the other. You either believe in the reality of *sin* or you don't—*that* is the important moral distinction—not whether you are good or bad. Puritanism does not believe in sin: it merely believes that certain things must not be done.'[24] Eliot's 'Puritan' mother nevertheless prepared the way for his interest in Catholic forms by her own tolerant interest. One of her poems beckons the stranger to the stately Cathedral with its art treasures, its sweet music, and fragrant incense. 'Must not the Lord be near?' she asks. 'Wilt thou not pause to kneel?'[25]

Eliot regretted the cultural impoverishment which he felt resulted from the Reformation. 'Milton's celestial and infernal regions are large but insufficiently furnished apartments filled by heavy conversation,' he said, 'and one remarks about Puritan mythology an historical thinness.'[26] Of all the reformed churches the Church of England retained the closest connection, in formal creed and ritual, with the ancient Roman Church. Eliot, with his interest in a revival of the Catholic tradition, found it freshest in the prayers and sacraments of the Anglo-Catholic inheritors of the Oxford Movement which, a hundred years before, had attempted to revive within the Church of England the best aspects of the Roman Church. For Anglo-Catholics the pulpit was less significant than the sacraments; faith centred on the altar and the confessional which had the advantage of being constant, free from the local limitations of individual pulpits, exempt from the pulpit's competition with mass media, and unimpaired by the fallibility of individual clergymen which had so troubled the learned congregant in 'Mr. Eliot's Sunday Morning Service'. The Anglo-Catholics were a strong and dominant party within the Church at that time and Eliot saw a place for himself there, among people who demanded of themselves a regulated personal life of high sanctity and service.

Why should someone who was not born an Anglican not go directly to Rome? Firstly, Eliot felt that Anglo-Catholicism, unlike Roman-Catholicism, would allow his mind scope. The Anglican Church acknowledges that the truth of the scriptures is only dimly traced and must be verified by individual judgement. The believer takes, at best, only a modest step amidst the encircling fog.[27] Eliot's other consideration was his growing attachment to the English past. His confessor said that he saw his conversion as a return to the religion of the remote English ancestors he recalled in 'East Coker'.[28] Eliot was drawn to the Anglican Church through his historical imagination, associating its creation with the reign of Elizabeth rather than with that of Henry VIII. He used to recall with pleasure its flourishing under Elizabeth and the scholar-clerics who had dignified it in the seventeenth century.

By 1925 it was clear to Eliot that he must make some deliberate change. That year his many anxieties came to a head—another near-fatal illness for Vivienne in the winter of 1924–5, the *Criterion* in danger, and his new collected edition of poems which seemed to him merely an ejection of things he wanted to get out of the way.[29] His anxieties came at him from different areas of his life, but together they urged him to a new resolution, at the end of 1925, to close this unhappy period in his life and begin anew.[30] The stresses of 1925 seem to have been practical ones, but together they encouraged him to change his life in a decisive way. Eliot quoted Orestes saying that furies were hunting him down and he must move on.[31]

His first thought was to leave his wife. By 1925 Eliot was finally convinced that his marriage was doomed. In ten years nothing had really changed—her condition and their relations had only deteriorated.[32] One of Vivienne's unpublished sketches provides an almost diabolically detached report of a husband's miserable homecomings from work. 'Anthony' comes in very quietly and hangs about in the hall for a minute, dreading his wife. 'There were many things he dreaded. That Ellison might have a headache, that she might be irritable and hate him, that she might be in despair or have with her her greatest friend who would have been quarrelling with her.' He moves almost stealthily to his study, hoping it will be empty, to find his wife lying in wait on the sofa.[33] Vivienne's moods and nervous states must have given her husband ample cause for self-pity, but I think their marriage was also blighted by something else, something in Eliot, that he half-recognized as the underlying cause of their troubles. What exactly it was, one can only conjecture from other fragmentary remarks in his poems and in Vivienne's sketches. He seemed to suffer from an inability to empathize with suffering outside his own experience. In a strange guilty poem he published in 1924 he said he could see eyes in a golden vision, but not eyes in actual life, in tears. The latter he saw only through a blank, almost sealed-off division. 'This is my affliction', he repeated, 'This is my affliction'.[34]

There is another picture of Eliot's curious detachment in a sketch by Vivienne called 'Fête Galante'. At a bohemian party, a lively girl called Sybilla encounters an American financier-poet. She describes him leaning with exaggerated grace against the fireplace, refusing to speak. Her portrait is rather like the one painted by Wyndham Lewis of T. S. Eliot a few years later— a heavy, slumbering, white face; long hooded eyes, unseeing and leaden-heavy; a large sleek head. She is fascinated, but recognizes that there is something strange about him. 'I like him, I like him', she muses, '—if only he would—What? What is wrong, what missing?'

If there is any truth in this sketch it is not surprising that Vivienne should have had a hopeless sense of exclusion. 'Sybilla'

15. Eliot in his new job as editor at Faber (March 1926)

16. Portrait of T. S. Eliot by Wyndham Lewis (1938)

is Eliot's Sybil in the epigraph to *The Waste Land*.[35] She who had directed Aeneas to the Underworld now withers eternally in a cage. There is a pathetic description of Vivienne Eliot in 1923, a convalescent—heavily powdered, shaky, and somewhat over-dressed—being driven into the country to enjoy Sunday afternoon tea with the Woolfs, where her husband pressed her to take medicine and Virginia lightly snubbed her small effort at conversation.[36] In the winter of 1924–5 she was struck down by a terribly painful illness just as she had begun, at last, to show signs of new morale.* All through 1924 she had been writing and publishing anonymously in the *Criterion*. In her husband's opinion she wrote 'EXTREMELY well' and with 'great originality'.† Her sketches of a dingy Parisian hotel and its inhabitants, a *thé dansant* in London, or a boring bohemian party where ballet dancers are shepherded in by a 'macaw', are all emotionally alive and critically observant, with a clever choice of detail reminiscent of Katherine Mansfield.

In 1925 Eliot wrote to Russell that the obvious alternative to their present life was that they should part—if only Vivienne could manage to live on her own. It is interesting that he did not complain of her illnesses but of the damaging relationship. He blamed partly himself—'living with me has done her so much damage'—and partly her emotional immaturity. 'I find her still perpetually baffling and deceptive', he wrote. 'She seems to me like a child of 6 with an immensely clever and precocious mind. . . . And I can never escape from the spell of her persuasive (even coercive) gift of argument.'[37] In 1927, no longer quite normal,[38] she went to a centre for nervous disorders at Divonne-les-Bains, near Geneva. A fellow-patient has recorded vividly his first sight of Vivienne 'as she walked almost as though in a trance along the wooded path. Her black hair was dank, her white face blotched—owing, no doubt, to the excess of bromide she had been taking. Her dark dress hung loosely over her frail form; her expression was both vague and acutely sad.'[39]

* Eliot wrote to Virginia Woolf that the disease was diagnosed as rheumatism, although the doctor admitted she had never seen anything like it. What with pain and near-delirium Vivienne hardly slept and it seemed to Eliot, at times, that she would die from exhaustion. Letter (n.d.), Berg Coll. (Leonard Woolf misdated this letter 1937: Eliot left Vivienne in 1933.)

† Letter to Russell (7 May 1925), *Autobiography*, ii. 174. Although there is a suggestion of collaboration with T. S. E. and Irene Fassett in Vivienne's diary (27 Mar. 1935), Vivienne's manuscripts in the Bodleian Library show that she conceived and wrote almost everything.

In the end Eliot did not leave his wife until 1933, but he made several other attempts to change his life. He went to beg help from Geoffrey Faber, who agreed to take him into his new publishing firm in the autumn of 1925; here he found work that was closer than banking to his literary interests. There is a photograph of Eliot in Bloomsbury in 1926 in his new role of elegant young publisher: his bowler hat very straight, he leans casually on his tightly-rolled umbrella. He also moved to a pleasanter neighbourhood, 57 Chester Terrace in S.W. 1. Then in 1927 he joined the Church of England and, in November, exchanged American for British nationality.

In 1914 Eliot might have become a Christian in a mood of passionate assent; by 1927 he had hesitated too long for such a mood to be possible. What he needed now was essentially a haven from the turmoil of 'heaven and damnation / Which flesh cannot endure.'[40] Forced to mute his longing for religious extravagance (because 'these wings are no longer wings to fly'), hoping no longer to recover the 'infirm glory'[41] of private intuition, 'the one veritable transitory power'[42] of his youth, he now aspired only to keep his soul alive by regular prayer.[43] In 1926 he began to attend regularly at early-morning Communion. He learnt the morality of patience ('teach us to sit still')[44] and that 'humility is the beginning of anything spiritually or even culturally worthwhile'.[45] In the years immediately preceding his conversion Eliot no longer sought the visionary 'silence' of his youth, nor waited, like Gerontion, for the heavens to open, but began to think of religion as a long-term regimen. Under the influence of Bishop Andrewes and St. John of the Cross he moved away from his mother's revelatory moment of 'truth' towards more moderate goals of 'prayer, observance, discipline, thought and action.'[46]

On 13 November 1926 Eliot asked Stead if he might be confirmed in the Church of England.[47] He wished for absolute secrecy; he hated, he said, dramatic public conversions. As a Unitarian, Eliot had never been baptized in the name of the Trinity, so Stead arranged for his baptism in his own village of Finstock, in the Cotswolds. Eliot's godfathers were to be B. H. Streeter, a theologian of Queen's College, Oxford, who did much to recommend the Church to educated agnostics, and Vere Somerset, a historian, a fellow of Worcester (the college with which Stead was associated). On 29 June 1927 the doors of Finstock Church were firmly locked against idle spectators, and Stead poured the waters of regeneration over Eliot's head.

Next morning Eliot was taken to the Bishop of Oxford, Thomas Banks Strong, at Cuddesdon. In his private chapel the Bishop laid his hands on Eliot's head and said: 'Defend, O Lord, this thy Servant with thy heavenly grace, that he may continue thine forever.'

The third, and for Eliot probably the most important, ceremony only came nine months later when he made the first confession, in about March 1928, after finding a spiritual director in Father Underhill. Eliot said that 'the recognition of the reality of Sin is a New Life'.[48] All his adult life he had been haunted by a sense of guilt—most frequently, judging by his poems, sexual guilt and withdrawal of self—which now found relief. Eliot wrote to Stead of his extraordinary sense of surrender and gain, as if he had finally crossed a very wide, deep river, never to return.[49] He liked Underhill but sometimes felt he needed the severer disciplines of a priest called Whitby. He wanted something more ascetic, more violent, more 'Ignatian'.[50] One of his first tasks was to come to terms with celibacy and to find it easy for the first time.[51] In his poem, 'Animula', he speaks of 'denying the importunity of the blood' and living solely for 'the silence' after the blessing.[52]

Eliot's penitent in 'Ash Wednesday', turning and turning on the winding stair, acts out the two mental 'turns' Andrewes prescribed for a conversion: a turn that looks forward to God and a turn that looks backward to one's sins, sentencing oneself for the past.[53] In this sermon 'Of Repentance', preached on Ash Wednesday, 1619, Andrewes gives an exhaustive analysis of the demands which conversion must make on the most developed and sensitive conscience—the weighing of motives, the '*hatred of sinne*', the guard against hypocrisy.[54]

There is always a public and a private side to conversion. Eliot was impatient to fix his identity and be made wonderfully anew. He announced his conversion as an achieved goal much as the American Puritans would give public testimony of faith before being received into the communion of saints. As a public figure in the thirties he took it upon himself to call for the religious reform of society at school prizegivings and church conclaves. The private self lagged behind. In 'Ash Wednesday' and the Ariel poems, written between 1927 and 1931, Eliot wonders if he does

not belong with those who espouse Christianity officially without
being properly committed, whose ostentatious piety is 'tainted
with a self-conceit',[55] who 'are terrified and cannot surrender', and
who 'affirm before the world and deny between the rocks'.[56]

Eliot did not make it easy for his contemporaries to understand
his conversion. In 1928 he announced rather curtly that he was an
'Anglo-Catholic in religion'. It sounded oddly wilful and insistent
and, furthermore, was coupled with dogmatic beliefs in royalism
and classicism. Eliot rashly gave the impression that all these
beliefs were of equal importance to him. He did not make it clear
that his royalism and classicism were subsidiary to his Christianity and should be taken in a special way. By royalism Eliot did
not mean George V or any living ruler but an ideal similar to Sir
Thomas Elyot's, a hope that the majesty, propriety, and responsibility of an ideal ruler would reform people from above. He
believed, like Maurras, that church and king should work together.[57] The king, he said later, 'had not merely a civil but a
religious obligation toward his people'.[58] Similarly, Eliot invoked
classicism to uphold a Christian education. 'If Christianity is not
to survive', he wrote, 'I shall not mind if the texts of Latin and
Greek languages become more obscure and forgotten than those
of the language of the Etruscans.'[59]

It seemed to many of Eliot's contemporaries that he wilfully
averted his eyes from social problems between the wars and took
refuge in obsolete institutions. *TLS* called Eliot a kind of traitor.
Edmund Wilson deplored 'the unpromising character' of the
ideals and institutions he invoked and the 'reactionary point of
view'.[60] The *Manchester Guardian* said that only an American
expatriate could go so far in the direction of the right.

These critics were baffled because, perhaps naturally, they
assumed Eliot was allying himself to an institution whose mass
appeal was rather weak between the two wars.[61] But for Eliot
belief was 'something detached from the temporal weakness or
the corruption of an institution'.[62] Like many religious thinkers
he put together a faith which answered private needs and then
attached that to an institution which he believed to carry the
living stream of Christianity but which needed reform. Eliot's
attachment to Anglicanism had this dual aspect. He saw means of
support and self-correction within the English traditions; at the
same time he brought something of himself to the Anglican

Church, a spirit more vehement, more dogmatic and zealous. As Newman remarked: 'It is not at all easy . . . to wind up an Englishman to a dogmatic level.'[63] The average layman was more concerned with the demeanour of the vicar than with theology and reform. Eliot's dogmatic orthodoxy, his concern with damnation, his intolerance in his earlier years for ordinary sinners, his sense of civilization's decay and doom, his intuitions of a 'promised land beyond the waste'—all this suggests a lingering Puritan strain, rather different from the equable, mild-mannered temper of the gentlemen-clergymen with whom Eliot began to associate and to whose habits he wholly conformed.

Eliot's temperament craved an exacting moral code. Chastity, austerity, humility, and sanctity, he said he must have—or perish.[64] This code did not, of course, conflict with the aims of Anglo-Catholics, but it was *sui generis*. To express his ideals of virtue Eliot fastened on an English institution that was particularly mild in its minimal demands and set about reforming it from within. During the thirties he called upon Anglicans for a stricter theology, for discipline and asceticism, for a religion not 'watered down and robbed of the severity of its demands'.[65]

A tireless Calvinist, Robert Lowell called Eliot, who harried his pagan English public with godliness and austerity.[66] The English perhaps served Eliot as the lost tribes, as the Indians had served the religious energies of the Puritans and as the Westerner had served the missionary zeal of Eliot's grandfather in mid-nineteenth-century St. Louis and his uncle in late-nineteenth-century Oregon. Lowell recognized in Eliot's attraction to Anglicanism the authentic colour of the New Englander who would preach a more rigorous code than that which prevailed and enjoy its proprieties of form and the introspective mood it induced. If Eliot's mask suggested England, his inbent eye recalled the New England divines.

Eliot's public was, I think, partially justified in its unfriendly reaction to his faith. He had misled it by defamiliarizing the message of *The Waste Land* and then baffled it by his odd attachment to the Anglican Church. The hostility Eliot evoked, however, seems excessive and probably lay outside Eliot personally, in the age itself. Edmund Wilson deplored the forced mating of New England temper with the Anglican mode, yet admitted at the same time the unfriendliness of their age to anything religious.[67]

Eliot joined a church which, for him, retained the façade of the Elizabethan Establishment, a national church reinforced by secular power. Beside support for his private life, he found strength also in a sense of community and tradition. Living communities in America are based less on natural ties of kinship and familiarity as on a shared theory. Whether the group be based on religious belief, a political platform, or an academic field, there will be a strong emphasis on creed and jargon, a strictness within the ranks combined with a fair degree of intolerance for the uninitiated. To a non-American such groups will hardly seem communities because of the impermanence of personal and local ties. The members share no past and, very likely, no future. All they have in common—and this they will insist on—is the label. Eliot pinned on his Anglican label in the preface to *For Lancelot Andrewes*. He brought to the Church of England the American's capacity to commit himself to an idea with a fervour that seems at once strained and brave, wilful and yet attractive in its sheer vitality of moral passion. Yet in his thorough and permanent identification with the English past and locale in 'East Coker' and 'Little Gidding', which celebrate communities based on family ties, and in his acceptance of pastoral responsibility in *The Idea of a Christian Society*, Eliot became more genuinely English than any American before him.

Eliot's attachment to Anglicanism may be justified from an ideological as well as a personal angle. He discarded popular ideologies of social change—extremist politics and liberal optimism—as solutions to cultural despair, and offered as an alternative the idea of a community knit together by religious discipline. Liberal humanism, Eliot felt, could work only for a few highly-developed individuals who lived in the aftermath of a strong religious tradition. Babbitt's doctrine of the 'inner check' was too subtle and private to be the masses' alternative to the encroaching chaos of the thirties. Men like Russell and the Huxleys, who believed in a civilized but non-religious mentality, had too naïve expectations of human nature. Eliot was not against liberalism or democracy *per se*; he simply feared that they would not work: 'It is not that the world of separate individuals of the liberal democrat is undesirable', he wrote, 'it is simply that this world does not exist.' Eliot saw the masses, with their illusion of freedom,

manipulated by a society organized for profit which would influence them by any means except their intelligence.[68] He thought
that unless there was an ideal that could comprehend all of life,
namely Christianity, the masses would find the burden of thought,
each man alone, so difficult that they would come to crave simplified monistic solutions, like the racist solution of Nazi Germany.

Eliot saw in the English Church decency, common sense, and
a capacity for compromise that, he felt, might provide a proper
corrective to the faddist modern mind. He deplored the kind of
lazy, facile mind that advocated ruthless reforms and leapt across
all existing reality to some utopian ideal—through fascism or
communism—what he called 'the gospels of this world'. In
1910 already, Gide had prophesied that the weakness of the
twentieth-century mind would be in 'locating the ideal of perfection, not in equilibrium and the middle path, but in the extreme
and exaggeration'.[69] Eliot thought he found a responsible and
rational answer in the *via media* of Elizabethan Anglicanism and
praised its talent for compromise, its moderation and flexibility.
'In a period of debility like our own,' he wrote, 'few men have
the energy to follow the middle way in government; for lazy or
tired minds there is only extremity or apathy, dictatorship or
communism, with enthusiasm or indifference.'[70]

In the thirties Eliot was criticized for his refusal to turn the
Criterion into a forum for writers with radical social ideas. It
seemed to many that he was simply aligning himself with a crass,
old-fashioned conservatism. Although Eliot did discount the
sweeping ideologies for social change then current, his own
'scheme for the reformation of society' was not old-fashioned.
He saw that the future lay with the lower middle class, who
would be the most numerous and whose taste would be indulged.
He assumed that the lower middle class would have inferior
taste, but he did not kick against this. Instead he proposed a
reformation of society set at a low level: 'a social minimum', he
called it. There would be rural communities where Christian values
would not be fervently upheld but would be assimilated into
humdrum lives as mere behaviour and habit. He proposed communities small enough to consist of a network of direct personal
relationships, so that people would watch over one another. He
felt that a renewed sense of community would energize society,
although he admitted that the rural ideal did not fit very well into

the twentieth-century urban-industrial scene. Eliot also felt there should be a place for a spiritual élite, not to command or compel other people, but to preserve the best standards of thought, conduct, and taste so that people should have a sense of higher forms of life towards which they might, if they so wished, aspire.

It has not been customary to take much notice of Eliot's ideological position, yet it seems, from a historical distance, far more reasonable than the sweeping ideologies fashionable in his day. His modest ideal was men's virtue and well-being in community for all, and for a few, the divine beatitude. He wanted a community that would enrich the individual's sense of dignity, and he was indifferent to twentieth-century social schemes in which the individual was of small worth. Only one or two recognized the reasonableness of Eliot's position. In 1940 Lionel Trilling wrote that, although Eliot might have deceived himself in considering the Church an effective force for social reform, he had provided one moderate answer that favoured morality and human dignity, rare in his time.[71]

The difficulty in studying Eliot's life lies not in his religious search, which seems quite straightforward, but in isolating what was innovative and original in his vision of the world from what was idiosyncratic and sometimes distorted. William James pointed out how each temperament makes religion according to its needs.[72] If one is humane, one's religion tends to be comforting; if one is self-absorbed and obsessed with a darker life, one's religion tends to exalt self-sacrifice and drastic cures. Eliot braced himself for 'cords and scourges and lamentation' and 'a whole Thibet of broken stones / That lie, fang up, a lifetime's march.'[73] His nature, like that of his early hero, the martyred Saint Narcissus, was drawn by Christianity's martyrdoms and feats of asceticism rather than by its more compassionate humane goals. He certainly knew, after his conversion, moments of singing happiness, recorded in the lyrical parts of 'Ash Wednesday' and 'Marina'; he may, late in life, have discovered the comforting face of religion, but most of his life was spent in the shadow of its torments rather than its blessings.

Eliot was sensitive to the power of evil in human hearts and felt that his conception of sin, in a twentieth-century world dedicated to material, political, and sexual cures, was itself a triumph. He felt the devil not so much in social wrongs, but within, and believed that the chief purpose of civilization was to cope with the notion of original sin.* This defensible point of view found an unhappy focus in Eliot's routine identification of women with sin. He regarded lust as the most corrupting of all sins and, as a young man, he wished the flesh could be denied, burnt away by that refining fire he so often invoked. Soon after his conversion he wrote savagely that those who 'suffer the ecstasy of the animals' may look forward only to death.[74]

Eliot always acknowledged and derided the idiosyncratic element in his philosophy. Although he presented himself as an exemplary figure, he frankly included his personal flaws. Eliot had an extraordinary drive for perfection, and in his early years hunted for signs that he had been singled out in a special way. He wished to be God's ambassador, but admitted again and again in his early years that he could not honestly claim the credentials. Even in his light-filled moments he retained a degree of modesty or hesitation. Because of his distance from God—a distance reinforced by his times—the approach had to be willed, doggedly and alone. Eliot's mental isolation perhaps brewed the eccentric elements in his early life—the distrust of women and the narrow self-absorption. Eliot's personality was self-centred enough to assume that the world and its vicissitudes—its women, its wars, seasons, crowds—existed as signals for his private conduct. The isolation and the absence of signs, of which Eliot complained in 'Gerontion', brewed also a certain wilfulness. Eliot's poetic record did not concentrate on the beatific vision but on himself, his determination to be recognized and chosen.

Eliot passed his youth walled-in by shyness and vast ambition. His adult life may be seen as a series of adventures from the citadel of his self in search of some great defining experience. He made expeditions across a perilous gap that divided him from the great world, and ventured into society, into marriage, into religious communion. He tried to maintain the polite, even curiosity of an explorer far from home, but each time had to withdraw—shuddering from the contact—to his citadel, where he would then labour to record, as precisely as possible, his strange encounters. It was soon apparent to Eliot that the religious

---

* 'La vraie civilisation', Eliot once quoted from Baudelaire, '. . . est dans la diminution des traces du péché originel.' *SE*, p. 381.

encounter was the most commanding of his experiences but, ironically, with this perception the gap seemed to widen, to become ever more difficult to cross. By 1925, it had become clear to him that if he were to cross the gap successfully he would have to abandon his citadel, and plunge into a journey of no return. The plunge came with his first confession in 1928; during the thirties he adapted to living in an Anglican clergyhouse; at last, with the genuine state of self-abnegation recorded in *Four Quartets*, came the chance to commune with God on Little Gidding's holy ground.

At each stage of his career Eliot defined his identity and measured his distance from enlightenment. There was, in his poetry, a persistent self-portraiture—from the languid, well-dressed gentleman in 'Spleen', who waited impatiently on the doorstep of the Absolute, to Prufrock, whose impulse to assault the universe with a prophetic truth beat beneath his anxiously correct façade; and from the phantom pilgrim searching the city for a miraculous cure for depression to the anxious penitent patiently climbing the purgatorial stair. One developing personality redefined, in each poem, the position won in the previous poem. From the start, Eliot was preoccupied with his own special fate, but he was uncertain how to characterize himself. He sensed his identity as a 'shadow of its own shadows, spectre in its own gloom'.[75] Eliot haunted his poems like an irresolute ghost seeking shape and form and visible role. When at length he was sure of his best self, he suddenly revealed a preacher, his outlines distinct, his feet firmly planted on an Anglican platform.

One of the persistent features of Eliot's early years is his displacement in his time. He derided his contemporaries' faddist political solutions, their smug rationalism, their meaningless toys—horoscopes and porcelain collections—their boring stereotyped parties, their magazine-styled romances. Eliot saw the children of the early twentieth century as an alien people clutching cheap gods. Like a prophet he denounced those who sat 'in the sty of contentment', and those who glittered 'with the glory of the hummingbird' and, above all, those who supported a predatory commercial society.[76] He had seen in his youth in America the hypertrophy of the motive of profit as a public ideal and the gross misuse of money. In 1939 he foresaw that these evils were more tenacious than those that provoked the Second

World War. In 1939 his rhetoric seemed irrelevant; several decades later his denunciations seem pertinent:

> Surely there is something wrong in our attitude towards money. The acquisitive, rather than the creative and spiritual instincts, are encouraged. The fact that money is always forthcoming for the purpose of making more money, whilst it is so difficult to obtain . . . for the needs of the most needy, is disturbing to those who are not economists. I am by no means sure that it is right for me to improve my income by investing in the shares of a company, making I know not what, operating perhaps thousands of miles away, and in control of which I have no effective voice. (Postscript, *ICS*, p. 76)

He also criticized the exhaustion of natural resources by unregulated industries ('exploiting the seas and developing mountains') and warned that 'a good deal of our material progress is a progress for which succeeding generations may have to pay dearly. . . . . For a long enough time we have believed in nothing but the values arising in a mechanized, commercialized, urbanized way of life: it would be as well for us to face the permanent conditions upon which God allows us to live upon this planet.'[77]

Eliot had little hope that a civilization smugly assembled on congeries of banks, industries, and insurance companies, would listen to his exhortations. He wrote that God commanded him to 'prophesy to the wind, to the wind only for only / The wind will listen.'[78]

Eliot wilfully adopted roles unlikely to charm the audience of his day, of pilgrim and preacher. The models of manhood by which he measured himself—Augustine, Lazarus, Ezekiel, Elijah, Parzival—were heroes of other, more religious ages. The cultural anecdotes in *The Waste Land* temporarily deluded Eliot's postwar audience into adopting him as a child of their times. The 'lost' generation followed him willingly to the brink of cultural despair, but wondered at his inclinations when he went beyond it. He ventured alone in search of the lost ideals of religious communities, and occasionally bethought himself of his generation and called back urgent exhortations. These sounded odd in their ears—dogmatic, wilful, and irrelevant.

Through his personal record Eliot tried to give back to the early twentieth century a world in which men lived by fresh visions and to restore the moral dimensions of a universe in which visions belonged. Eliot himself enjoyed only infrequent, and often frustrating, moments of revelation—the silence between the waves, the silence in the streets of Boston, the ring of silence in the Parisian attic—but these were sufficient to initiate in him a new sense of the meaning of life. He used to experience a vision not as pleasure but as a sudden relief from an intolerable burden. It was as if strong habitual barriers were broken down. 'Some obstruction is momentarily whisked away', he said.[79] Although the vision commanded Eliot's life and dictated his message, he tended, in his published poetry, to gloss over it and to concentrate on the doubts and struggles that followed. These were easy to communicate, while the vision, he realized, was essentially incommunicable. The habitual barriers re-formed very fast.

Eliot showed great courage and persistence in defending his faith as an inescapable human need and in pointing out that what was objectionable to one generation was simply what it was not used to. After moving in intellectual circles he experienced, in his identification with the church, an odd but exhilarating feeling of intellectual isolation.[80] When he was presented with the Emerson–Thoreau medal, in 1959, he was called the spiritual heir to a line of 'come-outers', New Englanders who spoke out for their private convictions, who braved misunderstanding, and welcomed the solitude of original insight. Eliot set himself to rediscover modes of experience absent from the world into which he was born: the saintly life, the Christian community, religious fear and hope. If he could not quite live the saintly life himself, if he could not speak directly to his contemporaries, he still hoped his story would benefit generations to come, 'in a world of time beyond me'.[81] He consigned his deeds to oblivion, but proffered his love to the choice souls of the future, 'the posterity of the desert'.[82] In 'Song for Simeon' he hoped that they would acknowledge and re-enact, with greater success, his lonely watch. They would praise God and suffer derision and discover light upon light, mounting the saints' stair.

Eliot's Reading in Mysticism (1908–14)

SOME of Eliot's student notes survive from his years at Harvard, about forty cards in the Houghton Library, recording his reading in philosophy. The majority of the cards show his interest in mysticism and the psychology of religious experience. In the following selected list I have omitted numerous journals of the day and asterisked those books from which he took more than brief notes.

AMES, E. S. *The Psychology of Religious Experience*. Boston, 1910.

BOURIGNON, ANTOINETTE. (She was a Franco-Flemish Quietist, 1616–80. Eliot cites the title as 'Vie'. Possibly this was Von der Linde's edition of *Das Licht der Welt*, 1895, or a biography by MacEwen, 1910.)

BURNET, J. *Early Greek Philosophy*. London, 1908.

CALDECOTT, A. *The Philosophy of Religion in England and America*. London, 1901.

CUTTEN, G. B. *The Psychological Phenomena of Christianity*. London, 1909.

DELACROIX, H. *Essai sur le mysticisme spéculatif en Allemagne au XIVᵉ siècle*. Paris, 1910.

DUMAS. *L'Amour mystique*. Rev. ed., 1906.

INGE, W. R. *Christian Mysticism*. London, 1899.

—— *Personal Idealism and Mysticism*. London, 1907.

—— *Studies of English Mystics*. London, 1906.

JAMES, WILLIAM. *The Varieties of Religious Experience*. London, 1902. (Eliot's notes are from the chapter on Mysticism.)

JANET, PIERRE. *Névroses et idées fixes*. Paris, 1898.

—— *Obsessions et psychasthénie*. Paris, 1903.

JEFFRIES, RICHARD. *The Story of My Heart*. 2nd ed. London, 1891.

JEVONS, F. B. *An Introduction to the History of Religion*. London, 1896.

JONES, RUFUS M. *Studies in Mystical Religion*. London, 1909.

LADD, G. T. *The Philosophy of Religion*. 2 vols. New York, 1905.

LEUBA, J. H. 'Les tendances fondamentales des mystiques chrétiens'. *Revue philosophique*, juillet, 1902.

MURISIER, E. *Les Maladies du sentiments religieux*. Paris, 1901.

NORDAU, MAX. *Degeneration*. London, 1895. (Eliot notes that this book seeks to undermine mysticism.)

PATRICK, G. T. W. *Heraclitus of Ephesus*. Baltimore, 1889.

POULAIN, A. *Les Grâces d'oraison.* n.d.

PRATT, J. B. *The Psychology of Religious Belief.* New York, 1907.

RAUWENHOFF, L. W. E. *Religious Philosophy.* n.d.

RÉCÉJAC, E. *Essai sur les fondements de la connaissance mystique.* Paris, 1897.

ROUSSELOT, P. *Les Mystiques espagnols.* Paris, 1867.

STARBUCK, E. T. *The Psychology of Religion.* 2nd ed. London, 1901.

SUSO, H. *Life of Henry Suso,* by Himself. Transl. by T. F. Knox. London, 1913.

UNDERHILL, EVELYN. **Mysticism.* London, 1911. (Eliot took copious notes.)

WOODS, J. H. *Practice and Science of Religion: A Study of Method in Comparative Religion.* New York, 1906.

—— *The Value of Religious Facts.* n.d.

Dating The Waste Land *Fragments*

THE manuscript of *The Waste Land* is a hoard of fragments accumulated slowly over seven and a half years. Only in the seventh year were the fragments transformed into a major work. In order to trace the growth of *The Waste Land* through all the stages of its composition, I first grouped the fragments according to the different batches of paper Eliot used and then established a tentative chronological order by means of a variety of clues, many of which are provided by Valerie Eliot's clear and well-annotated facsimile edition of the manuscript.

When Eliot was still at Harvard in 1914 he wrote three visionary fragments on the same Linen Ledger quadruled paper, punched for filing: 'After the turning . . .', 'I am the Resurrection and the Life . . .', and 'So through the evening . . .'. Valerie Eliot dates the handwriting '1914 or even earlier'. These fragments should be read in conjunction with other poems of that time which were not included in the *Waste Land* manuscript but which presage *Waste Land* material: 'The Burnt Dancer', 'The Love Song of Saint Sebastian', 'Oh little voices . . .', and a religious poem of 1911, 'The Little Passion', which Eliot revised in 1914 and copied into his Notebook.

In the summer of 1914 Eliot went to Oxford to read philosophy and there, a few months later, he wrote 'The Death of Saint Narcissus'. His first draft has the watermark 'Excelsior Fine British Make', the same paper used for 'Mr. Apollinax'. Both poems must have been written by January 1915 for, on 2 February, Eliot alluded to them in a letter to Pound ('I understand that Priapism, Narcissism etc are not approved of . . .').

No more fragments were written until some time after Eliot's marriage to Vivienne Haigh-Wood in June 1915, but in January 1916 Eliot wrote to his Harvard friend, Conrad Aiken, that he had '*lived* through material for a score of long poems in the last six months'.

Between 1916 and 1919 Eliot wrote another batch of fragments introducing new themes—the threatening wife and London. It might be possible to be more specific about the date of 'The Death of the Duchess' by matching the paper with that of non-*Waste Land* manuscripts but, in the absence of other clues, the paper evidence is inconclusive. The paper matches that of an unpublished 1916 review of H. D.'s translation of choruses from *Iphigenia in Aulis*. It also matches a draft of 'Gerontion', which Eliot sent to John Rodker in the summer of 1919. Possible evidence for an earlier date is a 1918 reference by Pound (on a draft of 'Whispers of Immortality') to a Duchess who is outraged by Grishkin's animality. But there is no doubt that the poem was done by 1919: Valerie Eliot has found a letter written to Eliot in 1919 expressing admiration for it and referring also to Mr. Bleistein in 'Dirge'.

A phrase from the 'Duchess', 'bound forever on the wheel', links the poem with 'London', whose inhabitants are bound on the wheel. 'London', 'Dirge', 'O City City', 'The river sweats . . .', and 'Elegy' were all written on Hieratica Bond small notepad sheets. The form of 'Elegy' points to Eliot's quatrain period, 1917–19; also the theme of death by water and the name Bleistein appear in other poems of 1918 and 1919. A drowning, similar to Bleistein's, involving the disembodiment and transformation of a Phoenician sailor, appears in 'Dans le Restaurant' (1918), which was later translated with alterations and added to *The Waste Land*. It is impossible, so far, to date the Hieratica cluster exactly, but 1918 seems a reasonable guess. The earliest date would be the spring of 1917 when Eliot began his career as bank clerk in the City, for 'O City City' and 'London' are clearly associated with that experience.

The turning-point between a hoard of fragments and a unified poem comes about through 'Gerontion', which was written in May–June 1919. Eliot did not include 'Gerontion' in the manuscript and I shall not discuss it here except to say that Eliot saw 'Gerontion' as a prelude to *The Waste Land* but submitted to Pound's advice to exclude it. Towards the end of 1919 Eliot wrote to his New York benefactor John Quinn and to his mother in Boston that he wished to write a long poem he had had in mind for some time.

I have remained in two minds about the sequence of *The Waste Land*'s composition during 1921. One hypothesis is that Eliot did almost all the work of that year in one continuous stretch, while on sick-leave from October to December. The second hypothesis is that parts I and II were done earlier, possibly in the spring of 1921. There is no doubt that 'Song to the Opherian' was written earlier in 1921 for it was published in April in *The Tyro* under the pseudonym, Gus Krutzsch. Eliot used his Harvard typewriter and British Bond paper for the *Waste Land* copy. Parts I and II of *The Waste Land* use the same typewriter and paper, though the paper of 'Song' is slightly yellower, perhaps a different batch. On 9 May 1921, Eliot wrote to Quinn that he had a 'long poem' in mind and 'partly on paper' which he wished to finish. More significant in this letter is the remark on Vivienne's absence at the seaside. Vivienne and Eliot would have been separated when he wrote part II as the top copy was mailed back and forth. (Vivienne wrote 'wonderful wonderful' next to her husband's graphic description of the tormented couple and 'Send me back this copy and let me have it' on the verso of the second sheet.)

On 2 May Eliot mentioned to Robert McAlmon and on 9 May to Quinn that he was reading the latter part of *Ulysses* in manuscript. The original opening scene of part I of *The Waste Land* is a Boston version of the visit to Night-town. The name, 'Krutzsch', in this scene recalls the recent 'Song'.

Although the above clues seem to point to a spring date for parts I and II, a letter from Pound to John Quinn, on approximately 22 October, casts some doubt. Pound was in the habit of commenting on Eliot's latest poems, even prospective poems, to Quinn, but there is no mention in the October letter of the first two parts of a major poem, only a comment on Eliot's health. If in fact Eliot had finished those polished and complete typescripts before October 1921 he would surely have shown them to Pound at that early autumn meeting in London, just before his departure for Margate.

My guess is that on 12 October Eliot went to Margate with the old fragments, 'Song', and no more than a few new scattered lines or passages. Using an office typewriter and yellowish paper with a 'Verona' watermark Eliot typed his title-page with the epigraph from *Heart of Darkness*, a short lyric, 'Exequy', and, in duplicate, a long episodic section which combines the old City fragments with portraits of unappealing Londoners. Eliot called it 'The Fire Sermon' because he planned to assault these worldly sinners with the Buddha's sermon at the end of another Hieratica fragment, 'The river sweats . . .', to be appended to 'The Fire Sermon' as a finale. Hugh Kenner noted that the absence of a part number to 'The Fire Sermon' suggests it must have antedated any decision about the amount of *Waste Land* material that should precede it.

On 12 November Eliot left Margate, spent a week in London with his wife, then passed through Paris on 18 November when presumably Pound jotted pencilled comments on the Verona sheets and 'Song'. Eliot spent the rest of November and December at the sanatorium in Lausanne where he wrote two new sections, parts IV and V, a rough draft of 'Venus Anadyomene', and a fair copy of 'Dirge', all on the same quadruled paper. The question remains whether he could also have composed parts I and II in Lausanne, and since these were typed it becomes a question whether or not Eliot took his Harvard typewriter with him. It would seem common sense to take a typewriter, even a heavy one, but there is no doubt, as Helen Gardner points out, that in Lausanne Eliot does something unusual. He carefully transcribes his fair copies ('Dirge' and part IV) by hand. Further evidence that Eliot may not have taken his typewriter is that when he stops in Paris on his way home part IV is typed on a borrowed (unidentified) machine and part V on Pound's machine.

Turning the question around, other evidence remains that parts I and II were written late, particularly the Sosostris scene. Grover Smith noted that the name comes from 'Sesostris the Sorceress' in Aldous Huxley's *Crome Yellow* and, since this was published only in November 1921, it seems unlikely Eliot could have written this before his stay in Lausanne. Even if *Crome Yellow* was circulated in manuscript prior to publication it was only completed in August, which makes the spring date for part I impossible. In any case, Mme Sosostris's wicked pack of cards is a unifying device, a late attempt to draw the fragments together with a parade of the poem's characters. It must have been written after Eliot conceives of the merchant in 'The Fire Sermon' and the phrase 'death by water' in part IV.

With Vivienne in Paris and Eliot in Lausanne, there is again an opportunity for the top copy of part II to be mailed back and forth. Eliot then returned to Paris early in January 1922 and showed part II to Pound for the first time—for Pound pencilled '1922' in exasperation next to Eliot's anachronistic reference to a closed carriage. (It is worth noting the pencil since Pound habitually used pencil for a first reading of Eliot's manuscripts, and ink for a second reading.) Pound corrected part I only once, whereas he corrected 'The Fire Sermon' on two occasions, 18 November and early January. Eliot must have had British Bond paper with him for, when Pound cut the line '(Those are pearls that were his eyes. Look!)' from Mme Sosostris's prophecy, Eliot—reluctant to let it go—scribbled a late fragment, beginning with the same line, on British Bond.

The final doubt remains: if parts I, II, and III were done before Eliot went abroad, are parts IV and V enough to justify the impression, given by Pound and Eliot, that the substance of the poem was done at Lausanne?

The story of *The Waste Land*'s composition in 1921 remains, as yet, unresolved. There are two possible hypotheses and one can do no more at present than weigh one body of circumstantial evidence against the other. Probably, somewhere in Eliot's unpublished manuscripts or correspondence there lies the decisive clue which, sooner or later, must be found.

A Note on The Waste Land *and* Ulysses

I T is one of the commonplaces of modernism to note *The Waste Land*'s debt to *Ulysses*, both of which were published in 1922. Eliot published the earlier chapters of *Ulysses* in the *Egoist* in 1919, and in the spring of 1921 read the later chapters in manuscript. It is easy to point to Eliot's specific borrowings, to the parodies of different English styles in imitation of 'Oxen of the Sun', and to Eliot's tamer Boston version of the visit to Night-town, but I do not think that Eliot was profoundly influenced by Joyce.

Eliot's specific borrowings, almost always from the 'Proteus' and 'Hades' episodes of *Ulysses*, reinforce his own sense of horror at the prospect of decay and death. They are essentially embellishments to the poem and came, with one exception, only late in the history of *The Waste Land*'s composition. From 'Proteus' came the dog vulturing the dead in part I of *The Waste Land*. Like Joyce in 'Hades' Eliot aligns the living with the dead. Flesh interfuses with dead matter in the suburban gardens of Eliot's London as in Joyce's Dublin graveyard, and the decomposition of miserable people becomes part of everyday consciousness. Eliot adapts Bloom's thoughts as he walks about the graveyard ('How many! All these here once walked round Dublin') to the Dantean 'so many, / I had not thought death had undone so many'. Bloom thinks of a corpse planted rather than buried, and of the gardener digging the weeds which represent the body's sole form of revival. 'That corpse you planted,' Eliot's observer asks one of the mechanical workers sarcastically, 'has it begun to sprout?'

The funeral procession in 'Hades' passes the canal with the gas-works. Joyce's words 'rattle his bones', referring to the body in the coffin, are picked up by Eliot in 'The Fire Sermon':

> But at my back in a cold blast I hear
> The rattle of bones, and chuckle spread from ear to ear.

In the drowning of Phlebas the Phoenician in part IV, the sea current which 'picked his bones in whispers' is a new addition from Joyce's graveyard where the obese rat nibbles corpses: 'One of those chaps would make short work of a fellow', Bloom observes. 'Pick the bones clean no matter who it was.' In a similar drowning scene in the manuscript fragment, 'Dirge', Eliot like Stephen Dedalus resists having to share humanity with the dehumanized drowned object. 'Five fathom out there', Stephen muses. 'Full fathom five they father lies. . . . Bag of corpsegas sopping in foul brine. . . . God becomes man becomes fish becomes barnacle.' Eliot's corpse becomes a sea-object, in time indistinguishable from the life of the sea.

The rejection of history in part V of *The Waste Land* may be aligned with Stephen Dedalus's distaste for history as a tale too often heard or a nightmare from which one tries to awake. 'I hear the ruin of all space,' thinks Stephen, 'shattered glass and toppling masonry, and time one livid final flame.' The difference is that when Eliot contemplates the ruins of time, he conceives of an alternative timeless realm which he later calls the 'other Kingdom'.

Eliot imitates the kind of polluted, rat-ridden, decomposing modern city he found in Joyce's Dublin. But whereas for Eliot this means hell and nothing else, Joyce's imaginative exuberance allowed for multiple responses. In *The Art of T. S. Eliot*, Helen Gardner deftly summed up the differences between Eliot and Joyce, and the publication of the manuscript bears out her view that *The Waste Land* moves in the opposite direction to *Ulysses*. The earliest source material for *The Waste Land* shows Eliot consistently leaning towards an escape from the sordid reality of daily life through 'aetherial rumours'. When Eliot discussed *Ulysses* with Virginia Woolf in 1922, he said that there was no 'great conception' and that Joyce's stream of consciousness often did not tell as much as some casual glance from the outside.

Source Notes

CHAPTER I. EARLY MODELS

1. Diary (19 Sept. 1920), Berg Collection, New York Public Library.
2. Letter to Alfred Kreymborg (30 May 1925), Alderman Library, Univ. of Virginia at Charlottesville.
3. 'The *Pensées* of Pascal', *SE*, p. 360.
4. Eliot to William Force Stead (9 Aug. 1930), Osborn Collection, Beinecke Library, Yale Univ.
5. 'Ben Jonson', *SW*, p. 118.
6. 'A General Introduction for my Work', *Selected Criticism*, ed. A. Norman Jeffares (London: Macmillan, 1964), p. 255.
7. R. L. Rusk, *The Letters of Ralph Waldo Emerson*, vol. 4 (New York, 1939), pp. 338–9.
8. *Paris Review* interview with Donald Hall, rpr. *Writers at Work*, ed. Van Wyck Brooks, 2nd series (N.Y.: Viking, 1963).
9. Charlotte Champe Eliot, *William Greenleaf Eliot* (N.Y.: Houghton Mifflin, 1904), p. 336.
10. Sixty-page typescript, Olin Library, Washington Univ., St. Louis. I should like to thank the Archives Supervisor, Beryl H. Manne, for prompt help.
11. Frank Morley, 'A Few Recollections of Eliot', *Sewanee Review*'s T. S. Eliot memorial issue (1965), rpr. *T. S. Eliot: The Man and his Work*, ed. Allen Tate (N.Y.: Dell, 1966), pp. 90–113.
12. Address, Washington University (1953), rpr. 'American Literature and the American Language', *CC*, p. 45.
13. 'Dry Salvages', *CP*, p. 191.
14. 'From a Distinguished Former St. Louisian' [part of a letter from Eliot to M. C. Childs], *St. Louis Post-Dispatch* (5 Oct. 1930).
15. 'Dry Salvages', *CP*, p. 195.
16. T. S. Eliot, 'Why Mr. Russell is a Christian', *Criterion*, 6 (Aug. 1927), 179.
17. All photographs mentioned in this chapter, mostly by Eliot's brother, Henry Ware Eliot, Jr., are in the Eliot Collection, Houghton Library, Harvard Univ.
18. The manuscript (n.d.) is in Special Collections, Butler Library, Columbia Univ.
19. H. W. H. Powel, Jr., 'Notes on the Life of T. S. Eliot 1888–1910' (M.A. thesis, Brown Univ., 1954), p. 28.
20. St. Louis letter from 'Margery' to Mary von Schrader and Randall Jarrell (n.d.), Berg Coll.
21. Letter (Apr. 1910), Eliot Coll., Houghton Library.
22. Obituaries, Eliot Coll., Houghton Library.
23. 'The Three Kings', Scrapbook, Houghton Library.

24. 'Charade of the Seasons', Houghton Library.

25. *Daedalus*, 89 (Spring 1960), 421–2.

26. Robert Giroux, 'A Personal Memoir', Allen Tate's collection, pp. 337–44.

27. Preface to James B. Connolly's *Fishermen of the Banks* (London: Faber, 1928). Eliot had Faber reprint this book, one of his favourites as a child, originally called *Out of Gloucester* (1902).

28. Ibid., p. 267.

29. *Harvard Advocate*, 87 (May 25, 1909), 115–16.

30. See L. M. Little, 'Eliot: A Reminiscence', *Harvard Advocate* (Fall 1966), p. 33.

31. *UPUC*, pp. 78–9.

32. *CC*, pp. 43–60.

33. Quoted by Herbert Howarth, *Notes on Some Figures behind T. S. Eliot* (London: Chatto & Windus, 1965), pp. 1–2.

34. Levy and Scherle, *Affectionately, T. S. Eliot* (N.Y.: Lipincott, 1968), pp. 53–4.

35. Rusk, op. cit.

36. Letter to Middleton Murry (6 Nov. 1931), Berg Coll.

37. Pearl Hogrefe, *The Life and Times of Sir Thomas Elyot, Englishman* (Iowa State University Press, 1967).

38. 'East Coker', *CP*, pp. 182–3.

39. Ephraim Eliot, *Historical Notices of the New North Religious Society in the Town of Boston, with Anecdotes of the Reverend Andrew and John Eliot* (Boston: Phelps and Farnham, 1822).

40. *NDC*, p. 115.

41. *SW*, p. 32.

42. Eliot's cousin, Frederick May Eliot, told this to Powel: 'Notes on the Life of T. S. Eliot', p. 25.

43. Levy and Scherle, op. cit., p. 121.

44. *SE*, p. 380.

45. Published in *The Unitarian* (Aug. 1887).

46. Letter to Bertrand Russell (22 June 1927), Russell Archive, McMaster Univ. See also review of Middleton Murry's *Son of Woman: The Story of D. H. Lawrence*, *Criterion*, 10 (July 1931), 771.

47. Introduction to *Revelation*, ed. John Baille and Hugh Martin (London, 1937).

48. Letter to Murry, op. cit.

49. *A Sermon* preached at Magdalene Chapel (Cambridge, England, 1948), p. 5.

50. H. B. Parkes, 'The Puritan Heresy' in *The Pragmatic Test: Essays on the History of Ideas*, ed. Henry Bamford (San Francisco: Colt, 1941).

51. *The Education of Henry Adams* (Cambridge, Mass.: Riverside, 1961), p. 34.

52. 'The Relationship between Politics and Metaphysics', a talk to Harvard's Philosophical Society, quoted by John Soldo in 'The Tempering of T. S. Eliot' (Harvard dissertation, 1973), p. 166.

53. 'Democratic Vistas', rpr. *Leaves of Grass and Selected Prose*, ed. John Kouwenhoven (N.Y.: Modern Library, 1950), pp. 467–9.

54. *ASG*, p. 16.
55. Letter to Herbert Read (1928), quoted in Allen Tate's collection, p. 15.

CHAPTER 2. A NEW ENGLAND STUDENT

1. 'Nature', *Ralph Waldo Emerson: Selected Prose and Poetry*, intro. Reginald L. Cook (N.Y.: Holt, Rinehart, 1964).
2. *The Listener* (19 Dec. 1946), p. 895.
3. *SE*, p. 358.
4. *The American Scene* (1904; rpr, ed. Leon Edel, Indiana Univ. Press, 1968), p. 232.
5. *Selected Writings*, ed. Jacques Barzun (N.Y.: Minerva Press, 1968), pp. 135–7.
6. *Anti-Intellectualism in American Life* (1962; rpr. N.Y.: Vintage, 1966), p. 191.
7. *Letters*, ii. 466.
8. 'The Genteel Tradition in American Philosophy', *Selected Critical Writings of George Santayana*, vol. ii, ed. Norman Henfrey (Cambridge Univ. Press, 1968), pp. 95–6.
9. Henry James, *The American Scene*, p. 246.
10. *Letters*, ii. 466.
11. These poems were written in Oxford in 1915. *CP*, pp. 20–2.
12. 'Henry James: The Hawthorne Aspect', *Little Review* (Aug. 1918), rpr. in *The Shock of Recognition*, ed. Edmund Wilson (N.Y.: Random, 1955; London: W. H. Allen, 1956), p. 860.
13. *Letters*, ii. 414.
14. 'Dante', *SW*, p. 169.
15. *The Education of Henry Adams*, p. 307.
16. Part of this letter (May 1914) is published in *Memoirs of Lady Ottoline Morrell*, ed. Robert Gathorne-Hardy (N.Y.: Knopf, 1964; London: Faber, 1963), p. 255.
17. H. W. H. Powel, Jr., 'Notes on the Life of T. S. Eliot 1888–1910', p. 61.
18. These memories, above and below, are from Conrad Aiken, 'King Bolo and Others' in *T. S. Eliot: A Symposium* edited by Tambimuttu and Richard March, p. 20. (Hereafter called 60th birthday coll.)
19. *Harvard Advocate*, 89, No. 5.
20. Eliot's relationship with Copeland is described by J. Donald Adams, *Copey of Harvard* (Boston: Houghton Mifflin 1960), pp. 153–4, 159–64.
21. A holograph address on Politics and Metaphysics read before Harvard's Philosophical Society, Houghton Library.
22. Eliot's philosophy notes, Houghton Library.
23. 'The Humanism of Irving Babbitt', *SE*, p. 426.
24. *TLS* (29 Dec. 1927), pp. 981–2.
25. BBC talk (1932). Eliot gave a series of weekly talks in March and April entitled 'The Modern Dilemma'.
26. Charlotte Champe Eliot, 'Not in the Flesh, But the Spirit', Scrapbook, Eliot Coll., Houghton Library.

27. Two 'Song's and 'Before Morning', *Poems Written in Early Youth*, pp. 10, 18, 19.
28. 'Song', first published in the *Advocate* (24 May 1907).
29. 'Circe's Palace', *Poems Written in Early Youth*, p. 20.
30. 'Song', *Poems Written in Early Youth*, p. 22.
31. Eliot recalled this scene in an address to the Mary Institute in St. Louis in 1959. Published in *From Mary to You*, p. 135.
32. *Poems Written in Early Youth*, p. 21.
33. 60th birthday collection, pp. 21–2, and *Ushant* (Boston: Little, Brown, 1952), pp. 173–4.
34. 'Opera', Berg Coll.
35. *CP*, p. 25.
36. *Poems Written in Early Youth*, pp. 24–5.
37. Autograph letter to Thomas Lamb Eliot (7 Mar. 1914), Reed College Archives, Portland, Oreg., quoted by John Soldo.
38. *SE*, p. 380.
39. 'Pour le livre d'amour'.
40. Francis Scarfe, 'Eliot and Nineteenth-Century French Poetry', in *Eliot in Perspective*, ed. Graham Martin (London: Macmillan, 1970), pp. 45–62.
41. Quoted by Symons, *The Symbolist Movement in Literature* (1899; rpr. N.Y.: Dutton, 1958), p. 56.
42. Howarth, p. 105.
43. *Life* (15 Jan. 1965), p. 92.
44. *Poems Written in Early Youth*, p. 26.
45. *Life* (15 Jan. 1965), p. 92.
46. 'Conversation Galante', 'Nocturne', and 'Humoresque'.
47. Adams, *Letters*, ii. 313.
48. Eliot Coll., Houghton Library.
49. The graduation ceremony and the Orator's speech are described in the *Boston Evening Transcript* (24 June 1910).
50. 'Goldfish (Essence of Summer Magazines) I–IV', Berg Coll.
51. 'Mandarins, 1–4', dated Aug. 1910, Berg Coll.
52. *The Listener* (19 Dec. 1946), p. 895.
53. *WL*: I, *CP*, p. 54.
54. 'Burnt Norton': I, *CP*, p. 176.
55. 'Marina', *CP*, p. 105.
56. Quoted by Symons, p. 58.

CHAPTER 3. BEYOND PHILOSOPHY

1. See *The Wings of the Dove* (1902; rpr. London: Bodley Head, 1969), p. 115.
2. *La France libre*, 8, No. 44 (15 June 1944), 94–9.
3. *Paris Review* interview with Donald Hall, rpr. in *Writers at Work*, intro. Van Wyck Brooks, 2nd series (N.Y.: Viking, 1963), pp. 91–110.
4. Conversation (2 May, 1921), recorded by Robert McAlmon, *Being Geniuses Together 1920–30*, ed. Kay Boyle (N.Y.: Doubleday, 1968), pp. 8–9.
5. Eliot's notes from the Bergson lectures are in the Eliot Coll., Houghton Library.

6. Henri Bergson, *An Introduction to Metaphysics* (1903), transl. T. E. Hulme (1912; rpr. N.Y.: Liberal Arts Press, 1955), pp. 49–50.

7. Holograph poem, 'Fourth Caprice in Montparnasse' (dated Dec. 1910).

8. Holograph poem, 'Interlude in London' (dated Apr. 1911).

9. See holograph poem, 'Interlude: in a Bar' (dated Feb. 1911).

10. See 'Rhapsody on a Windy Night', *CP*, pp. 16–18.

11. Bergson, *An Introduction to Metaphysics*, p. 25.

12. 'The American Scholar', *Ralph Waldo Emerson: Selected Prose and Poetry*, p. 65.

13. 'Burnt Norton': II, *CP*, p. 177: 'The dance along the artery / The circulation of the lymph / Are figured in the drift of stars.' See Thoreau's *Walden*.

14. The second part of 'He said: 'this universe is very clear . . .,' an untitled, two-part, holograph fragment on the verso of the debate of the constellations (dated Mar. 1911).

15. 'Dante', *SW*, p. 170.

16. *Ushant*, pp. 157, 186–7.

17. Third Prelude and 'Prufrock's Pervigilium'.

18. 'Cyril Tourneur', *SE*, p. 166.

19. 'Pascal', *SE*, p. 368.

20. 'Experience', *Ralph Waldo Emerson: Selected Prose and Poetry*, p. 253.

21. 'Faith', Scrapbook, Houghton Library.

22. 'Giordano Bruno in Prison' (1890), Scrapbook.

23. *An Introduction to Metaphysics*, pp. 25–6.

24. Eliot, 'London Letter', *Dial*, 73 (Sept. 1922), 331.

25. I have preferred Eliot's date (1912, mentioned in a letter to Stead on 12 Nov. 1931) to Aiken's dates (1913, 1914), since the latter seems to have had a less reliable memory.

26. See reviews of the *Catholic Anthology* (1915).

27. Virginia Woolf's Diary (Sept. 1920), Berg Coll.

28. *The Family Reunion*, Part I, Scene ii, *Collected Plays*, p. 80.

29. See Eliot's introduction to Josef Pieper, *Leisure: The Basis of Culture* (1952; rpr. N.Y.: Mentor-Omega, 1963; London: Collins, 1965), p. 12, and 'Views and Reviews', *NEW* (June 1935), pp. 151–2.

30. Quoted by Brand Blanchard, 'Eliot in Memory', *Yale Review* (Summer 1965), pp. 637–40.

31. Eliot, review of *Ethical Studies*, *TLS* (29 Dec. 1927), pp. 981–2, rpr. 'Francis Herbert Bradley', *SE*.

32. 'Commentary', *Criterion*, 3 (Oct. 1924), 2.

33. *Vanity Fair* (U.S.A.) (Feb. 1924), pp. 29, 98.

34. *Appearance and Reality*, rpr. intro. by Richard Wollheim (O.U.P., 1969), p. 486.

35. Ibid., p. 487.

36. 'Interlude in a Bar', Notebook.

37. *Appearance and Reality*, p. 431.

38. Ibid., p. 114.

39. Ibid., p. 217.

40. Ibid., p. 408.

41. *KE*, p. 145. (Eliot's dissertation was eventually published under the title, *Knowledge and Experience in the Philosophy of F. H. Bradley*.)
42. *Appearance and Reality*, p. 229.
43. Ibid., p. 228.
44. Ibid., p. 297.
45. Ibid., p. 229.
46. *KE*, pp. 24, 165.
47. *KE*, p. 143.
48. *KE*, pp. 147, 148, 162, 163, 164. I am indebted to A. Walton Litz for drawing attention to Eliot's 'half-objects', a term not to be found in Bradley.
49. Harry Todd Costello, *Josiah Royce's Seminar 1913–1914*, ed. Grover Smith (New Brunswick, N.J.: Rutgers Univ. Press, 1963), pp. 121, 138, 173–5.
50. *KE*, p. 31.
51. *KE*, p. 143.
52. *KE*, p. 144.
53. *KE*, pp. 143, 163.
54. *KE*, p. 55.
55. *KE*, pp. 147, 120.
56. *KE*, pp. 53–4, 31.
57. *Vanity Fair* (U.S.A.) (Feb. 1924).
58. 60th birthday coll., p. 20.
59. Receipts are in the Eliot Coll., Houghton Library.
60. Holograph, 'The Relationship between Politics and Metaphysics', written in 1913 or shortly after (it discusses Walter Lippman's *A Preface to Politics*, 1913), Eliot Coll., Houghton Library.
61. The programme is in the Houghton Library.
62. Edition of the *FQ* manuscripts.
63. Eliot's letters are sequestered at Princeton University until 2020.
69. This fragment is added to 'Do I know how I feel? Do I know what I think . . .'
65. *CP*, p. 26. John Hayward dated the poem 1911. See Gardner, *The Art of T. S. Eliot* (London: Faber, 1949), p. 107.
66. See Leon Edel, *Henry James: The Untried Years 1843–1870* (London: Rupert Hart-Davis, 1953), pp. 330, 332, 335.
67. *facs. WL*, p. [12].
68. Eliot's introduction to Josef Pieper's *Leisure*. Also, *NEW* (6 June 1935), pp. 151–2.
69. Eliot, *George Herbert, Writers and Their Work*: No. 152 (British Council, 1962), p. 24.
70. Eliot told this to Kristian Smidt, *Poetry and Belief in the Work of T. S. Eliot* (London: Routledge, 1961), p. 11.
71. *Adelphi*, 27, No. 2 (1951), 106–14.
72. Josiah Royce, *The Problem of Christianity*, rpr. (Univ. of Chicago Press, 1968), p. 215.
73. *Josiah Royce's Seminar*, pp. 76, 78.
74. Ibid., pp. 83, 85.
75. Ibid., p. 119.

76. 'Dry Salvages': V.
77. From 'Pro Peccatis suae Gentis' (published in the *Christian Register*).
78. Holograph index cards, 'Notes on Philosophy', Houghton Library.
79. *Mysticism* (1911; rpr. London: Methuen, 1945), p. 271. The quotation is from the chapter on Voices and Visions.
80. Letter to Paul Elmer More, Special Collections, Princeton.
81. 'The Complete Works of T. E. Hulme' (about five poems) were printed as an appendage to *Ripostes of Ezra Pound* (London: Stephen Swift, 1912), p. 64. Grover Smith points out the connection between 'Conversion' and 'The Death of Saint Narcissus' in *T. S. Eliot's Poetry and Plays*, p. 34.
82. 'John Ford', *SE*, p. 173.
83. Holograph index cards and *Mysticism*, pp. 279–81.
84. Letter to Aiken, quoted in 60th birthday coll., p. 23.
85. *The Scarlet Letter*, Centenary Edition of the Works of Nathaniel Hawthorne, Vol. I (Ohio State Univ. Press, 1962), pp. 142–5. See also 'The Minister's Virgil', pp. 147–58.
86. Unpublished lecture on Henry James at Harvard (Spring 1933), quoted by F. H. Matthiessen, *The Achievement of T. S. Eliot*, 3rd edition (N.Y.: O.U.P., 1958), p. 9.

CHAPTER 4. ELIOT'S ORDEALS
I should like to thank Elspeth Kennedy for translating Eliot's manuscript poems in French.
1. There is a letter, dated Feb. 1914, from C. R. Lanman about the possibility of a travelling fellowship.
2. Holograph poem, 'Afternoon', Notebook.
3. Typescript poem, 'In the Department Store', laid into Notebook.
4. Letter to Henry Ware Eliot, Jr. (8 Sept. 1914), mentioned by Grover Smith, *T. S. Eliot's Poetry and Plays*, p. 30.
5. Brand Blanchard, 'Eliot in Memory', *Yale Review* (Summer 1965), pp. 637–40.
6. Eliot, letter to the Secretary of the Merton Society (24 June 1963), Merton College Library, Oxford.
7. 60th birthday coll., pp. 22–3.
8. Ezra Round, *Paris Review* interview (1962), rpr. in *Writers at Work*, p. 47.
9. Ibid., p. 48.
10. Ezra Pound, *Selected Letters 1907–1941*, ed. D. D. Paige (1950; rpr. N.Y.: New Directions, 1971), p. 40.
11. Ibid., pp. 40–1.
12. Introduction, *Literary Essays of Ezra Pound*, ed. T. S. Eliot (N.Y.: New Directions, 1968; London: Faber, 1954), p. xii.
13. 'Ezra Pound', *NEW* (31 Oct. and 1 Nov. 1946), pp. 27–8, 37–9, rpr. *Ezra Pound: A Collection of Critical Essays*, ed. Walter Sutton (Englewood Cliffs, N.J.: Prentice-Hall, 1963), pp. 18–19.
14. Letter (20 June 1922), Quinn Collection, Manuscript Division, New York Public Library.

15. Wyndham Lewis, 'Early London Environment', 60th birthday coll., pp. 24–32.

16. *Paris Review* interview, *Writers at Work*, p. 95.

17. *Selected Letters*, p. 40.

18. To Quinn (11 Apr. 1917), Quinn Coll.

19. Pound to Wyndham Lewis (July 1916), *Selected Letters*, p. 86.

20. Eliot to Quinn (Oct. 1923), Quinn Coll.

21. To William Carlos Williams (1920), *Selected Letters*, p. 158.

22. Graham Martin drew attention to this comment from 'Four Meetings', in his Introduction to *Eliot in Perspective*, p. 22.

23. Letter to Perry, quoted by Edel, *Henry James: The Untried Years*, p. 264.

24. To H. L. Mencken (1916), *Selected Letters*, pp. 97–8.

25. To Harriet Monroe (1922), ibid., p. 183.

26. Editorial, *Little Review* (May 1917).

27. Letter to Quinn (15 Nov. 1918), Quinn Coll.

28. Review of *ASG*, *NEW* (1934).

29. To Quinn (Apr. 1918), *Selected Letters*, p. 134.

30. Review, *International Journal of Ethics*, 27 (July 1917), 543.

31. Review, *Int. J. Ethics*, 27 (Oct. 1916), 112.

32. Review, ibid. 115–17.

33. Election sermon (1765), Eliot Coll., Houghton Library.

34. *SE*, p. 373, and *ASG*, p. 56.

35. See Ronald Schuchard, 'Eliot and Hulme in 1916', *PMLA* (Oct. 1973), 1083–94.

36. *Grantite Review*, 24, No. 3 (1962), 19.

37. Review, *Int. J. Ethics*, 27 (July 1917), 542.

38. 'Ode' (dated July 1918), published in *Ara Vos Prec* (1920).

39. *Int. J. Ethics*, 27 (Oct. 1916), 127.

40. Vivienne lists '12 unbound poems by V.H.E.' in an inventory of her possessions. These are not among her manuscripts in the Bodleian Library. Eliot published the best of her sketches and one poem, pseudonymously, in the *Criterion*.

41. My impression is based on Vivienne's diaries and manuscripts in the Bodleian Library, Oxford. I am also indebted to comments by Sir Herbert Read, Conrad Aiken, Aldous Huxley, and Bertrand Russell. (See Allen Tate's coll., Huxley's *Letters*, Russell's *Autobiography*, vol. ii, and *Life*, 15 Jan. 1965.)

42. 'Dante' (1920), *SW*, pp. 165–6, and 'Dante' (1929), *SE*, pp. 207–8.

43. *SE*, p. 380.

44. *Milton Graduates Bulletin* (1933), p. 8.

45. To Ottoline Morrell (July 1915), *Autobiography*, ii. 61.

46. Diary (26 Dec. 1935).

47. Wyndham Lewis, 60th birthday coll., pp. 24–32, and *Blasting and Bombardiering* (London: Eyre & Spottiswoode, 1937), p. 284.

48. Bernard Bergonzi makes an enlightened comment on the sense of erotic failure in Eliot's early poetry as a projection of a common human problem, in *T. S. Eliot* (N.Y.: Collier, 1972), p. 22.

49. 'Ode'.

50. *facs. WL*, p. [22].

51. 'Thé Dansant', *Criterion*, 3 (Oct. 1924), 78.

52. To Henry Ware Eliot, Jr. (Sept. 1916), *facs. WL*, p. xi.

53. *facs. WL*, p. [26].

54. Vivienne Eliot, 'Letters of the Moment—I', *Criterion*, 2 (Feb. 1924), 220–2.

55. Diary (1919), Berg Coll.

56. Letter to Quinn (12 Mar. 1923), Quinn Coll.

57. Vivienne Eliot, Diary (3 Oct. 1934).

58. Footnote by Grover Smith, *The Letters of Aldous Huxley* (London: Chatto & Windus, 1969), p. 232.

59. 'Letters of the Moment—I'.

60. 'The Death of the Duchess', *facs. WL*, p. [104]. The title of a later version was 'In the Cage'.

61. Sir Herbert Read, Allen Tate's coll., p. 23.

62. Diary (1 Sept. 1934).

63. Extracts from letter quoted in Sotheby's 'Catalogue of Nineteenth-Century and Modern Autograph Letters', for sale on 4 Dec. 1973.

64. To Ottoline Morrell (Nov. 1915), *Autobiography*, ii. 64.

65. Virginia Woolf, Diary (Sept. 1933).

66. Diary (10 May 1934).

67. *Autobiography*, ii. 7.

68. *Kangaroo* (1923; rpr. N.Y.: Viking, 1970), p. 220.

69. *The Years* (N.Y.: Harcourt; London: Hogarth Press, 1937), pp. 300, 340–1.

70. Pound to Quinn (10 Aug. 1918), Quinn Coll.

71. *Milton Graduates Bulletin* (1933).

72. Levy and Scherle, p. 26.

72. Charlotte Eliot, Poem, Eliot Coll., Houghton Library.

74. Letter to Russell (18 Jan. 1916), Bertrand Russell Archive, McMaster Univ.

75. Letter to Julian Huxley (29 Dec. 1916), *Letters*, p. 117.

76. Letter to Carrington (May 1919), Michael Holroyd, *Lytton Strachey: A Biography* (Baltimore: Penguin, 1971), p. 364.

77. Diary (26 Dec. 1935).

78. Clive Bell, 'How Pleasant to Know Mr. Eliot', 60th birthday coll., p. 15.

79. *Selected Letters*, pp. 166–7.

80. Eliot first visited Hogarth House on 15 Nov. 1918, bringing three or four poems which he hoped the Woolfs would publish.

81. A. Huxley, *Letters*, p. 141.

82. *Laughter in the Next Room* (Boston: Little, Brown, 1948; London: Macmillan, 1949), p. 38.

83. *Ushant*, p. 215.

CHAPTER 5. THE WASTE LAND TRAVERSED

1. Epigraph to *facs. WL*.

2. *SE*, p. 180. I am indebted to Ronald Schuchard for pointing this out.

3. 'The Three Voices of Poetry', *OPP*, pp. 110–11. The quotations below are from this essay.

4. *facs. WL*, pp. [108–14]. The three are written on the same quadruled paper, punched for filing, and with a 'Linen Ledger' watermark (used by several paper companies in America). Valerie Eliot dates the handwriting '1914 or even earlier', p. 130.

5. For the religious significance of the upside down posture, see Jonathan Smith, 'Birth Upside Down or Right Side Up?', *History of Religions. An International Journal of Comparative Historical Studies*, 9 (May 1970), 281–303.

6. A review of a new edition of Donne's sermons, *Athenaeum* (28 Nov. 1919), p. 1252.

7. *SE*, p. 204.

8. Paul Delaney, *British Autobiography in the Seventeenth Century* (N.Y.: Columbia Univ. Press, 1969).

9. Peter Anson, *The Call of the Desert* (London: S.P.C.K., 1964) cites as his source Eusebius, *Historia Ecclesiastica*, VI. 9.

10. Letter, Bertrand Russell Archive, McMaster University.

11. See George Williams, *Wilderness and Paradise in Christian Thought* (N.Y.: Harper, 1962), for a detailed study of the Biblical desert experience and its imaginative recreation by various individuals and groups through history.

12. John Higginson's preface to Cotton Mather's *Magnalia Christi Americana* . . . (1702), ed. Thomas Robbins (Hartford, 1853–5), i. 13–18.

13. *Inferno*, VI.

14. *Confessions*, III. See *WL*: III for the same allusion: 'To Carthage then I came'.

15. *Paris Review* interview.

16. Part of letter quoted in *facs. WL*, p. x.

17. Part of letter quoted in *facs. WL*, p. xiii.

18. Letter, Bertrand Russell Archive, McMaster University.

19. Letter quoted by E. Martin Browne, *The Making of T. S. Eliot's Plays* (London: C.U.P., 1970), pp. 106–8.

20. 'Poems', Berg Coll.

21. *facs. WL*, p. [116].

22. *facs. WL*, pp. [48–52]. The river is again associated with an injured woman in a later poem which describes a man haunted at night by the reproach of 'a face that sweats with tears' looking up from the surface of a blackened river ('The wind sprang up at four o'clock', *CP*, p. 134). 'The surface of the blackened river / Is a face that sweats with tears' recalls the diction of 'The river sweats. . .'.

23. *The Teaching of the Compassionate Buddha*, ed. E. A. Burtt (N.Y.: Mentor, 1955), pp. 96–8.

24. 'The Present Hour', published in the *Christian Register*, Eliot Coll., Houghton Library.

25. *facs. WL*, p. [36].

26. *Grace Abounding to the Chief of Sinners*, ed. Roger Sharrock (London: O.U.P., 1966), p. 16.

27. *facs. WL*, p. [34].

28. London Letter to the *Dial* (June 1921).

29. See *facs. WL*, p. [36] for the first draft and p. [30] for the second draft which Pound cut. Valerie Eliot provides a most useful note on Eliot's allusion to the City of God, *facs. WL*, p. 127.

30. Extracts from Eliot's letters to Strachey are to be found in Michael Holroyd, *Lytton Strachey: A Biography* (Baltimore: Penguin, 1971), pp. 775–6.

31. In an autograph letter to John Rodker (1 June 1919) Eliot says that 'Gerontion' is half finished (Alderman Library, Charlottesville). I should like to thank the reference librarian, Kendon Stubbs, for useful information.

32. Noted by Valerie Eliot, *facs. WL*, p. xviii.

33. 'A Sceptical Patrician', *Athenaeum* (23 May 1919), pp. 361–2. Eliot rightly considered this one of his best essays (letter to Quinn, 9 July 1919).

34. 'The Preacher as Artist', *Athenaeum* (28 Nov. 1919), p. 1252.

35. Ibid.

36. See Daniel B. Shea, *Spiritual Autobiography in Early America* (Princeton, N.J.: Princeton University Press, 1968; London: O.U.P., 1969): Chapter 3, 'Traditional Patterns in Puritan Autobiography'.

37. 'Self-Reliance', *Selected Prose and Poetry*, op. cit., p. 178.

38. See Leonard Woolf, *Downhill All the Way* (London: Hogarth, 1967), p. 111.

39. Letter to Quinn (9 May 1921), quoted by Valerie Eliot in *facs. WL*, p. xxi: '. . . He was "wishful to finish a long poem" (as he still described *The Waste Land*) which was now "partly on paper".'

40. Eliot to Quinn (21 Sept. 1922), Quinn Coll.

41. (3 Oct. 1921), *facs WL*, p. xxi.

42. Letter, Russell Archive, McMaster University.

43. Letters to Julian Huxley (26 and 31 Oct.) and to Aldington (6 Nov.) are quoted by Valerie Eliot, *facs. WL*, p. xxii.

44. Letter to Quinn from Paris (22 Oct. 1921) Quinn Coll. Pound habitually reported on Eliot's literary progress to Quinn, and if he had seen any of *The Waste Land* he would surely have mentioned it in his letter.

45. Included in letter to Eliot (24 Jan. 1921), *Selected Letters*, p. 170.

46. *Collected Shorter Poems* (1958; rpr. London: Faber, 1973), pp. 203–22.

47. I should like to thank Gillian Smee for pointing out these words in *The Cocktail Party*, 1. iii, *Collected Plays*, p. 169.

48. *facs. WL*, p. [100]. Eliot uses Arnaut Daniel's words from the *Purgatorio*, XXVI.

49. The influence of the Russian ballet was suggested by Herbert Howarth in *Notes on Some Figures Behind T. S. Eliot*, pp. 306–10.

50. See Eliot's London Letters in July and October to the *Dial*, 71 (July–Dec. 1921), 214, 452–3, and 'A Commentary', *Criterion*, 3 (Oct. 1924), 5.

51. *Josiah Royce's Seminar*, ed. Grover Smith, p. 89.

52. 'Easter', Eliot Coll., Houghton Library.

53. Letter to Pound (Jan. 1922), *Selected Letters*, p. 171.

54. See Lionel Trilling, *Sincerity and Authenticity* (Cambridge, Mass: Harvard; London: O.U.P., 1972), pp. 11–12, 108.

55. Hugh Kenner noted the 'sequence of personal pasts' in *Eliot in His Time*, p. 38.

56. I owe this observation to Fiona McArdle.

57. *The Autobiography of Bertrand Russell*, ii. 254.

58. Malory, *Works* (London: O.U.P., 1973), p. 531.

59. 'Experience', *Selected Prose and Poetry*, pp. 234, 242.

60. Typescript address, 'The Bible as Scripture and as Literature', read in King's Chapel, Boston (1 Dec. 1932), Eliot Coll., Houghton Library.

61. According to Valerie Eliot (*facs. WL*, p. 129), this statement, which Eliot made in his essay on Pascal, was autobiographical and referred to his writing of 'What the Thunder Said'.

62. From Gerard de Nerval, 'El Desdichado'.

63. *TLS* (20 Sept. 1923), rpr. Casebook Series on *WL*, ed. C. B. Cox and Archibald P. Hinchliffe, 33–8.

64. *Selected Letters of Ezra Pound*, p. 170. Pound's two January letters and Eliot's one reply rpr. here pp. 169–72.

65. *facs. WL*, p. [8].

66. Ibid., p. [6].

67. See *facs. WL*, p. [100]. Pound wrote in January that 'the sovegna doesn't hold with the rest'.

68. The letter is paraphrased by Nicholas Joost, *Scofield Thayer and 'The Dial'* (Carbondale, Ill., 1964), p. 159.

69. The doubts are half-phrased and abruptly dismissed in the taped interview (1959) with Donald Hall, Eliot Coll., Houghton Library.

70. Letter to Eliot (26 Feb. 1923); B. L. Reid, *The Man From New York: John Quinn and his friends* (N.Y.: O.U.P., 1968), p. 580; and *facs. WL*, p. xxvi.

71. The rough draft is scribbled on the back of the discarded Fresca fragment, *facs. WL*, p. [24].

72. *Selected Letters of Ezra Pound*, p. 171.

73. London Letter to the *Dial*, 72 (Apr. 1922), 510–13.

74. Aiken, Prefatory Note, 'An Anatomy of Melancholy'. There may be some confusion as to the date of these lunches. Aiken says that they took place *before* Eliot went to Lausanne but says also it was the winter of 1921–2. I think his 'winter' date is correct. He mentions one of these lunches in a letter dated 15 Feb. 1922 in the Chapin Library, Williams College, Mass. I should like to thank the Custodian, H. Richard Archer, for useful information.

75. Eliot's idea for a sequel is cited in a letter from Charlotte Eliot to her brother-in-law, Walter Lamb Eliot (7 May 1923): 'He has had for some time the plan for another poem in his mind.' Eliot Coll., Houghton Library.

76. See Quentin Bell, *Virginia Woolf: A Biography*, vol. 2 (N.Y.: Harcourt; London: Hogarth, 1972), p. 173.

77. 'A Note on Poetry and Belief', first published in Wyndham Lewis's *Enemy*, 1 (Jan. 1927), 15–17.

CHAPTER 6. CONVERSION

I should like to thank the Revd. Peter Mayhew for correcting some misconceptions about Anglo-Catholicism.

1. Preface to the 1928 edition of *SW*, p. vii.

2. *SW*, p. 31: 'Romanticism is a short cut to the strangeness without the reality, and it leads its disciples only back upon themselves.'

3. Paul Elmer More, 'An Absolute and an Authoritative Church', *Criterion*, 8 (July 1929), rpr. in *The Catholic Faith* (Port Washington, N.Y.: Kennikat, 1972), pp. 169–205. Eliot said in the *Princeton Alumni Weekly*, 37 (5 Feb. 1937), 373–4, that P. E. More had come 'by somewhat the same route, to almost the same conclusions' as his own and had provided the kind of help which English theologians could not give him. I am indebted to Ronald Schuchard for sending an extract from this piece.

4. *The Catholic Faith*, p. 203.

5. Interview (Dec. 1974).

6. AW: II, *CP*, p. 88.

7. *Criterion*, 3 (April 1925), 364.

8. Eliot mentioned his inability to write in a letter to Mark Van Doren (Jan. 1925), Special Collections, Columbia Univ.

9. 'Fête Galante', *Criterion*, 3 (July 1925), 557–63.

10. *The Wings of the Dove* (London: Bodley Head, 1969), pp. 119–20.

11. Thomas Merton, Introduction to *The Wisdom of the Desert* (1960; rpr. London: Sheldon, 1974), p. 23.

12. Letter to Bonamy Dobrée (1936), quoted in Dobrée's 'T. S. Eliot: A Personal Reminiscence', Allen Tate's coll., p. 81.

13. *SE*, p. 142.

14. See Virginia Woolf's letter to Lytton Strachey mentioning Eliot's becoming desperate (n.d.), Berg Coll., and Pound, *Selected Letters*, pp. 172, 173, 196.

15. Letter (12 Mar. 1923), Reid, *The Man From New York*, p. 582.

16. Letter (7 May 1925), quoted in Russell's *Autobiography*, ii. 174.

17. Vivienne Eliot, Diary (Nov. 1934).

18. Cable to Quinn (2 Apr. 1923), Quinn Coll.

19. Quotation and comment from 'Lancelot Andrewes', *SE*, pp. 305–6.

20. *SE*, pp. 306–7.

21. 'The *Pensées* of Pascal' (1931), *SE*, pp. 360–1.

22. M. B. Rickett recalled this comment made by Eliot at the Anglo-Catholic summer school of sociology at Keble College, Oxford (July 1933). Taped by the Revd. Peter Mayhew in 1974.

23. Quoted by Barbara Tuchman, *The Proud Tower* (N.Y.: MacMillan; London: Hamilton, 1966), p. 146.

24. The date stamp is obscured, but the envelope is among Vivienne's manuscripts of about 1923–4 in the Bodleian Library.

25. 'Charade of the Seasons'.

26. 'Blake', *SW*, p. 157.

27. See Newman's hymn, 'Lead, Kindly Light'.

28. Interview (Dec. 1974).

29. Letter to Leonard Woolf (17 Dec. 1925), Berg Coll.

30. Ibid.

31. Epigraph to 'Sweeney Agonistes', *CP*, p. 111.

32. Implied in a letter to Russell (21 Apr. 1925), *Autobiography*, ii. 173.

33. MS. in Bodleian Library.

34. 'Eyes that last I saw in tears', *CP*, p. 133.
35. Cyril Connolly pointed out the connection in a *Times* review. The epigraph is from the *Satyricon* of Petronius.
36. Virginia Woolf, Diary (1923), Berg Coll.
37. Russell, *Autobiography*, ii. 174.
38. Eliot to Russell (5 Oct. 1927), Russell Archive, McMaster Univ.
39. Robert Sencourt, *T. S. Eliot: A Memoir* (N. Y.: Dodd; London: Garnstone Press, 1971), p. 124.
40. 'Burnt Norton', *CP*, p. 178.
41. AW: I, *CP*, pp. 85–6.
42. AW: I.
43. Eliot to William Force Stead (10 Apr. 1928). This and other letters to Stead, mentioned below, are in the Osborn Collection, Beinecke Library, Yale Univ.
44. AW: I.
45. Remembered by M. B. Rickett and recorded on tape by the Revd. Peter Mayhew.
46. 'Dry Salvages', *CP*, p. 199.
47. I take the details of Eliot's entry into the Church from Sencourt, pp. 127, 131, 132, and from Eliot's letters to William Force Stead.
48. 'Baudelaire', *SE*, p. 378.
49. To Stead (15 Mar. 1928).
50. To Stead (10 Apr. 1928).
51. To Stead (2 Dec. 1930).
52. *CP*, p. 103.
53. *Sermons*, ed. G. M. Story (Oxford: Clarendon, 1967), pp. 122–3.
54. Ibid., p. 129.
55. 'The Cultivation of Christmas Trees', *CP*, p. 107.
56. AW: V. See Elisabeth Schneider, 'Prufrock and After: The Theme of Change', *PMLA* (Oct. 1972), 1110–13, for good insights into the subjective statements in the 1927–31 poems.
57. *The Monthly Criterion*, 6 (July 1927), 73.
58. 'John Bramhall', *SE*, p. 316.
59. 'Modern Education', *SE*, p. 459.
60. *Axel's Castle* (N.Y.: Scribner, 1931), p. 126.
61. Roger Lloyd, *The Church of England 1900–1965* (London: SCM Press, 1966), p. 457.
62. 'The Church as Action', *NEW* 7 (19 Mar. 1936), 451.
63. *Apologia Pro Vita Sua*, p. 185.
64. 'Christianity and Communism', *Listener* (16 Mar. 1932), pp. 382–3.
65. 'The Church as an Ecumenical Society', address to the Oxford conference on church, community, and state, 16 July 1937. (Typescript in Houghton Library.) See also 'Thoughts After Lambeth', *SE*, pp. 328, 329.
66. *Harvard Advocate* (Dec. 1938), p. 20. Written when Lowell was a freshman.
67. *Axel's Castle*, pp. 126–7.
68. *ICS*, p. 32.
69. *Journals*, I, ed. Justin O'Brien (rpr. N.Y.: Vintage, 1947), p. 136.

70. 'John Bramhall', *SE*, p. 316. See also Eliot's essay on Bishop Andrewes (1926) and his 'Thoughts After Lambeth' (1931).
71. Review of *ICS*, *Partisan Review* (Sept.–Oct. 1940).
72. *The Varieties of Religious Experience*, pp. 368–9.
73. 'Song for Simeon' and 'The Family Reunion', II. ii.
74. 'Marina', *CP*, p. 105.
75. 'Animula', *CP*, p. 103.
76. 'Marina'.
77. 'The Rock', *CP*, p. 157, and *ICS*, pp. 48, 49.
78. AW: II.
79. *UPUS*, p. 145.
80. *SE*, p. 325.
81. 'Marina'.
82. AW: II.

Biographical Sources

PROBABLY all the more important Eliot manuscripts are now available, and Faber has published facsimiles of the manuscripts of *The Waste Land* and *Four Quartets*. There are manuscripts that are completely sequestered, notably at Princeton University an overwhelming number of letters to Emily Hale, but others may be seen with Mrs. Eliot's permission: for example, the collection of index cards at the Houghton Library, Harvard, on which Eliot, as a young man, made notes from books that had interested him (see Appendix I), and two holograph essays, one on Henri Bergson (*c.* 1912) and the other on the relationship between politics and metaphysics (*c.* 1914).

Of those manuscripts readily available to scholars, those in the New York Public Library's Berg Collection are the most valuable for a study of Eliot's early years. Most important, here, is the *Waste Land* manuscript and the holograph Notebook in which Eliot in his youth made fair copies of numerous poems, most of which he never published. Luckily he dated them, so that, despite his frugal impulse from time to time to fill up unused blank spaces, a sequence may be reconstructed. The Notebook contains a draft of 'Prufrock' with a section that was excised before publication. The Berg Collection's acquisition (which came from John Quinn's estate) also includes a folder of early poems, some holographs but most of them in typescript. Here, too, are a few curious unpublished poems as well as drafts of published poems—in the case of 'Whispers of Immortality' about seven drafts.

Eliot was too guarded to be a great writer of letters, but Virginia Woolf evoked a fair degree of candour. Their correspondence is in the Berg, as well as the Woolf diaries which provide the most intelligent portraits of Eliot in his first years in London.

The Houghton Library's Eliot collection is vast and has the advantage of comprehensiveness. First in importance are the writings of Eliot's mother, Charlotte Champe Eliot, her immense Scrapbook and her published volumes: *Easter Songs* (Boston: James H. West, n.d.), *Savanarola* (London: Faber, 1926), and the biography of Eliot's impressive grandfather, *William Greenleaf Eliot* (N.Y.: Houghton Mifflin, 1904). A good source of biographical information is the Library's nine boxes of Eliot family documents, photographs, personal letters, and out-of-the-way newspaper clippings, most of which were collected by Eliot's elder brother, Henry Ware Eliot, Jr.

For Eliot's problems, financial and marital, during his first years in London see his letters to John Quinn and, more revealing, Ezra Pound's letters to Quinn, both of which are in the Manuscript Division, New York Public Library. Eliot's letters to Pound at the Beinecke Library, Yale University, are rather too mannered to be of much biographic interest. More valuable, here, is the little-known correspondence with William Force Stead, which forms a background to Eliot's growing attachment to Anglicanism during the 1920s, his conversion, his first confession, and his acceptance of celibacy. These letters are in the Beinecke's Osborn Collection.

Eliot's letters to Bertrand Russell are in the Russell Archive at McMaster University, Hamilton, Ontario; the best parts are quoted in Russell's *Autobiography*. Serious students of Eliot's life will want to see the rather dull typescript Autobiography of his father, Henry Ware Eliot, in the Olin Library, Washington University, St. Louis; a large collection of letters from Eliot to various less intimate friends at Princeton University; and a very small collection of letters to John Rodker at the Alderman Library, University of Virginia at Charlottesville, which deals with Eliot's writing and attempts at publication in 1919.

Eliot's first wife, Vivienne, left her diaries to the Bodleian Library, Oxford. They are not as significant as one might hope, for all but one were written before and after she lived with Eliot. Yet they are a fascinating document of moods, character, and behaviour. The Bodleian Library also has drafts and fragments of her attempts at fiction in the early twenties, some of which Eliot published in the *Criterion*.

I should like to thank the curators of the above-mentioned collections for permission to examine the manuscripts, in particular Mr. Osborn for courteous help, Dr. Lola Szladits of the Berg Collection for letting me examine the paper of the *Waste Land* manuscript, and Professor Donald Gallup, Eliot's bibliographer, for useful comments on my dating of the *Waste Land* fragments (see Appendix II).*

PRINTED SOURCES

Eliot's essays in literary biography, 'The *Pensées* of Pascal' and 'Baudelaire', together with the collected editions of poems and plays and in particular *The Family Reunion*, are probably more revealing of his inward life than any existing memoir. For a curious self-characterization, see Eliot's 'Eeldrop and Appleplex, I', *Little Review*, 4 (May 1917), 7–11,

---

* An additional thanks to William Ingoldsby, the cataloguer of the Conrad Aiken Collection, Huntington Library, and to Helen Gardner for her transcripts of Eliot's 1914–16 letters to Aiken which contain much of personal and literary interest.

and also the strange 'Ode', published once only, in *Ara Vos Prec* (London: Ovid, 1920).

Donald Gallup's bibliography shows what a prolific reviewer Eliot was during his first few years in London. Short as they are, some of his pieces in the *Athenaeum*—'A Sceptical Patrician' (23 May 1919) and 'The Preacher as Artist' (28 Nov. 1919)—and some of his London Letters to the *Dial* (Vol. 70, Apr. 1921, 448–53, and June 1921, 686–91; Vol. 71, Aug. 1921, 213–17, and Oct. 1921, 452–5; Vol. 72, Apr. 1922, 510–13; Vol. 73, Sept. 1922, 329–31) are of more enduring interest than the dogmatic 'Tradition and the Individual Talent', with its theory of impersonality which, as Ronald Schuchard's articles suggest, has tended to obscure the personal nature of Eliot's poetry.

Eliot often talked more freely to children. Two obscure school addresses are interesting for their reminiscences: one at Milton Academy, Milton, Mass., on 17 June 1933, which is printed in the *Milton Graduates Bulletin* 3 (Nov. 1933), 5–9; the other at the centennial of the Mary Institute, St. Louis, on 11 Nov. 1959, which is printed in *From Mary to You* (St. Louis, 1959), pp. 133–6. See also an informal interview with Eliot in the *Grantite Review*, 24, No. 3 (1962), 16–20, and the fine *Paris Review* interview, rpr. in *Writers at Work*, ed. Van Wyck Brooks, 2nd series (N.Y.: Viking, 1963). Eliot also reminisced, this time about his family in St. Louis, in a 1953 address rpr. in *CC*, 'American Literature and the American Language'. Occasional recollections may be found in his various prefaces to books by other writers. For memories of America see his Preface to E. A. Mowrer, *This American World* (London: Faber, 1928); for memories of Harvard's Philosophy Department in the early years of this century see his Introduction to Josef Pieper, *Leisure: the Basis of Culture* (rpr. N.Y.: Mentor-Omega, 1963).

There have been numerous memoirs by people who knew Eliot in one way or another. The best have been cameos which do not venture beyond immediate knowledge. An amusing collection was edited in honour of Eliot's sixtieth birthday by Richard March and Tambimuttu (London: Editions Poetry, 1948), containing lively memoirs by Conrad Aiken ('King Bolo and Others'), Clive Bell ('How Pleasant to Know Mr. Eliot'), and Wyndham Lewis ('Early London Environment'). Another good collection was edited by Allen Tate after Eliot's death, *T. S. Eliot: The Man and his Work* (N.Y.: Dell, 1966; London: Chatto & Windus, 1967), with interesting memoirs by Frank Morley, Sir Herbert Read, Bonamy Dobrée, and Robert Giroux.

There are numerous books and articles which are not about Eliot but contain glimpses of him. The best known are Bertrand Russell's *Autobiography*, vols. 1 and 2 (Boston: Little, Brown, 1967–9; London: Allen & Unwin); Ezra Pound, *Selected Letters 1907–1941*, ed. D. D.

Paige (rpr. N.Y.: New Directions, 1971); and Leonard Woolf, *Downhill All the Way* (N.Y.: Harcourt, 1967). A less known but very vivid image of Eliot as a newcomer to London's literary scene may be found in Iris Barry, 'The Ezra Pound Period', *The Bookman* (Oct. 1931). Witty anecdotes of Eliot as an undergraduate may be found in Donald J. Adams, *Copey of Harvard* (Boston: Houghton Mifflin, 1960), and Conrad Aiken, *Ushant* (Boston: Little, Brown, 1952). There is a rather snide picture of angelic coldness in Richard Aldington, *Life for Life's Sake* (N.Y.: Viking, 1941). Finally, some rare close-ups of the Eliots may be discerned in Vivienne Eliot's sketches: 'Letters of the Moment—I and II', *Criterion*, 2 (Feb. and Apr. 1924), 220–2, 360–4; 'Thé Dansant', *Criterion*, 3 (Oct. 1924), 72–8; 'A Diary of the Rive Gauche' and 'Necesse est Perstare?', *Criterion*, 3 (Apr. 1925), 425–9, 364; 'Fête Galante', *Criterion*, 3 (July 1925), 557–63.

There are several full-length memoirs, all written with an uneasy blend of effusion and condescension. They are based on no more than a slight acquaintance with the man and show little feeling for his work. They are *Affectionately, T. S. Eliot* by William Turner Levy and Victor Scherle (N.Y.: J. B. Lippincott, 1968); Robert Sencourt, *T. S. Eliot: A Memoir* (N.Y.: Dodd; London: Garnstone Press, 1971); and T. S. Matthews, *Great Tom* (N.Y.: Harper; London: Weidenfeld & Nicolson, 1974). The latter does uncover the important relationship with Emily Hale and has collected some honest information about her.

H. W. H. Powel, Jr. did pioneering biographic work in his Brown University master's essay, 'Notes on the Life of T. S. Eliot, 1888–1910' (1954), followed by John Soldo with his informative Harvard dissertation, 'The Tempering of T. S. Eliot 1888–1915' (1972). The most imaginative source of biographic facts is still Herbert Howarth's *Notes on Some Figures Behind T. S. Eliot* (N.Y.: Houghton Mifflin, 1964; London: Chatto & Windus, 1965).

Index

Adams, Henry, 8, 13, 17–19, 30, 33, 90; and 'Gerontion', 101

'After the turning', 58–9, 87–8. *See also The Waste Land*

'Afternoon', 65

Aiken, Conrad, 21, 26, 31, 32, 43, 45, 47, 66, 85, 166, 167; TSE's confidant, 61 n., 63, 64, 67, 72, 95, 117

Aldington, Richard, 67, 104, 118, 167

America, 2, 12, 14, 16, 25, 31–2, 68, 85, 90, 93, 101, 134, 138–9; moral fervour, 12, 90, 94; new world idea, 7, 37, 111; work ethic, 82. *See* New England background

Ancestors, Stearns, 4–6, 71; Eliot, 3, 8–11, 71

Andrewes, Lancelot, 103, 125, 130, 131

Anglicanism, *see* Church of England

'Animula', 9, 131

Artworks (inspired poems), Manet, *La Femme au perroquet*, 26; studies of St. Sebastian, 61 n.

'Ash Wednesday', 24, 28, 57, 90, 119, 121, 131, 136

Athenaeum articles, 101, 102, 103, 166

'Aunt Helen', 17–18

Babbitt, Irving, 19, 22, 134

Ballet, Russian, 107–8

'Barcarolle', 34

Baudelaire, 30, 137 n., 165

'Bel Esprit' fund, 124 n.

Bell, Clive, 83, 84, 122, 166

Bergson, Henri, 29, 38, 40–1, 43, 46–7, 55

Bleistein (character), 105, 144

Bloomsbury Group, 83–5

Böhme, Jacob, 60

Boston, *see* New England background

'The *Boston Evening Transcript*', 18

Bradley, F. H., and TSE's dissertation, 49–54, 65, 107

Briggs, Dean, 19

Browning, 'Porphyria's Lover', 28

Bubu de Montparnasse, *see* Charles-Louis Philippe

Buddha, 98–9, 111, 145

Bunyan, 92, 99

'The Burial of the Dead', 91, 94, 111

'The Burnt Dancer' (1914), 59, 143

'Burnt Norton', 35, 39, 41, 55–6

Cape Ann, *see* New England background

'Caprices in North Cambridge' (1909), 19

Chapin, Samuel, 4–5

Chapman, John Jay, 16, 19

Christ, 42, 61, 70, 109–11, 115

Christianity, piety of TSE's nurse, 3; piety of family, 4–6, 9–12; martyrdom's appeal, 61–3, 91–3, 136; martyrdom as alternative passion, 72, 74, 96, 97–9; TSE's state of 'partial belief', 69–70; TSE's blasphemy, 39, 70–1; TSE's definition of, 12, 69, 136; in *The Waste Land*, 86–95, 97–104, 108–15; in 'Exequy', 116; TSE's 'belief', 118; intuition versus 'the accumulated wisdom', 120–1, 130; monastic position, 122–3; humility, 121, 130, 137; the convert, 130–3; need for Christian community, 57–8, 135–6

Church of England, 1, 16, 138, 140; personal basis of TSE's attachment, 130–4; ideological basis, 134–6; 125–7, 132; *via media*, 134–6, 165

Churches, Anglican, 70, 99–100, 116, 126, 130

'Circe's Palace', 26

Cobden-Sanderson, Richard, 125

Conrad, *Heart of Darkness*, 109–11

'Conversation Galante', 23, 26, 27, 29

'Convictions' (1910), 27

Copeland, 21, 167

Cousin Harriet (character), 18

'Cousin Nancy', 17

Cousins, Abigail, 26, 32; Frederick, 21, 32, 70; Martha, 26, 32; William Greenleaf Eliot II, 32

Criterion, 118; P. E. More's essay, 120, 127, 135; Vivienne's sketches, 129, 165, 167

Cunard, Nancy, 79